THE

LAMBRETTA

BIBLE

All models built in Italy:
1947-1971

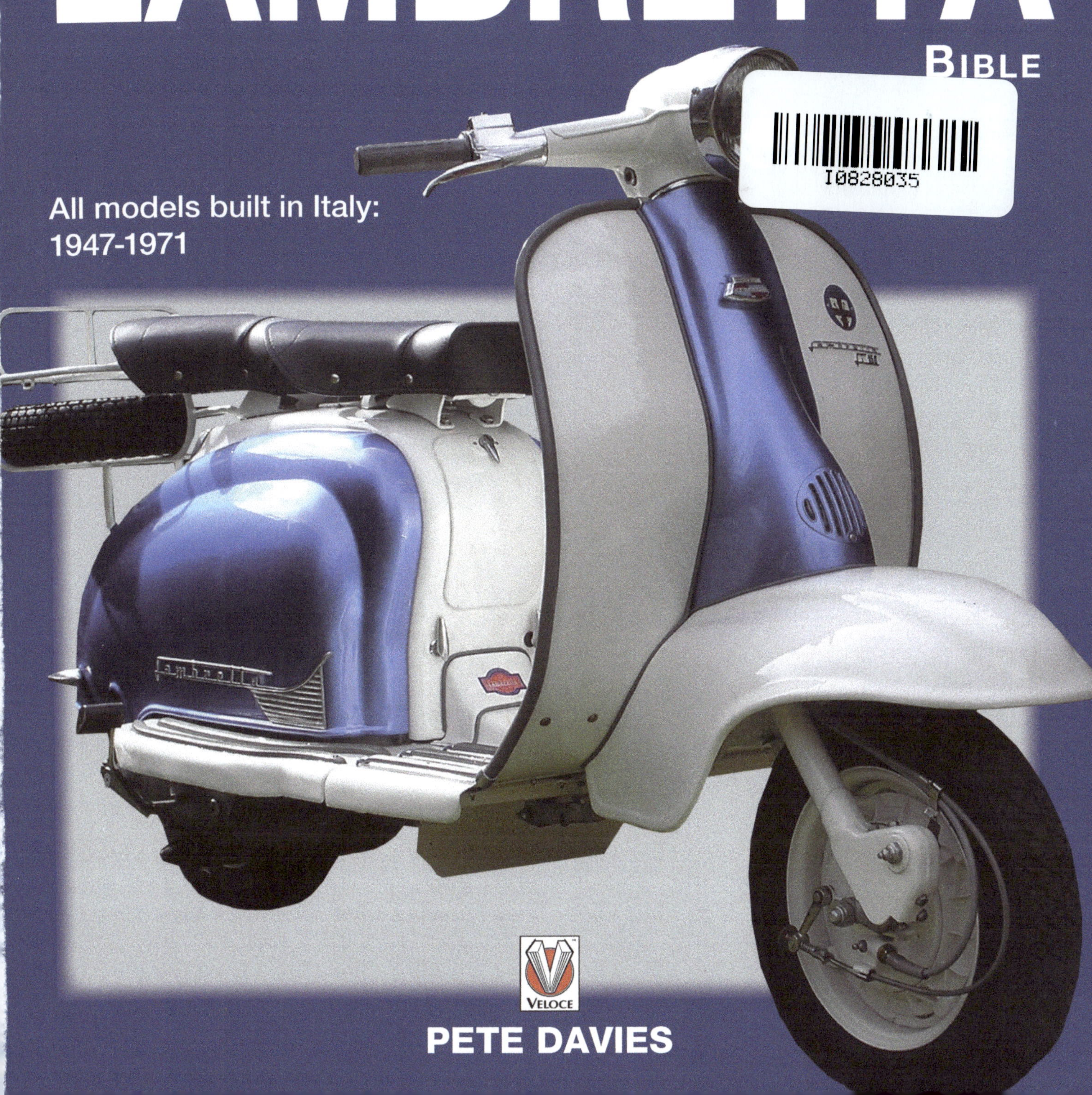

VELOCE

PETE DAVIES

First published in May 2008, reprinted March 2009. Revised updated edition published October 2013. New paperback edition published April 2016, reprinted July 2016 & February 2017 by Veloce Publishing Limited, Veloce House, Parkway Farm Business Park, Poundbury, Dorchester, Dorset DT1 3AR, England. Phone 01305 260068/fax 01305 250479/e-mail info@veloce.co.uk/web www.veloce.co.uk or www.velocebooks.com.
ISBN:978-1-787111-39-4/UPC:6-36847-01139-0

British Library Cataloguing in Publication Data – A catalogue record for this book is available from the British Library. Typesetting, design and page make-up all by Veloce Publishing Ltd on Apple Mac. Printed and Bound by CPI Group (UK) Ltd, Croydon, CR04YY.

Contents

Introduction & acknowledgements

Introduction

2007 saw the first publication of this book, and I guess many will ask why a revised edition has been published. The answer is quite simple – in the intervening six years, new material has been found which has been added to the original content. My aim always was, and always will be, to provide *Lambretisti* everywhere the fullest information that I can on the Innocenti-built machines, whilst at the same time providing a more British view of them. With this edition of the book I have included new photographs, new road test reviews, and new information from Lambretta Concessionaires. Where appropriate, text has been updated from the original book and new text added, and in many cases new 'Did You Know?' and 'What The Tester Said' sections have been provided. This includes the weight of each machine and the total production figures, along with the months of most and least production. I have added these to show that despite huge outputs the factory also had months of low production even back in the 1950s.

In respect of the Innocenti factory production of the Lambretta, it's worth bearing in mind that manufacture of Lambretta scooters started in October 1947 and ended in April 1971. During that time, 1,975,374 Lambretta scooters were produced (this figure excludes mopeds and Lambros). That figure equates to 6890 machines per month, with the most being made in March 1960 – a total of 16,400 Series 2 machines.

For those who have not read the original book, I should explain that my reason for writing this work is to try and put 'under one roof' as much information as possible about the Italian-built Lambrettas and the machines prepared and modified by Lambretta Concessionaires,

Alan Kimber on his Rallymaster at the 1961 ISDT. (Courtesy Power & Pedal)

Right from the start Innocenti was interested in seeing its scooters set speed records. This advert dates from June 1957. (Courtesy Smees Advertising Agency)

along with those dealer specials prepared by the main UK dealers in the 1960s and early 1970s. The machines prepared and modified by Lambretta Concessionaires, which include the Scottish 6 Days Trials machines, the Rallymaster, the Amphi-scooter and the dual controlled Lambretta, have not, to my knowledge, been covered in any other book. Likewise the dealer specials, which include the Horners Hornet, Rafferty Newman's Wildcat, the PJ Oakley Mk 3 SX 200, Supertune (Lowline, Rallye and Avanti machines), and the Arthur Francis built S and Super S Types, have also never been covered in any book. Although many of those have been the subject of magazine articles by myself and others, in view of their popularity now amongst *Lambretisti* worldwide, a book covering them is long overdue.

This book contains as much history as can be gleaned from the sources available to me. This will enable the reader to trace the background, development, history and modifications of all of these machines from their inception until the end of their production. Much of the information was obtained from dealer sheets sent by the Centro Ricambi at Innocenti – however, it must be borne in mind that Innocenti, like most motor manufacturers, would fit the parts it had available at any one time (for example, the Series 3 Li 125 had rear light units manufactured by Aprilia, Carello and CEV – all used during production). This of course inevitably leads to some variation over any specification listed by the company. However, conflicting information abounds, even in extant factory sources, and inevitably some questions will remain unanswered and new ones will be raised. 'Intelligent' guesses have sometimes, of necessity, had to be made to try and set matters straight, but hopefully these deductions will not cause further frustration.

Added to the material that came from the Centro Ricambi is a new chapter, one which deals with the information supplied by Lambretta Concessionaires to the extensive UK Lambretta Dealer and Lambretta Service Agent network. This provides an almost unique British perspective on Lambretta and how it was promoted and sold within the UK. As with most original paperwork – even that from the 1950s and 60s – there are gaps, and where possible I have tried to obtain any missing information.

In writing and researching this book, I have realised that a great deal of detail is still missing. Factory records have long since been lost or destroyed, employees of both the factory and the dealers involved are no longer around, and a huge pool of information in the form of correspondence files, specification books, memoranda, drawings, blueprints and other ephemera have long since gone. However, this book will answer many questions, and is hopefully a distillation into one coherent record of all of the information available. Please note that any information in respect of paint schemes is, in the main, kept to those used by the Innocenti factory. The material from Lambretta Concessionaires does cover paint schemes used by Concessionaires, BUT we do not know the exact paint codes for these colours.

Throughout the book I have used excerpts from numerous road tests that were written during the 1950s, '60s, and '70s. These have been included to give you, the reader, a feel for what testers at the time thought of the various Lambretta models. Since writing the original version of this book, I have updated many of these. Unfortunately there are some machines for which I could find no road tests, and others where there were quite a few. In order to provide the fullest amount of information, I have included excerpts from all those I could source. This edition also includes the testers' thoughts on the various dealer specials.

Italian riders line up at the start of the 1963 Milan – Taranto event. (Courtesy Innocenti Motor Coporation)

Readers with new information are invited to contact me via Veloce Publishing so that, one day, perhaps the full story of the Lambretta and the role it played on the worldwide scooter scene can be told.

Acknowledgements

When the Milanese Innocenti plant closed its doors in 1971, most of the factory records were destroyed or lost. The once bustling company had become the scene of industrial problems, and intervention by BMC revealed a lack of care and interest in the Lambretta product. I doubt if, when the factory doors shut, any thought was given to saving for posterity records and documents.

This book would have been much less enlightening had it not been for the help, advice and information freely given by those who worked for Lambretta Concessionaires (including the late Rex White), and the various dealers who produced dealer specials during the 1960s and 70s. Some brochures and leaflets survive, along with the memories of those who were involved and have provided much of the detail in this book.

There are a number of people who have specifically helped in the production of this revised edition of the book, not least Stuart Owen, Doug Miller, John 'Brano' Branson, Ann Weir, Christine Jackson, Johnny Lambrettista, Andy Carney, Ian Newman, Tony Tessier, Peter Oakley, Malcolm Pike, David Ashmead, Gill Beecham, Barry Hart, Roberto Morelli, Steve Grant, Brendan Horgan, Ron Moss, Paul Brierley, and many others too numerous to mention individually. Also organisations such as the National Motor Museum, and AWL Limited (which allowed the use of the Lambretta logo). I am grateful to all of them, and owe them a great deal for the time and effort they have put into providing information and assistance with this book's production.

Ultimately this book exists due to the influence of one person, Kev Walsh (ex-General Secretary of the Lambretta Club of Great Britain), without whom it would not exist. Some years ago, Kev encouraged me to submit write-ups on the various Lambretta scooters for use in the LCGB magazine, *Jetset*. I happily obliged, and what started as a series of small articles set me off on a quest to find more detailed information on the various Lambretta scooters. My quest was further enhanced by my being appointed the Vehicle Registrar for the LCGB. The six years that I spent as the LCGB's Vehicle Registrar also spurred me on to find ever more detailed information. It should be quite clear, then, that without the impetus from Kev and my role within the LCGB I would probably not have amassed the quantity of information that I have. To Kev and the LCGB Committee members who helped and supported me, I again would like to say a big thank you.

On a final note, I would like to dedicate this book to a number of *Lambretisti* who are no longer with us: Andy Astill, Pete Mullinder, Rex White, Dougie Bedford, John Manns, Martin Darroch, Peter Agg, Don Noys, Neville Frost, Eric Tudor, Frans Hollander, Mike Karslake, Terry Frankland, Pete Robinson, and the man who started it all, Ferdinando Innocenti. Every single one of them gave so much to the world of Lambretta that we know now. They paved the way for us to carry on the Lambretta tradition, and the world is a poorer place without them. What I can say is that they all shared information and inspiration with me, and for that I am eternally grateful. This book is therefore a tribute to them all.

Pete Davies
British Lambretta Archive

uno

A brief history of the Innocenti company

Ferdinando Innocenti began experimenting with possible applications for metal tubes in 1920 and, during that and the following decade, he undertook many projects, his Rome-based company, Fratelli Innocenti, producing tube scaffolding in 1933. In 1934 the World Cup was held in Italy and Innocenti was given the profitable task of building the new spectator stands.

The company had two factories – one in Rome and one in Milan – with smaller branch offices in Genoa, Naples, Bologne, Trieste, Cagliari, Palermo, Padua and Florence. Within the company four

An aerial view of the factory showing how expansive it was. (Courtesy Innocenti Motor Corporation)

divisions dealt with different areas: building; agriculture; industry; mechanical industry. In 1935 Innocenti decided to concentrate most of its production at the Milan factory.

During the Second World War, Innocenti supplied the bodies for 150kg and 250kg aeroplane bombs, this additional wartime production necessitating an increase in worker numbers at the Milan factory, with a plant for the construction of seamless tubes being completed in 1942. By the spring of 1943, the factory's workforce totalled some 7000 people.

When war ended, Ferdinando's plans for the company were threefold: firstly, he wanted to produce a low cost vehicle for the working classes; secondly, build machinery and industrial plants; and, finally, develop sintering processes. The low cost vehicle was to be the Lambretta, an idea which evolved from the small bikes used by British paratroopers. Ferdinando thought that there may be a lot of interest in such a vehicle, which would quickly provide a means of transport for the masses. He had a meeting with the Italian designer, Corandino D'Ascanio, but the two had different ideas about vehicle design; later, D'Ascanio went on to design the Vespa.

Another meeting was held with the designer, Pierre Luigi Torre (who was to become the father of the Lambretta scooter), but production of the scooter was delayed due to difficulty in obtaining supplies, and power shortages, coupled with the fact that the scooter was a new product for the company.

Twenty-five Lambretta scooters were nearing completion when two scooters and one van were shown at the 1947 Paris Exhibition. Throughout Italy trade agents were working to gain orders; 3300 were secured with supply planned for March 1948. However, instead of 150 Lambrettas being built daily as scheduled, poor organisation and lack of finances meant that actual production was just ten machines, although, by the following spring, this had risen to fifty machines per day.

By the end of 1948, 125M (Model A) production reached seventy a day. During the autumn, exports began to the United States and Argentina, as well as work on a successor to the Model A – the Model B – with production scheduled for 1949. By the end of October 1948, 9660 Model As had been produced. The company accounts of February 1949 showed a loss of 800 million lira. However, during the first three months of Model B production (which addressed many of the A's faults) this loss had dropped to 200 million lira, thanks to high sales of the new scooter.

Production was now more organised, and seventy machines a day were leaving the line in January 1949, rising to 150 a day by July that year. Increases in production were

J Range & Luna Line machines lined up in 1970.

Engine assembly in 1970.
(Courtesy Innocenti Motor Corporation)

planned, and sales surpassed all expectations as more models were introduced. By the time Model D production began, more than 8000 machines a month were being built, a total of 96,000 machines in 1952, 16,000 of which were exported.

Manufacturing licences had been granted to NSU in Germany, and a similar agreement was reached in France with SIT Lambretta. In 1955, Innocenti obtained a contract for the building of a factory in Venezuela. In the five year period between 1958 and 1963 Italy experienced an industrial boom, and production increased further at Innocenti. In 1959 the British Motor Corporation became involved with Innocenti and agreement was reached for the production of Austin 900 and Austin A40 cars.

In 1966, Ferdinando Innocenti died and was succeeded by his son, Luigi. Luigi's stint as head of Innocenti came at a time of change in Italy, with industrial unrest causing almost weekly strikes at the company. By this time most traditional scooter users had traded in their machines for small cars, the resultant decrease in demand meaning production of new models was not viable. Undeterred by this, Innocenti sought new designs; in 1967, Italian designer, Nuccio Bertone, was assigned the task of improving the Lambretta's design.

Bertone came up with the GP (DL) range and the Luna line. However, despite these attempts to refresh the Lambretta's design, Innocenti management was aware that the end of scooter production was just a matter of time.

In 1971, Luigi Innocenti left the company due to health problems, and the company was sold to Leyland. The plants were emptied and the assembly lines of the GP (DL) models sold to Scooters India Limited. The Innocenti company did continue but only in motorcar manufacture. During a relatively short history of scooter production and by the time the factory doors closed in 1971, a total of 2,147,914 Lambrettas (excluding mopeds and Lambros) had been built by Innocenti.

due

2

Model A to LC 125

In 1947 no-one could have doubted that a new scooter was on its way, with Italian radio station RAI broadcasting adverts to promote the arrival of the first Lambretta scooter. In fact, this first foray into scooter advertising saw Innocenti advertising a product that hadn't even been built. To ease public curiosity a wooden prototype of the forthcoming Lambretta was displayed. This new scooter was eagerly awaited and many dealers placed orders for it, and, in October 1947, the first examples of the model 125 M (or Model A) began to roll off of the production line. Initially though, the numbers weren't enough to keep up with demand. In fact by the start of 1948 the production line was only producing 50 scooters per day. This had improved by the summer of that year when Innocenti realised that they had built too many Model A machines and started to export them to Argentina where they were also eagerly snapped-up by Italian expatriates who wanted a piece of the homeland.

In October 1948 the engineers at Innocenti started to design a successor to their first scooter, along with providing minor design changes to the Model A. In December 1948 Innocenti presented the Model B Lambretta which had many improvements over the inaugural machine. These improvements included rear suspension, larger wheels and a gear change that was now

Front cover and opposite, top: inside pages of the 125M brochure; the model was launched in 1947. (Courtesy Innocenti Motor Corporation)

Lambretta 125m gioiello della meccanica moderna, il più pratico ed economico mezzo di trasporto

Telaio in acciaio, cambio di velocità con preselettore, trasmissione rigida con giunto elastico, sono garanzie della grande robustezza, del perfetto funzionamento, dell'integrità e della lunga durata del Motor-scooter Lambretta.

Sedile in gomma piuma su molle, forcella elastica su supporto antivibrante, pneumatici Pirelli a larga sezione, rendono estremamente confortevole viaggiare su Lambretta.

Rapida chiusura del portabagaglio, sistema di scappamento reso assai silenzioso, impianto di illuminazione di sicura efficacia, concorrono a completare l'organica praticità del Motor-scooter Lambretta.

CARATTERISTICHE DELLA Lambretta 125m

Telaio in lamiera di acciaio
Motore monocilindrico a due tempi
Cilindrata cmc 125 (mm 52x58)
Potenza effettiva CV 4,3 a 4000 giri
Lubrificazione a miscela: 5 % di olio
Trasmissione rigida con parastrappi
Frizione a dischi multipli
Cambio a tre velocità, comando a pedale
Accensione e impianto di illuminazione a mezzo di volano magnete
Altezza del sedile da terra cm 66
Freni a tamburo sulle due ruote
Pneumatici Pirelli 3,5x7 a bassa pressione
Peso circa Kg 55
Velocità 65/70 Km orari
Capacità serbatoio lt 6 - riserva lt 0,8
Consumo 1 lt di miscela ogni 50 Km
Autonomia circa 300 Km

COLORI DI SERIE

1 2 3 4 5 6

situated on the handlebars, as opposed to the foot gear change found on the Model A. As with the Model A, the Model B also received minor modifications during its production run and, by 1950, Innocenti were ready to launch another new model. The Model C was announced in the magazine *Notiziario Lambretta* alongside an enclosed model the LC (or Lusso C to give it its full name). The Model C and the LC saw Innocenti now building its scooters with sectional tubing for the frame, which for the LC meant that the scooter's bodywork could be bolted to it. Along with this change in design came a reduction in price which made the Model C affordable to many more people. Although some Model B Lambrettas had been privately imported to the UK, it was the Model C that saw official imports begin along with imports of the Model C. Constant improvements and refinements saw Innocenti's production increase from a total of 9669 Model A machines to 87,500 Model C scooters. By November 1951 Innocenti's total output for all of the machines from the Model A to the LC was some 174,683 scooters.

The Model A was radical in design but easy to operate, with a tubular frame that consisted of two sections. Economical and quick, it gave 110 miles to the gallon (89 kilometers per litre), and a top speed of 40-45mph (65-70kph). (Courtesy Roberto & Kimberley Morelli)

The 125 M/Model A

Cost (when new): 156,000 lira
Dimensions: Length 1620mm, width 650mm, height 880mm, weight, 72kg
Total production: 9669
Month of least production: October 1947 – 22 machines
Month of most production: September 1948 – 1750 machines

Even with the Model A, there was a desire to race. (Courtesy Rimini Lambretta Centre)

A Mark 2 Model A with a Tittarelli sidecar. (Courtesy Rimini Lambretta Centre)

A year after Piaggio had started production of the Vespa, Innocenti presented the world with the 125M, subsequently known as the Model A Lambretta. Between October and December 1947 a total of only 152 Model A machines were built. However, by the end of October 1948 a further 9517 examples had rolled off of the Milan production line. During its production the Model A saw some evolution as Innocenti worked on improving its first production scooter.

Interestingly, despite being built in 1947, the paperwork endorsed by the General Inspectorate of Civil Motorisation and Transport states that the design is in line with Act number 183 dated 29th October 1951.

Overall, the Model A was both economical and quick, providing 110 miles per gallon (39 kilometres per litre) and producing a top speed of 40-45 miles per hour (65-70 kilometres per hour). The scooter was radical in its design, but easy to operate. The frame was of a tubular design and consisted of two sections. The front end comprising a pressed steel main section connected to the steering head, which held the front forks. The rear section comprised two chromed tubes surrounding the fuel tank and connected to a pressed steel toolbox. The 123cc engine was direct air-cooled and shaft-driven, with a Dell'Orto MA 16 carburettor fitted. The gearbox was a three-speed item that was operated by foot via a rod mechanism, a system which was dropped on all subsequent Lambrettas. The suspension was basic, consisting of nothing at the rear of the scooter and only two bushes in the front forks. Early Model A machines had wheels featuring three nuts clamping the split rims together and fixing the wheel to the hub, but this arrangement caused a minor problem when the rider came to change the wheels as the tyre had to be let down in order for the wheel to be changed. Stopping power came in the form of drum brakes.

Production changes

1st version (running from frame 5001 to 6900 approximately): These first Model A machines had a mechanical horn which was operated via a pedal control. The seat was square in shape and made of leather. The rear toolbox had a key and ignition off switch. The wheel rims on this model were chrome items. The stand had a metal blade spring and a straight gear pedal was fitted. The light switch was a brown item.

2nd version (running from frame 6900 to 11,000 approximately): The horn was now an electronic item, the seat was triangular in shape and covered in imitation brown leather. The toolbox had no key and the wheels were now simply painted silver. A coil return spring was fitted to the stand and an inclined gear pedal used. The light switch was now a beige coloured item. Later models built within this production run had the brake pedal fitted on the left-hand side of the legshields.

3rd version (running from frame 11,000 to c.14,700): A larger front seat was now fitted with a central spring and was now covered in brown imitation leather. The saddle support was made of light alloy. The stand was now a cast iron item.

Did you know?

Model A returns to Milan. In 1968, to celebrate

the 21st birthday of the Lambretta, Ken Peters (who worked for Arthur Francis in Watford) and Peter Lumley (editor of *Scootering & Lightweights* magazine) undertook a journey to Rimini for the 21st Lambretta birthday rally. Ken rode a Model A while Peter rode a Super Starstream. Months prior to the trip the Model A had been languishing in a disassembled state in the workshop at Arthur Francis' establishment. The Model A, a 1947-built machine, was rebuilt and renovated within the workshop. The Model A completed the trip to and from the rally, even traversing the Gotthard Pass and on its return to England it had clocked up 1500 miles in 5 days.

What the tester said

A road test of the Model A was conducted by *Motorcycling* magazine in 1948; however I have been unable to locate a copy of it.

November 1948 saw the introduction of the Model B. Innocenti had learnt lessons from its production of the Model A, and its successor incorporated improved mechanical and structural design. (Courtesy Roberto & Kimberley Morelli)

The Model B

Cost (when new): 170,000 lira
Dimensions: Length 1680mm, width 650mm, height 900mm, weight, 60kg
Total production: 35,014
Month of least production: November 1948 – 464 machines
Month of most production: September 1949 – 3356 machines

Unveiled in November 1948 the Model B looked like its predecessor the Model A, however, Innocenti had learnt lessons from its production of the Model A. The Model B now incorporated improved mechanical and structural designs. The biggest change was effected upon the scooter's suspension which was now a coil spring and damper mounted horizontally under the engine and a knuckle joint providing suspension at the rear. The front suspension came in the form of a spring in the front forks. The main design of the frame saw Innocenti using a central tubular frame with chrome double tubes bent over the fuel tank and engine (thus supporting the driver and pillion seats). The three-speed gear change was improved from the Model A foot-operated system and was now a Teleflex system using a handlebar mounted twist grip which was located on the left-hand side of the handlebars. Ride, stability and smoothness came with the introduction of eight inch wheels. On the legshields Innocenti mounted a speedometer which was driven by a cog on the front wheel. The 123cc engine fitted to the Model B produced 4.3bhp with a top speed of 44mph. Fitted to the engine was a Dell'Orto MA 16 carburettor.

The Model B was a popular machine and was

The Model B's front suspension took the form of a spring in the front forks. (Courtesy Roberto & Kimberley Morelli)

With the Model B, Innocenti again used a central tubular frame with chrome double tubes bent over the fuel tank and engine (thus supporting the driver and pillion seats). (Courtesy British Lambretta Archive)

used in racing circles, and even achieved success in setting world speed and endurance records. The racing Model Bs had a special exhaust and an enlarged fuel tank along with a larger carburettor. Engines were modified and a lighter frame used with a streamlined cowling over the front wheel.

Throughout its production run the Model B was exported worldwide to countries such as Australia, India and Egypt.

It is interesting to note, that although the scooter was not officially imported into the United Kingdom, in the May 1959 edition of *Motorcycle Mechanics* the Model B Lambretta is listed, stating this was the original Lambretta first imported into this country in 1950-51. Most of them were used for sales demonstrations, but there were still a number about and on the second-hand market. In 1968 a Model B (bearing the registration 'LLN 521') appeared on the Lambretta Concessionaires stand at the Belle Vue show, as part of a 20 Year Revolution display.

Production run changes

1st version (to frame 20,000): Heel-operated brake pedal. Internal clutch control. Light switch on headlamp. Cylindrical rubber stops between fuel tank and toolbox. Kickstart lever with vertical spline.

2nd version (to frame 40,000): Toe-operated brake pedal. External clutch control. Light switch on right-hand lever (on the first 5000 of this version). Earth switch on frame. Fuel tank and toolbox rubber strap eliminated. Kickstart with horizontal spline.

3rd version (to end of production): Toolbox support buffers eliminated. Internal rear suspension leverage increased.

Did you know?

Beaulieu Model B. 1960 saw one of the first two Lambretta scooters that had been imported in 1948, offered to the National Motor Museum. The original owner had reluctantly decided that he needed something more modern so got in touch with Lambretta Concessionaires and they found that the scooter was in almost showroom condition. Concessionaires took the machine on and Derek Miller (Lambretta Sales Manager) handed the scooter, bearing the registration 'DPR 872,' over to Graham Walker, head of the motorcycle section at the museum.

What the tester said

"The engine transmission unit, comprising the 125cc two-stroke engine, clutch, three-speed gearbox and final shaft-drive is as neat and sturdy a production as one could wish to see. Forming an integral part of the main frame the unit is made accessible by merely unscrewing two bolts, disconnecting the petrol line and swinging up the pivoted 'superstructure' which contains the rear mudguard, the petrol tank and luggage boot. These two latter components are respectively concealed under the saddle and pillion – yes, a pillion on a '125.'" – *Motorcycling* July 21st 1949

The Model C

Cost (when new): £125 13s 6d

Dimensions: Length 1730mm, width 730mm, height 920mm, weight 70kg

A 1950s illustration of a Model C. (Courtesy Innocenti Motor Corporation)

Production: 87,500
Month of least production: February 1950 – 1870 machines
Month of most production: July 1951 – 5560 machines
Launched in February 1950 the Model C Lambretta was the first Lambretta officially imported into the United Kingdom. Innocenti had continued to learn lessons from their previous models, and now moved

A Model B at Beaulieu undergoes its 10-year test in the early 1960s. (Courtesy Scooter World)

Having learnt many lessons from previous models, Innocenti built the C using a single tubular frame design. (Courtesy Ryan & Abbi Israelsen)

Front suspension on the Model C was by way of a trailing-link.
(Courtesy Ryan & Abbi Israelsen)

As with the Models A & B, owners of the Model C utilised the scooter for racing.
(Courtesy Lambro Motori)

on to a single tubular frame design. With this new model came an increase in production with between 7000-8000 being assembled per month, as opposed to the 3000 per month figure for the Model B. Coupled with this was the machine's lower selling price, which further aided sales. The tubular steel frame housed the fuel tank below the front seat and a toolbox was fitted under the passenger seat. The bicycle style handlebars (which were initially those from the Model B) had a large round headlight fitted with a smaller round light being fitted at the rear of the scooter above the number plate. The engine block was now integral with the frame so that rear suspension was achieved by using a spring compressed by an axial tie-rod. At the front of the scooter a trailing-link was used to provide suspension. Stopping power was achieved by drum brakes at the front and rear, with the rear brake being foot-operated by a rod mechanism. The brakes were also uprated items which had the brake linings on the brake shoes and aluminium drums. To give a smoother ride with improved cornering, Innocenti fitted the Model C with 4.00 x 8 inch wheels.

The 123cc engine followed the lead set by the Model B and used a Teleflex gear changing system. Bore/stroke was kept at 52mm x 58mm producing 4.3bhp at 4200rpm with a top speed of 44mph. The Dell'Orto MA 16 carburettor that was found on the Model B was also retained on the Model C. It should be noted that a Zenith carburettor was fitted to some machines. One unusual feature of the Model C engine was the flywheel which had a plain face; engine cooling being achieved by the forward motion of the scooter. Ignition and lighting came via a Marelli flywheel.

Production of the Model C ceased in November 1951.

Production changes

See production changes for the LC 125

Did you know?

118mph Model C! On April 14th 1951 a specially prepared Model C, ridden by Romolo Ferri, completed a flying km at a speed of 118mph and a flying mile in 116.5mph. The engine was practically standard. However, it had been tuned, and now featured a rotary charger and the clutch had an extra plate fitted. The gearbox remained unchanged. As the rotary charger was fitted where the flywheel magneto would usually have been as an alternative form of ignition was employed, this was a simple circuit consisting of a coil and battery. A Dell'Orto carburettor was used.

A Model C with a Longhi sidecar attached. (Courtesy Rimini Lambretta Centre)

At maximum speed the engine produced 16bhp and revved to over 9000rpm. Covering the scooter was a streamlined shell which had been tested by Innocenti in a wind tunnel. A transparent panel in the front of the cover provided vision for the rider. The 3.00 x 12 inch tyres were specially prepared by Pirelli. The fuel was a mix of petrol (gasoline), benzole and methanol.

What the tester said

Despite extensive searching no road tests have been found for this model.

The LC Lambretta

Cost (when new): £145 13s 6d
Dimensions: Length 1740mm, width 730mm, height 920mm, weight, 80kg
Total production: 42,500
Month of least production: April 1950 – 399 machines
Month of most production: September 1951 – 2640 machines

Two months after the launch of the Model C, Innocenti introduced the LC Lambretta, with the initials standing for Lusso C. This was the company's first fully enclosed scooter, giving the

125 LC

A 1950s illustration of the LC 125. (Courtesy Innocenti Motor Corporation)

An LC 125 with a Frontalini sidecar attached. (Courtesy Rimini Lambretta Centre)

Once the Lusso C's sidepanels are removed the engine can be seen. (Courtesy Rimini Lambretta Centre)

scooter-buying public a glimpse of the future and, ultimately, Innocenti's long-term plan. The LC was a huge success in Europe and dominated sales in places such as Egypt and Morocco, with the bodywork protecting the rider and engine from weather and road debris. Again, the scooter utilised a single tubular frame on to which the bodywork was bolted. The 123cc engine unit was enclosed by side panels with the right-hand panel having an access flap so that the carburettor could be tickled in cold weather. The flap also enabled access for the rider to turn the scooter's fuel supply on or off. Further changes to the bodywork saw the legshields lengthened so that they went up to the handlebars. Rear footboards were now fitted and, under the rider's seat, there was a small toolbox. As with the Model C, the LC had 4.00 x 8 inch wheels fitted, along with the now uprated braking system.

The 123cc, three-speed engine unit was the same as that fitted to the Model C and, again, utilised the Teleflex gear change system. However, on the LC the cylinder had a cowling giving a direct and positive airflow over it, independent of any forward motion of the scooter. Unlike the plain-faced flywheel of the Model C, the LC had a flywheel with cast blades on it, making it, in effect, a fan supplying cooling air to the engine.

November 1951 also saw the end of LC production run.

Production changes (for both Model C & LC)

1st version (for those machines built in 1950): Irregular quadrangular box receiving the gear cable, engraved with 'Teleflex.' Model B-type handlebars, levers with 59mm x 10mm section lever mounts. Toolbox with single clasp only.
2nd version (for those machines built in 1951): Shield-shaped box with no writing on it. Smaller handlebar levers with 44mm x 10mm lever mounts. Reinforced rear damper mount.

Did you know?

1959 ACU Rally. In 1959 Birmingham Lambretta Club entered four scooters in that year's ACU Rally: 3 Li 150s and an LC. The LC being ridden by Geoff Biddle. Total mileage for the event was 600 miles, which all the scooters completed with some 20 minutes to spare. The LC provided no trouble for Biddle, unlike one of the Li machines for its rider.

What the tester said

Despite extensive searching, no road tests have been found for this model.

Model D & LD ranges

Whether used for social or sporting purposes, LD Lambrettas were popular (see also overleaf, top left).
(Courtesy Cambridge Lambretta Workshop/Power & Pedal)

Towards the end of 1951 Innocenti, launched two new scooters: the Model D and the LD (or Lusso D to give it its correct title). Again, Innocenti had looked at its previous scooters and changes were made to design and performance for the new models. Although, aesthetically, the Model D and the LD looked liked their predecessors, the Model C and LC, they were actually very different. The tubular frame had been slightly lengthened (the Model C being 1730mm long compared to the 1770mm of the Model D) in order to accommodate a new suspension set-up and other minor modifications. Along with this. Innocenti introduced other technical improvements to the scooter's engine. Again the Model D and LD featured shaft-drive, although the engine had been simplified. One noticeable improvement was concerned the suspension. Innocenti now used a torsion bar system at the front of the engine, providing improved comfort for the rider and flexibility for the engine. At the front of the scooter Innocenti improved the suspension by putting springs inside the fork tubes to act as shock absorbers. Improvements were also made to the exhaust which was revised and enlarged.

1953 saw Innocenti introducing numerous mechanical improvements to both the Model D and the LD, including improvements to the front brake, rubber engine mounts (to cut vibration) and the use of a Bowden cable for the rear brake. As well as these mechanical improvements, the

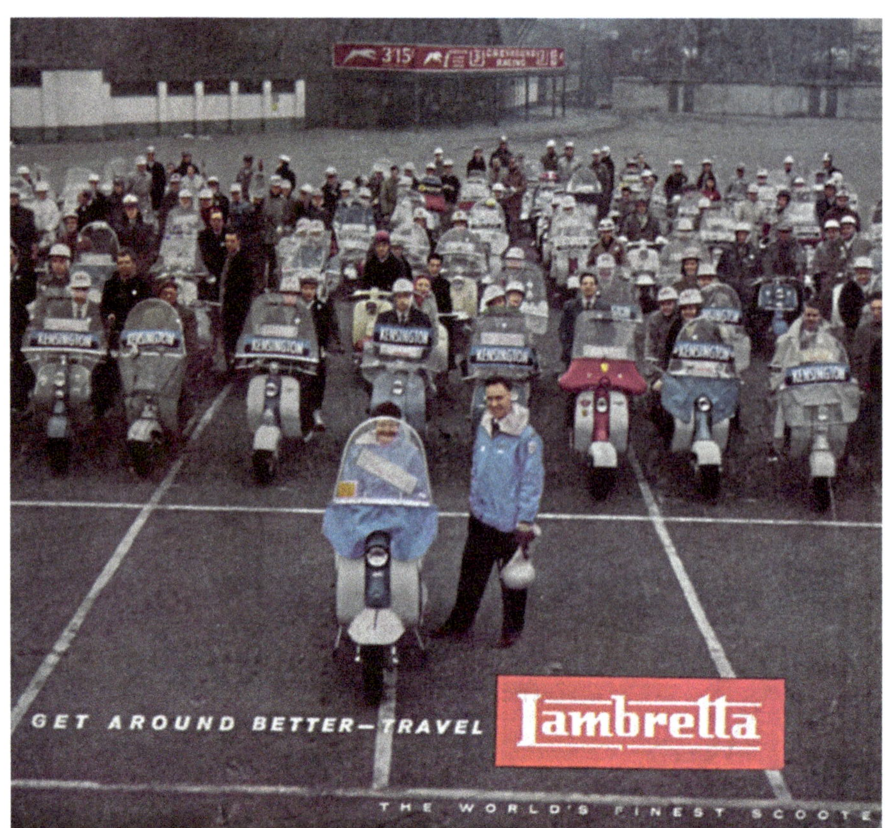

GET AROUND BETTER—TRAVEL
Lambretta
THE WORLD'S FINEST SCOOTE

36
MI-TA 2006

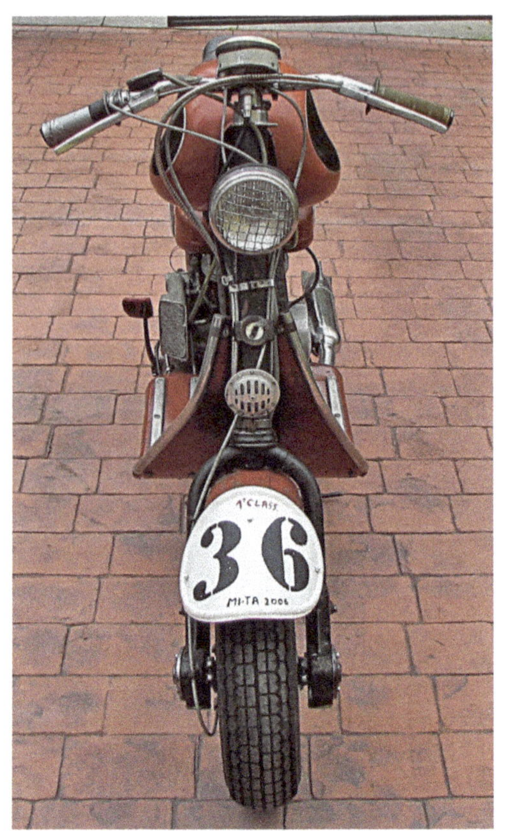

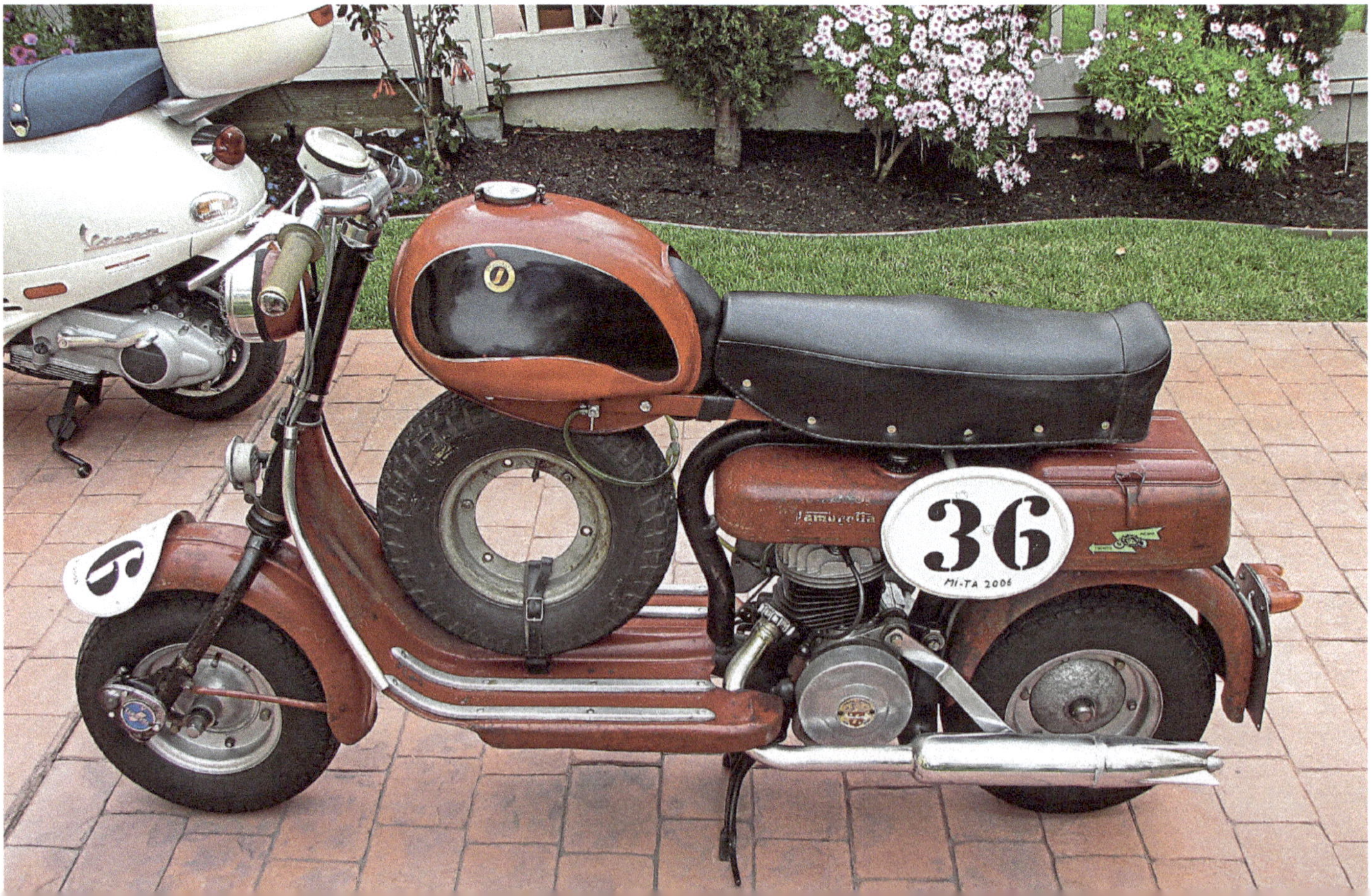
36
MI-TA 2006

Opposite, top right and bottom: Model D Lambrettas became popular with scooter racers in 1950s Italy. Note the spare wheel position on this machine, the addition of a larger fuel tank, and the use of a 'bench' seat.
(Courtesy Roberto & Kimberley Morelli)

bodywork of the LD was revised with the side panels now having kidney-shaped grilles and there was now a badge being fixed to the legshield to show the scooter's identity. Continued refinements meant that by 1954 further changes had taken place: the seats were now dark green (they had previously been brown) and an electric start version of the LD was introduced. This had larger seats and grey plastic sheathing covered the cables.

Up until 1954 the Model D had been dominant in terms of sales, although this was to change as the LD became the popular choice for scooterists. Innocenti didn't rest on its laurels though, and the Motosalone Internazionale di Milano was the venue for the company to announce the introduction of the Model D 150 and the LD 150. Along with the increase in engine capacity was a change from the Teleflex gear change system to double cable operation, an improved gearbox and forced air cooling for the engine were now features on both the Model D and the LD. By the end of 1954 production of the Model D 125 and the LD 125 ceased. Production of the 150cc versions continued with Innocenti bringing in continued improvements, especially to items such as the kick-start which was altered on a least four occasions.

By the end of 1955, partly as a result of export market requests, an electric start version of the LD 150 was produced and the introduction of the battery it required improved the overall performance and reliability of the machine. The following year saw a new LD 125 being introduced although in order to make it competitive in the market place, many economy measures took place such as cheaper seats being used, no protective sheathing for the control cables and a simplified electrical system. By the end of the year production of the Model D 150 had ceased.

Innocenti continued building and refining the LD 150 and, on 2nd February 1957, it unveiled a new LD 150 at the Centro Studi. Efforts had been made to make this model more reliable and part of this effort was the introduction of an epicyclical kick-start mechanism and a longer kick-start pedal. Other improvements included a handlebar cover that housed the horn and speedometer, better electrics, a larger rear light and the toolbox was now part of the frame, housed behind the passenger seat. An electric start version of this improved model was also unveiled, with the main change being the moving of the toolbox to a position behind the legshields so that the batteries could be housed behind the passenger seat. 1957 also saw (during March, May and June) 52 electric start LD 125s being built as a special order.

Production of the LD ceased in 1957 by which time sales of it and the Model D variants had helped to make Lambretta a household name worldwide. In 1959 Anthony Hutt and Graham Rex set off on a 20,000 mile journey from London to Australia on a Mark 3 LD 150, proving how much faith people had in these machines.

The Model D 125 (Mark 1)

Cost (when new): 135,000 lira
Dimensions: Length 1770mm, width 740mm, height 960mm, weight 70kg
Total production: 69,000
Month of least production: January 1953 – 459 machines
Month of most production: September 1952 – 6940 machines

December 1951 saw Innocenti introduce the 125 Model D, which sported a redesigned tubular frame but retained the fuel tank under the rider's seat and the toolbox under the passenger seat and short legshields. Unlike previous models, the front fork tubes now enclosed the front suspension springs and the rear suspension was provided by means of a torsion bar. The 123cc engine had a bore/stroke of 52mm x 58mm and produced 5bhp at 4800rpm and gave a top speed of 47mph. The engine featured a cast iron cylinder with an air-cooled aluminium cylinder head and a Dell'Orto MA 18 B3 carburettor. The ignition HT coil was built into the magneto as with on previous models. Finned drum brakes were fitted at the front and rear of the scooter. Production of the Model D 125 ceased in January 1953.

Production changes

1st Version: (December 1951 to mid 1952):
The handlebar was chromed steel with aluminium end caps. Small Model C-type front brake, rod actuated rear brake with a small pedal. Saddle frame with Model C-type conical tool tube, cap closed with a clip. Black, two position, light switch with chrome cover, horn with flower grille, smooth fork covers. Engine mounted on plain bearings. Earliest examples had rear toolbox that used a Model C-type clasp. Early 125 Ds had a second porthole on the engine cover, close to the torsion bar mount, that was intended to allow fitment of a return damper – though this facility was never utilised.

2nd Version (Mid 1952 to end of production): Larger rear brake pedal fitted and cable operation now used. Fork covers now had indents for larger bushes. Engine now mounted on silent blocks.

Did you know?
A 1966 Lambretta Club of Great Britain vintage run to Brighton saw a Mark 1 D 125 win the oldest machine award. The 13 year old scooter, owned by Christine Jackson of the Rakes Lambretta Club (Epping Forest), was first registered on 16th April 1953.

What the tester said
"Some criticism might be levelled against the weather protection. While the legshield-cum-footboard is adequate to protect the riders feet from road filth, the shield is too narrow and too short to afford sufficient defence against wind and rain. When riding in wet weather, full length leg and body waterproofs were required. Another criticism concerns the reserve fuel tap which, on average London roads, provided sufficient fuel for no more than one mile. No parking light is fitted." – *The Motor Cycle* February 26th 1953

The LD 125 (Mark 1)

Cost (when new): 158,000 lira
Dimensions: Length 1770mm, width 740mm, height 960mm, weight 85kg
Total production: 53,197
Month of least production: December 1951 – 137 machines
Month of most production: January 1953 – 7781 machines

Production of the LD 125 began alongside that of the Model D 125 in December 1951. However, unlike the Model D, the LD featured fully redesigned bodywork with legshields, footboards and side panels. As with the LC, the LD had a flap in the right-hand side panel which gave the rider access to the fuel tap, the choke and the carburettor. The side panels had two 'port holes' at the rear which had chrome ring trims. Single seats were fitted as standard. Handlebars were unenclosed items beneath which was an Innocenti badge. The LD 125 also used the same engine unit as that found on the Model D 125. The single seats were mid brown in colour and had an 'Aquila Continentale' badge on the rear. It is interesting to note that the rear seat could either be triangular or rectangular. Production of the Mark 1 LD 125 ceased in May 1953 when the last 689 machines rolled off of the production line.

Production changes
1st Version (December 1951 to mid 1952): The handlebar was chromed steel with aluminium end caps. Small Model C-type front brake, rod actuated rear brake with a small pedal. Black two position light switch with chrome cover, horn with flower grille, smooth fork covers. Engine mounted on plain bearings. Earliest examples had rear toolbox that used a Model C-type clasp. Early 125 LDs had a second porthole on the engine cover, close to the torsion bar mount, that was intended to allow fitment of a return damper – though this facility was never utilised. Side panels with two portholes with chrome rings, Lambretta script in aluminium on the legshield, Innocenti badge fitted above the headlamp.

2nd Version (Mid 1952 to end of production): Larger rear brake pedal fitted and cable operation now used. Fork covers now had indents for larger bushes. Engine now mounted on silent blocks.

What the tester said
"Fuel consumption for the journey was excellent, working out at almost 100mpg. This, despite the fact that the large frontal surface presented by the windscreen and shielding doubtless causes considerable drag, though the excellent protection they afford is adequate compensation. Moreover, they do not render the machine unmanageable even in gusty winds. The exhaust note tends to be noisy though not unpleasant. On the other hand the electric horn's note could be stronger and more tuneful with advantage. Another drawback is the absence of a parking light – surprising given in view of the fact that the Lambretta is primarily a town machine."
– *Motorcycling* February 19th 1953

The Model D 125 (Mark 2)

Cost (when new): 135,000 lira
Dimensions: Length 1770mm, width 740mm, height 960mm, Weight 70kg
Total production: 53,641
Month of least production: June 1953 – 0 machines
Month of most production: March 1954 – 5260 machines

Innocenti introduced the Mark 2 D 125 in April 1953 with the production run lasting until October 1954. In essence, the scooter was similar to its Mark 1 predecessor utilising the same frame (with shortened legshields, fuel tank under the front seat and toolbox under the passenger seat). The Mark 2 also utilised the same 123cc engine, which had a Dell'Orto MA 18 B2 carburettor fitted although there were no other significant changes. With a bore/stroke of 52mm x 58mm the engine produced 5bhp at 4600rpm giving a top speed of 47mph. The braking system was not uprated and

Although the Model D looked liked its predecessor, the Model C, it was actually very different. The tubular frame had been slightly lengthened by 40mm in order to accommodate a new suspension setup. (Courtesy Rimini Lambretta Centre)

Along with the increase in engine capacity came an improved gearbox and forced air cooling. (Courtesy Lambro Motori)

remained in the form of finned drum brakes at the front and rear of the scooter. However, the rear brake was now a cable-operated item as opposed to the rod-operated system found on the Mark 1 machine. The gearbox was still a three-speed item using a Teleflex hand change. The handlebars were redesigned but still had a bicycle-type appearance.

Production changes

Adjustable handlebar in aluminium with plastic levers. Front brake enlarged to 125mm. Passenger grab rail incorporated into rear saddle. Two-position light switch in ivory-coloured plastic. From February 1953 the horn had a traditional grille fitted. Toolbox supplied with lid that could be locked.

What the tester said

Despite extensive searching a road test has not been found for this machine.

The LD 125 (Mark 2)

Cost (when new): 158,000 lira
Dimensions: Length 1770mm, width 740mm, height

One noticeable improvement on the Model D was its suspension. Innocenti now used a torsion bar system at the front of the engine, providing improved comfort for the rider and flexibility for the engine. (Courtesy Lambretta Concessionaires)

At the front Innocenti improved the Model D's suspension by inserting springs inside the fork tubes to act as shock absorbers. (Courtesy British Lambretta Archive)

Popular throughout the 1950s the LD was a staple of club life. (Courtesy Lambro Motori)

960mm, weight 85kg
Total production: 78,468
Month of least production: February 1955 – 9 machines
Month of most production: June 1954 – 5767 machines

Two months after the launch of the Mark 2 Model D 125, Innocenti launched the Mark 2 LD 125. Mounted on its redesigned legshields, the Mark 2 machine carried a red and gold plastic shield-shaped badge that simply had the letters 'LD' on it. Early examples of this machine had a flap in the right-hand side panel, thus facilitating access to the choke, carburettor and fuel tap. Later models had the choke and fuel tap mounted on the frame behind the driver's seat. Underneath the right-hand panel, Innocenti fitted a small toolbox. Unlike the Mark 1 machines that had chrome 'port holes' on the side panels the Mark 2's side panels had kidney shaped grilles, which on the early machines were made of white plastic and on later machines chromed steel. The Mark 2 machine retained the same engine unit as its predecessor using a three-speed gearbox with a Teleflex hand change. Some of the early models had aluminium cowlings to aid cooling of the engine. On early Mark 2 machines the seats were fitted with brown covers, whilst later models carried green seat covers. Production of the Mark 2 LD 125 ceased in November 1956.

Production changes

1st Version (June 1953 to 1954): Adjustable handlebar in aluminium with plastic levers. Front brake enlarged to 125mm. Passenger grab rail incorporated into rear saddle. Two position light switch in ivory-coloured plastic. From Feb 1953 the horn had the traditional grille fitted. Early 1953 machines came fitted with Mark 1 side panels. The side panels were later changed and then had grilles fitted (initially grey plastic) instead of the two 'port holes.' Plastic red and gold LD badge fitted to the legshields.
2nd Version (1954 to mid 1955): Exhaust with chrome expansion box. Beige plastic grilles on side panels. Three notch gear change. Floorboard runners with rubber inserts. On early examples the ignition HT coil was inside the flywheel magneto.
3rd Version (mid 1956 to end of production): Exhaust without expansion box and two brass inspection caps. Side panel air vents now in chromed metal. Five notch gear change. Chromed steel handlebars. Control cables with lubricators. Cylinder intake manifold with central crest for the attachment screws.

Did you know?

1961 saw student Jeff Wharton completing a 4000 mile continental trip on his 1953 LD 125 (Mark 2). '6206 H' had a spotlight mounted on the front mudguard, ex-War Department panniers, and map holders amongst other modifications. Joining Jeff on the trip was his brother who rode a 1956 LD 150. The trip saw them crossing France, Belgium, Switzerland, Italy, Austria, Yugoslavia and Germany. The torsion bar suspension had to be replaced twice after Jeff broke it on (ironically) rough Italian mountain roads.

What the tester said

"Ease of riding is important in a vehicle intended to appeal to the lay public as well as to motorcyclists. Steering was light but accurate from a slow crawl up to the machines downhill maximum speed of over 50mph and the low centre of gravity gave excellent stability. Hands off riding was easy at any speed above 15mph. The combination of a good steering lock, outstandingly smooth transmission (the engine had only to be under light load to two-stroke evenly) and a 14.3 to 1 bottom gear endowed the Lambretta with excellent traffic threading manners and amply compensated for the small capacity of the engine." – *The Motorcycle* 6th May 1954

The Model D 150 (Mark 2)

Cost (when new): £134 4s 1d
Dimensions: Length 1770mm, width 740mm, height 960mm, weight 75kg
Total production: 33,758
Month of least production: October 1954 – 18 machines
Month of most production: March 1955 – 4411 machines

A move to a larger capacity 148cc engine saw Innocenti launch the Model D 150 in October 1954. The Model D frame was retained. The 148cc engine had a bore/stroke of 57mm x 58mm and produced 6bhp at 4800rpm, giving a top speed of 50mph. A cowling was now fitted round the cylinder and a fan on the flywheel provided forced air cooling for the engine. Gone was the Teleflex gear change, replaced by a two cable set-up. Coupled with this, the rear brake was also now cable-operated unlike the previous rod set-up. The refinements to the model didn't stop there, the exhaust being redesigned with a separate chrome expansion pipe. A D150 badge was fitted on to the legshields which were also fitted with pressed aluminium floor runners. Suspension remained in the form of the tried and tested torsion bar system with an hydraulic damper at the rear and two rocker and two coil springs in grease-tight units at the front of the scooter. Production of the Mark 2 ceased in December 1955 with 2625 machines being built in the last month of manufacture.

Production changes

1st Version (October 1954 to mid 1955): Handlebar in aluminium Electrics (non battery) & without current rectifier, 14mm piston gudgeon pin. Cylindrical power socket at the flywheel. Three-speed gearbox. Smooth starter casing (small bush on the cover of the last examples made mid-1955). Exhaust with chromed expansion box.
2nd Version (mid 1955 to mid 1956): Electrics with battery and rectifier. Starter casing with three screw cover. Exhaust with chromed expansion box. Less inclined rear damper location.
3rd Version (mid 1956 to end of production): Silencer without expansion box, two brass inspection caps. 16mm gudgeon pin. Additional oil vent on final drive. Quadrangular power socket on flywheel attached with a screw. Control cables with lubricators at steering head. Cylinder intake manifold with central crest for the attachment screws. Chromed steel handlebars. Five notch gear change. Additional left-hand screw on the rear hub nut.

Did you know?

Model D climbs to the top of Ben Nevis! Saturday 15th June 1957 saw two brand new Mark 2 D 150s being ridden from Edinburgh-based Lambretta dealers, Alexanders, to Fort William by Geoff Parker and Lewis 'Ludo' Moore. The 140 mile trip essentially seeing the scooters being 'run in.'
On Sunday 16th, the pair (accompanied by 13 helpers) set off up a goat track that led up towards the summit of Ben Nevis. Due to the terrain the scooters had to be manhandled in temperatures exceeding 80 degrees Fahrenheit. At the 2000ft mark, Ludo Moore had to give up due to his scooter suffering from clutch slip. Geoff Parker carried on, and five hours later he reached the summit (4400ft). It then took a further two and a half hours to get the scooter back down the mountain.

What the tester said

"First impressions on taking over the machine were that the extra power was out of proportion to the small increase in cylinder capacity. Acceleration from standstill left most other vehicles well behind and the rapid changes made by the twist-grip controlled gear shift added to this fast getaway characteristic. The gear control has a more positive locating device than on the earlier machines and there is an audible click at each engagement so that there is no doubt about the gear being right home. Second gear takes the machine from walking pace to well over 30mph. Top can be engaged at around 10mph and the

[hand] grip brutally opened to achieve smooth acceleration without protest." – *The Scooter* May 1955

Mark 2 LDs sported a small toolbox underneath the right-hand side panel. (Courtesy Lambro Motori)

The LD 150 (Mark 2)

Cost (when new): £164 15s 2d
Dimensions: Length 1770mm, width 740mm, height 960mm, Weight 88kg
Total production: 110,186
Month of least production: November 1954 – 171 machines
Month of most production: February 1956 – 6990 machines

November 1954 saw production of a 150cc version of the LD. The frame was now deeper and the bodywork and panelling were utilised for strength. Mounted on the left-hand legshield was a blue and white shield-shaped badge which had '150' written in gold on it. The legshields had six aluminium runners fitted which had rubber inserts and end caps fitted. Situated behind the legshields was a glove box that housed the speedometer and a clock, with the toolbox being an integral part of the frame and situated above the rear mudguard. The fuel tap and choke lever were now located behind the rider's seat. As with the Mark 2 Model D 150, the LD 150 retained the same 148cc engine unit fitted with a Dell'Orto MA 19 B4 carburettor. Between 1956-57 some transitional LDs appeared that had Mark 2 front ends but sported Mark 3 bodywork. These also had a streamlined rear light unit and an improved engine. The last two months of production saw Innocenti manufacture 5718 machines solely for the UK market (840 being made in December 1956 and 4878 being made in January 1957).

Production changes

1st Version (October 1954 to mid 1955): Handlebar in aluminium. Electrics (non battery) and without current rectifier. 14mm piston gudgeon pin. Cylindrical power socket at the flywheel. Three-speed gearbox. Smooth starter casing (small bush on the cover of the last examples made mid-1955). Exhaust with chromed expansion box.

Situated behind the legshields on the Mark 2 LD was a glovebox that also housed the speedometer and a clock. (Courtesy Lambro Motori)

2nd Version (mid 1955 to mid 1956): Exhaust with chromed expansion box. Less inclined rear damper location. Beige plastic grilles fitted to the side panels.

3rd Version (mid 1956 to end of production): Silencer without expansion box, two brass inspection caps, 16mm piston gudgeon pin. Additional oil vent on final drive. Quadrangular power socket on flywheel attached with a screw. Control cables with lubricators at steering head. Cylinder intake manifold with central crest for the attachment screws. Chromed steel handlebars. Five notch gear change. Additional left-hand screw on the rear hub nut. Bump stops with screws supporting the side panels, longer side panel handles and side panel grilles in chromed metal.

Did you know?

Round the World LD. 1963 saw 23 year old Australian salesman Adrian Timothy reach the halfway mark of his 40,000 mile round the world trip on a Lambretta. The Mark 2 LD 150 had been bought by Adrian for £28. The halfway mark for him being Belfast. He planned to return back to Australia in 1967 by which time he hoped to have visited America and the Far East.

What the tester said

"The Lambretta LD provided economical, trouble-free transport – just as thousands of similar models are doing at this moment in half the countries of Europe. It would be a safe bet to prophesy enhanced popularity for the marque here, now that this latest and best Lambretta is generally available." – *Motorcycling* 1954

"Scooters are, by virtue of their large frontal area, normally fairly thirsty. However, few could quarrel with the steady overall average of 75mpg which the Lambretta returned over a 30 mile plus, twice daily run, each leg of which included 17 miles or so of London and its traffic and terminated with some 10 miles of blinding on open roads. With a gentler hand on the throttle, this figure – which was coupled with a 30mph road average – could easily be bettered as the test figures show. Powerful and penetrating, the headlamp gave a beam more than adequate for the machine's performance." – *Motorcycling* 24th March 1955

The Model D 125 (Mark 3)

Cost (when new): 135,000 lira
Dimensions: Length 1770mm, width 740mm, hight 960mm, weight 70kg
Total production: 500
Month of least production: May 1956 – 50 machines
Month of most production: May 1955 – 200 machines

With a production run of no more than 500 machines it was thought that the Mark 3 Model D 125 was brought into production as a special order in May 1955. However, a close look at the production figures shows that this wasn't the case. May 1955 was the first month of production for this model, which had no redesign or refinements: the standard Model D frame was used along with the standard 123cc engine which had a Dell'Orto MA 18 B4 carburettor. 200 machines left the Innocenti plant in May 1955, followed by 150 in June 1955, 50 in 1956 and finally 100 in November 1956 which was the last month of production for this model.

Production changes

No known production changes for this model.

Did you know?

Folding Model D. A folding Model D 125 was designed in November 1956 for use by the military. It had a 123cc engine which was basically that of the later model D's with a three-speed gearbox. The machine was capable of climbing up gradients of 1 in 4 and had a top speed of 42mph. The frame was the usual open D-type design, however, it was made from high tensile steel to take the stress of riding on rough terrain and being dropped from an aircraft. The frame could be folded in half so that it could be stored in containers prior to being air dropped. The scooter's tyres were 3.50 x 8 inch items. There was an adjustable support on the handlebars for an automatic weapon and a headlight could be fitted instantly. As far as is known, none of these machines (other than prototypes) were ever manufactured.

What the tester said

Despite extensive searching no known road tests have been found for this model.

The LDA 150 (Mark 2)

Cost (when new): £179 17s 6d
Dimensions: Length 1770mm, width 740mm, height 960mm, weight 94kg
Total production: 2020
Month of least production: January 1956 – 5 machines
Month of most production: September 1956 – 440 machines

Innocenti started production of an electric start LD 150 in September 1955. The 12 volt system on the scooter was facilitated by linking two six volt batteries side by side at the rear of the scooter. The only giveaway being a small 'hump' behind the rear seat. A rectifier was fitted under

The 12 volt system on the Mark 2 LDA was achieved by linking two six volt batteries side-by-side at the rear of the scooter. The only giveaway was a small 'hump' behind the rear seat. (Courtesy Roberto & Kimberley Morelli)

LDA models had the distinctive 'LD AVV' legshield badge. (Courtesy Roberto & Kimberley Morelli)

The Mayfair model was produced by Lambretta Concessionaires in the UK, with some additional extras: spare wheel; rear carrier; heel plates; footboard extensions and saver borders. (Courtesy Lambro Motori)

the rider's seat to help with cooling. The scooter's starter motor was actuated by a lever on the left-hand side of the handlebars. Innocenti used a redesigned starter motor on this model, and this was located under the footboards. Battery power now meant that the scooters horn and headlight could be powered without the engine running. The LDA again used the 148cc engine with no major modifications. Manufacture of the LDA 150 (Mark 2) ceased in November 1956.

Production changes

1st Version (mid 1955 to mid 1956): Electrics with battery and rectifier. Starter casing with three screw cover. Exhaust with chromed expansion box. Less inclined rear damper location. Beige plastic grilles fitted to the side panels.

2nd Version (mid 1956 to end of production): Silencer without expansion box, two brass inspection caps. 16mm piston gudgeon pin. Additional oil vent on final drive. Quadrangular power socket on flywheel attached with a screw. Control cables with lubricators at steering head. Cylinder intake manifold with central crest for the attachment screws. Chromed steel handlebars. Five notch gear change. Additional left-hand screw on the rear hub nut. Bump stops with screws supporting the side panels, longer side panel handles and side panel grilles in chromed metal.

Did you know?

In the UK Lambretta Concessionaires introduced a special version of the LDA called the 'Mayfair' which was available for £197. For this you got the standard LDA machine with some extras: spare wheel, rear carrier, heel plates, footboard extensions and saver borders.

What the tester said

"On really greasy roads the rear end may sometimes tend to slide a little, but the scooter does not attempt to lie down. The front wheel is much more lightly loaded, but grips well and both brakes are effective and constant in action. A big windscreen is not much help in attaining high speeds and scooters are greatly affected by a head wind. I would put the honest speed of this model at 45mph, though it can hold 50mph under favourable conditions. 30mph comes up on second speed and 20mph is the maximum on first. The fuel consumption varies between 75 and 100mpg, the latter requiring moderate speeds and flat roads." – *Autosport* February 1st 1957

"An electric starter with Bendix-type drive is a feature of a 148cc LDA Lambretta tested in the early period of the year. During the six week test, the machine was used nearly every day for running between a staffman's home in Surrey and his place of work in London – a distance of 15 miles – for shopping and for visiting friends, for running down to the letterbox. On every occasion the electric starter was used. It never failed and during the entire period the twin 6-volt Bosch batteries required no attention – not even topping up. The batteries are of a plastic case, lead acid type and housed in a compartment in the body rear pressing under the pillion seat. Access to them is gained merely by unscrewing one nut and raising a small pressed lever." – *The Motorcycle* February 21st 1957

The Model D 150 (Mark 3)

Cost (when new): £129 17s 6d
Dimensions: Length 1770mm, width 740mm, height 960mm, weight 75kg
Total production: 20,835
Month of least production: January 1956 – 130 machines
Month of most production: November 1956 – 4402 machines

The final Model D 150 came into production in January 1956 for a production run of a year, with October and November being the two busiest months (4215 and 4402 units respectively). The Mark 3 retained the by now familiar D model frame, although the model received some design changes. To keep in step with Italian law, the scooter was now fitted with a battery which powered the horn and parking lights. The rectifier for the battery being located between the toolbox and fuel tank. The rear shock absorber was anchored to the rear part of the engine. The three-speed 148cc engine unit had a bore/stroke of 57mm x 58mm and produced 6bhp at 4800rpm giving a top speed of 50mph. Engine cooling being provided via forced air from the flywheel/fan and a cowling that was fitted round the cylinder head.

Production changes

1st Version (January 1956 to mid 1956): Electrics with battery and rectifier. Starter casing with three screw cover. Exhaust with chromed expansion box. Less inclined rear damper location.

2nd Version (mid 1956 to end of production): Silencer without expansion box, two brass inspection caps. 16mm piston gudgeon pin. Additional oil vent on final drive. Quadrangular power socket on flywheel attached with a screw. Control cables with lubricators at steering head. Cylinder intake manifold with central crest for the attachment screws. Chromed steel handlebars. Five notch gear change. Additional left-hand screw on the rear hub nut.

Did you know?

1956 saw London Lambretta dealer, Jack Hornsby (Speedway of Acton), riding from London Airport to Lands End. The Mark 3 D 150 (registration number 'VPF 634') was entered by Hornsby in the 1956 Lands End Trial. Riding through Maidenhead, Reading, Newbury and Marlborough it was all going well until the first off-road section at Stoney Lane, when the scooter was skidding on loose stones. The second section was dealt with without issues. By the time Jack reached Cornwall and Lands End he'd ended up with a third class award, not the gold medal he wanted.

What the tester said

"Although the engine only claims 6bhp maximum the impression on the road is of much more power than this. The power is available from very low revs and the light weight of the machine indicates a very good power/weight ratio. Added to this is the factor of the weight, what there is of it, being very low down so that there is no top hamper at all. However much the Model D is leaned over at any speed, or standing still, the weight never takes charge and this means that starting, stopping and wriggling through traffic calls for no physical

A Mark 3 LD 150 seen here during a Lambretta sporting trial in the 1950s. (Courtesy Lambro Motori)

effort from the rider at all." – *Power & Pedal* with *The Scooter* August 1957

The LD 125 (Mark 3)

Cost (when new): £149 17s 6d
Dimensions: Length 1770mm, width 740mm, height 960mm, weight 88kg
Total production: 43,635
Month of least production: July 1958 – 8 machines
Month of most production: July 1957 – 4143 machines

The height of the late 1950s scooter boom saw the introduction of the Mark 3 LD 125 in January 1957, a month in which a mere 335 machines were manufactured. Continuing with the now tried and tested LD design, the Mark 3 machine did feature some changes. The frame underwent some refinement and modification. Previously the horn had been found on the horn casting, however, the Mark 3 machine came with a cover for the handlebars which housed the horn and the speedometer. The rear of the frame now featured an integral toolbox and the rear light unit was a larger item. The engine was where major modifications could be found. The 123cc unit had a bore/stroke of 52mm x 58mm and produced 8bhp at 4600rpm. A Dell'Orto MA 18 B3 carburettor along with an epicyclical kick-starter, which made starting the scooter a lot easier as it turned the engine over several times with one kick. The Mark 3 machine now also had an exhaust that was a one piece item. The front brake was also refined on this model and was a larger item than previously fitted: it also had a rain/water lip cast into it. Unlike the 150cc machine the LD 125 had metal floor strips and a chrome 'LD 125' badge was mounted on the left-hand side of the legshield. Production of the Mark 3 LD 125 ceased in July 1958.

Production changes

1st Version (January 1957 to May 1957): Insulating plates added to the inside wall of the air filter. Front wheel hub had no dust trap. Exhaust with two inspection ports and short tail pipe. Oil lubricated starter mechanism, curved kick start. Dark green 150 D-type front saddle (on early examples this was black with an 'Innocenti' badge on the rear.

2nd Version (May 57 to end of production): Air filter insulator plates not used. Front hub now featured a dust trap. Silencer no longer openable and longer tail pipe extended through as far as rear brake. Grease lubricated starter mechanism, unified ball grease nipples, flat kick start. Fuel tank with vent and fuel cap without breather hole. Li-style locking wheel nuts. Front seat frame without pronounced spring mounts and with no runner protection on the bolts.

What the tester said

Despite extensive searching no known road tests have been found for this model.

The LD 150 (Mark 3)

Cost (when new): £159 6s 2d
Dimensions: Length 1770mm, width 740mm, height 960mm, weight 88kg
Total production: 113,853
Month of least production: July 1958 – 452 machines

Introduced in 1957 was the LD 125 Mark 3 that had a production run of 43,635 machines. (Courtesy Smees Advertising Agency)

Month of most production: March 1957 – 9968 machines

Alongside production of the Mark 3 LD 125 came the production of the Mark 3 LD 150. Overall, this machine was a good seller for Innocenti with many months of high production during the 18 months of manufacture. The 150cc machine had the same frame refinements and modifications as the Mark 3 LD 125. The 148cc engine featured a bore/stroke of 57mm x 58mm and produced 6bhp at 4800rpm. Again, the engine benefited from the epicyclical kick starter. The Dell'Orto MA 19 B4 carburettor had an air filter which sucked air through the frame via an expandable rubber hose. This set-up gave the engine higher revs and was quieter into the bargain. Manufacture ceased in July 1958, the month of least production of this model.

Available in Britain was a variant of this model called the 'Riviera' (or 'LDB'), which was identifiable by a 'Riviera' badge on the front of the machine. Included with the scooter as standard options were: a windscreen, rear carrier, spare wheel, heel plate and footboard extensions. The Riviera was available in grey, American blue, red and a couple of two-tone variants where the body colour was grey and panels being either red or blue. It is not known how many Rivieras were produced.

As production of the Lambretta was in its infancy in India in the 1950s a total of 33,217 Mark 3 LD 150s were exported there from Italy.

Production changes

1st Version (January 1957 to May 1957): Insulating plates added to the inside wall of the air filter. Front wheel hub had no dust trap. Exhaust with two inspection ports and short tail pipe. Oil lubricated starter mechanism. Curved kick start. Dark green 150 D-type front saddle (black on early examples with an 'Innocenti' badge on the rear

2nd Version (May 57 to end of production): Air filter insulator plates not used. Front hub now featured dust trap. Silencer no longer openable and longer tail pipe extended through as far as rear brake. Grease lubricated starter mechanism, unified ball grease nipples, flat kick start. Fuel tank with vent and fuel cap without breather hole. Li-style locking wheel nuts. Front seat frame without pronounced spring mounts and with no runner protection on the bolts.

Seen here with a large number of accessories is a Mark 3 LDA. (Courtesy Cambridge Lambretta Workshops)

Did you know?

Pilgrimage By Scooter. 1958 saw brothers-in-law J. Campbell and A. O'Neill leaving Hindley, Wigan, for a pilgrimage to Lourdes. Their scooter of choice was the Mark 3 LD 150 which they had blessed by the parish priest of St Benedicts Church, Hindley, prior to their setting off on the 1000 mile trip.

What the tester said

"Towards the end of our 900 miles ownership, we tried for maximum speeds. They came like this: bottom 24mph (academic really, but it keeps our records straight), second, 38mph (creditable and useful for those long drags a fraction too steep for top); top 43mph (not so hot for a 150cc). That's the one real criticism we have on top speed. If it could be raised by say five mph – and assuming a proportionate gain in cruising speed to near 40mph – then the Lambretta would have even greater appeal." – *Scooter & Three Wheeler* July 1957

"Before any test can start the engine must run and

Back in the range and better than ever!

Lambretta

at
£122·10·0
Basic Price £98·15·9
P.T. £23·14·3
lowest priced scooter
in its class!

MODEL 'D' 150cc

Yes, back in time for summer scootering, Lambretta Concessionaires reintroduce the Model 'D' 150cc. Consider what you get for this latest and greatest Model 'D' phenomenal low price of £122·10·0 including tax: First to catch the eye—the smart grey cellulose finish; then there's the comfortable pillion seat, accessible luggage box and wonderfully economical—
over 100 m.p.g.
Backed by the Lambretta After Sales Service, you'll find travel *is* a pleasure when you ride a Model 'D'!

LAMBRETTA CONCESSIONAIRES LTD., 424/426 KINGSTON ROAD, RAYNES PARK, S.W.20

Reintroduced due to popular demand was the Mark 3 D 150. (Courtesy Smees Advertising Agency)

the first thing tested and found good on the new Lambretta was the kick-starter. It will no longer be necessary for riders who have stalled in traffic to get off the machine, dislodging the pillion passenger if any, and stand alongside to kick up again. The new starter pedal can be used from the astride position and gives a first time start, hot or cold, without effort, without kick back and without knocking the nylon on the edge of the footboard."
– *Power & Pedal* with *The Scooter* July 1957

The LDA 125 (Mark 3)

Cost (when new): £150 approx.
Dimensions: Length 1770mm, width 740mm, height 960mm, weight 90kg
Total production: 52
Month of least production: March 1957 – 2 machines
Month of most production: June 1957 – 33 machines

The Mark 3 electric start LD 125 came into production alongside the LD 125 and 150 machines. However, only fifty two of these machines were built and it is thought that they may have been part of a special order – manufacture of the scooter only taking place in March, May and June of 1957. The frame and bodywork characteristics were the same as those featured on the standard LD 125 and 150 scooters. However, the Mark 3, as with previous electric start LD's had a 12 volt system provided by two 6 volt batteries for the starter, lights and horn. The 123cc engine was exactly the same as that found on the standard Mark 3 LD 125.

Production changes

No changes known for this model.

What the tester said

Despite extensive searching no known road tests have been found for this model.

LDA 150 (Mark 3)

Cost (when new): £179 10s 0d
Dimensions: Length 1770mm, width 740mm, height 960mm, weight 90kg
Total production: 4076
Month of least production: November 1957 – 171 machines
Month of most production: September 1957 – 818 machines

The last LD model to come into production was the electric start LD 150 which came into production in April 1957 when 390 machines were manufactured. The production run for this machine being relatively short as production ceased in December that same year. The frame and bodywork was exactly the same as that found on the standard Mark 3 LD 150 except for the fact that the two batteries were hidden in a hump behind the passenger seat. The glovebox was therefore moved to a position behind the legshields. On top of this glovebox were two holes for two optional extras for the scooter, these being an ammeter and a clock. The engine unit remained that of the standard Mark 3 LD 150 with a Dell'Orto MA 19 B4 carburettor being fitted.

Production changes

No known changes for this model.

Did you know?

1958 saw the Blackburn Police force buying three LDA 150s. Supplied by Anelays of Blackburn, the three machines were handed over to Chief Inspector Walsh of the Blackburn Police force. The machines were all one colour and fitted with a windshield and a rack behind the rider. One of the machines had the registration 'JCB 660.'

What the tester said

Despite extensive searching no known road tests have been found for this model.

quattro

4

Model E & F Lambrettas

It is without doubt that the commercial success of the Mark 1 Model D 125 and LD 125 (some 147,468 machines) so encouraged Innocenti that it then looked into producing a more economical scooter and, in 1953, the company's designers came up with the Model E Lambretta. An entry-level scooter which had a selling price of just 108,000 lira. However, coupled with the low selling price came a number of mechanical faults, centred in the main around the unusual pull-cord starting mechanism. Unfortunately for Innocenti, the scooter was not the success that the company had hoped for and, coupled with this failure, was a drop in public confidence in the product. To counter this Innocenti went back to the drawing board and, just a month after the cessation of production of the Model E, the company presented the Model F, which was redesigned and now 4000 lira more expensive than the Model E. However, the Model F wasn't that different from its predecessor utilising the same frame, although the pull-cord starter of the Model E was now replaced with a kick-starter on the Model F. The re-think by Innocenti produced by far one of the most reliable Lambrettas to date, though it has to be noted that neither the Model E nor F were produced in large numbers. A combined production run of 24 months saw only 85,053 machines being made by Innocenti.

The Model E

Cost (when new): 108,000 lira
Dimensions: Length 1760mm, width 660mm, height: 950mm, weight 58kg
Total production: 42,352
Month of least production: December 1953 – 1540 machines

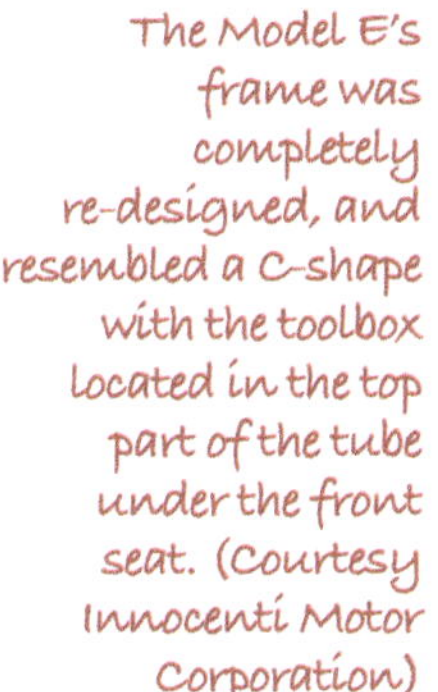

The Model E's frame was completely re-designed, and resembled a C-shape with the toolbox located in the top part of the tube under the front seat. (Courtesy Innocenti Motor Corporation)

Seen here in close-up is the pull-cord starter of the Model E. (Courtesy Lambro Motori)

Producing 3.8bhp at 4500rpm the 123cc engine unit had a bore/ stroke of 52mm x 58mm. The engine, which was fixed by a single bolt, was mounted with the driveshaft situated longitudinally reducing the number of transmission parts and improving the mechanical performance of the scooter. Innocenti took the unusual step of using a pull-cord starter (like those found on a chainsaw) mounted in front of the magneto on this model. The starter worked via a cord connected to a pulley and a ratchet concentric with the crankshaft and located on the flywheel magneto: the pulley being spring loaded for return. Fitted to the engine was a Dell'Orto MA 14 B2 carburettor. The torsion bar set-up that had been used on the Model D was retained on the Model E for the rear suspension. However, whereas the Model D had a trailing-link set-up on the front forks, the Model E had an elastic set-up. Unfortunately, mechanical problems with the engine saw Innocenti trying three different types of sparkplug and seven different types of magneto during production of this model. Manufacture of the Model E ceased in February 1954.

Month of most production: July 1953 – 7020 machines

The Model E was introduced by Innocenti in April 1953 (though it had been shown at the 1952 Milan Show) and none were ever sold in Britain. Innocenti had intended that the Model E would be an entry level scooter and therefore it was simpler in design than either the previous Model C or Model D scooters. This decision by Innocenti to build an economy model caused friction between the design and sales departments, as the aim was to keep the cost of the scooter low which resulted in the design department stating that a reliable scooter could not be built for less than 108,000 lira.

The frame was completely redesigned and resembled a 'C' shape with the toolbox located in the top part of the tube under the front seat. The single piece frame tube had the legshields (these being the shortened Model D-type), rear mudguard and number plate holder all welded to the frame. This simplification in the construction of the frame meant that it was lighter than that used on previous models (58kg compared with the 70kg frame of the Model D). The front forks were angled backwards and the shock absorbers were redesigned with blade springs wrapped around a split ring. The wheel rims were made from one piece of stamped metal. The fuel tank remained under the front seat with the usual toolbox located under the passenger seat. Innocenti retained the large headlight unit and the smaller rear light above the number plate.

Production changes

1st Version (from April 1953 to mid production): Ignition advance control with lever on the crankcase. Toolbox cover with no clips and only a central lock. Legshield and rear mudguard welded to the frame.
2nd Version (to end of production): Flywheel with automatic advance. Toolbox lid with lateral clasps and central lock. The legshields and rear mudguard were now fixed to the frame by means of screws. The front mudguard now had supplementary support struts. Last examples: exhaust silencer with right-hand exhaust.

What the tester said

Despite extensive searching no known road tests have been found for this model.

The Model F

Cost (when new): 112,000 lira
Dimensions: Length 1760mm, width 660mm, height 950mm, weight: 88kg
Total production: 32,701
Month of least production: March 1955 – 0 machines

The front suspension set-up of the Model E. (Courtesy Lambro Motori)

Month of most production: October 1954 – 4533 machines

March 1954 saw the introduction of the Model F Lambretta which continued the economy theme for Innocenti. The earliest Model Fs were simply Model Es that had the starter mechanism, footboards and transmission casings replaced, everything else being as that found on the Model E. The Model F's engine numbers simply had the bottom stroke of the E ground off to make an F. As with the Model E, no Model Fs were officially imported into the UK. However, a number did make it to the UK and, in fact, a Model F ridden by R Wilson, of the Watford Lambretta Club, competed in the 1965 Lambretta Club of GB economy test at Brands Hatch, returning 153.363mpg (against Innocenti's claim of 128mpg).

The three-speed 123cc engine of the Model F, produced 3.8bhp at 4500rpm and had a bore/stroke of 52mm x 58mm. Fitted to the engine was a Dell'Orto MA 14 C1 carburettor. Innocenti fitted an improved clutch which gave smoother gear changes. Rear suspension was the tried and tested torsion bar set-up. Though the Model F's front suspension set-up would see two types being used: some scooters being equipped with leading-link forks, whilst others had trailing-link forks. Stopping power came in the form of pressed steel drum brakes. One unusual feature of the Model F was that it was sold with a side stand as a standard fitment, with a centre stand being offered as an optional extra.

After just a few months of production a second version of the Model F was launched that had new forks and used the front mudguard from the Model D 125. The handlebars were raised to improve the riding position and the electrics were improved by using a high-powered coil and condenser fitted next to the magneto. A new dark green paint scheme was used on these models. Production of the Model F ceased in April 1955, a month that saw only 2 Model Fs being manufactured.

Production changes

1st Version (April to May 1954): Frame and seats as the Model E – dark green seats being used.
2nd Version (May 1954 to end of production): Seat frames as the Model D 150 with the front seat having chromed conical springs.

Did you know?

Show Winner. The 1963 London to Brighton run organised by the British Lambretta Owners Association saw 400 scooters take part. The Concours d'Elegance was held at the Withdean Stadium and in the class of machines up to 1955 a model F (registration number RXO 551), owned by J Edwards of the Croydon 41 Scooter Club, won the class, beating two of his fellow club members who had entered a Model C and a Model D.

What the tester said

Despite extensive research no road tests have been found for this model.

Similar to the Model E, but without the pull-cord starter, was the Model F. (Courtesy Rimini Lambretta Centre)

The Model F was available with trailing-link forks. (Courtesy Lambro Motori)

Fitted with a side stand as standard, the Model F didn't have a centre stand until later in production. (Courtesy Rimini Lambretta Centre)

Seen here with leading-link forks is an early Model F. (Courtesy Rimini Lambretta Centre)

cinque

5

Series 1 machines

1955 saw Piaggio present the Vespa GS 150 to the world and with the new Vespa came a challenge for Innocenti to produce a scooter that could rival it. The designers at Innocenti didn't simply look at increasing the engine capacity of the scooter, they looked at a complete redesign, moving away from the earlier open frame models and away from the smaller LC and LD machines. In due course Innocenti presented the world with the TV 175 (Series 1) which featured a completely redesigned frame and bodywork, along with larger wheels, a four-speed gearbox and numerous other changes. Eight months after the launch of the TV 175, Innocenti announced the Li 150 (Series 1) and two months later the Li 125 (Series 1). Although outwardly similar both Li machines differed in a number of ways, the Li 125 being a cheaper and less refined model and even the paint schemes that were offered for each model marked them apart. However, the Li machines did share one thing in common: a completely refined and redesigned engine unit that was different to that offered on the TV which had an engine casing which featured a kick-start in the centre. The February 1958 edition of *Motorcycling* stated – "With the introduction to the British market today of the new Lambretta TV 175 at the modest price

In 1955, Innocenti's rival, Piaggio, presented the world with the Vespa GS 150 – and a challenge to Innocenti to produce a scooter that could match it – which it did with the Series 1 TV 175 (also overleaf, top). (Courtesy Innocenti Motor Corporation)

of £209 17s 6d Lambretta Concessionaires Ltd., are offering a 170cc two-stroke powered luxury scooter that represents a considerable departure from previous Innocenti practice.

In November 1958 *Motorcycling* said of the introduction of the Li 150 and Li 125 machines – "The general specification is more luxurious for the Li 150 than its utilitarian and junior brother, but both differ in many major respects from the standard Lambretta which has revolutionized the pattern of personal transport in the past decade." The Li Series 1 machines were also chosen by a number of English Police forces, mainly for use in rural areas. In 1959 the Hampshire and Isle of Wight police obtained two more machines for their rural beat officers, these were fitted with a single seat and a large windscreen. The sidepanels and horn casting being painted blue.

The TV 175

Cost (when new): £209 17s 6d
Dimensions: Length 1825mm, width 710mm, height 1070mm, weight 120kg
Total production: 18,858
Month of least production: January 1959 – 8 machines
Month of most production: June 1959 – 1891 machines

On the 10th April 1957 the new

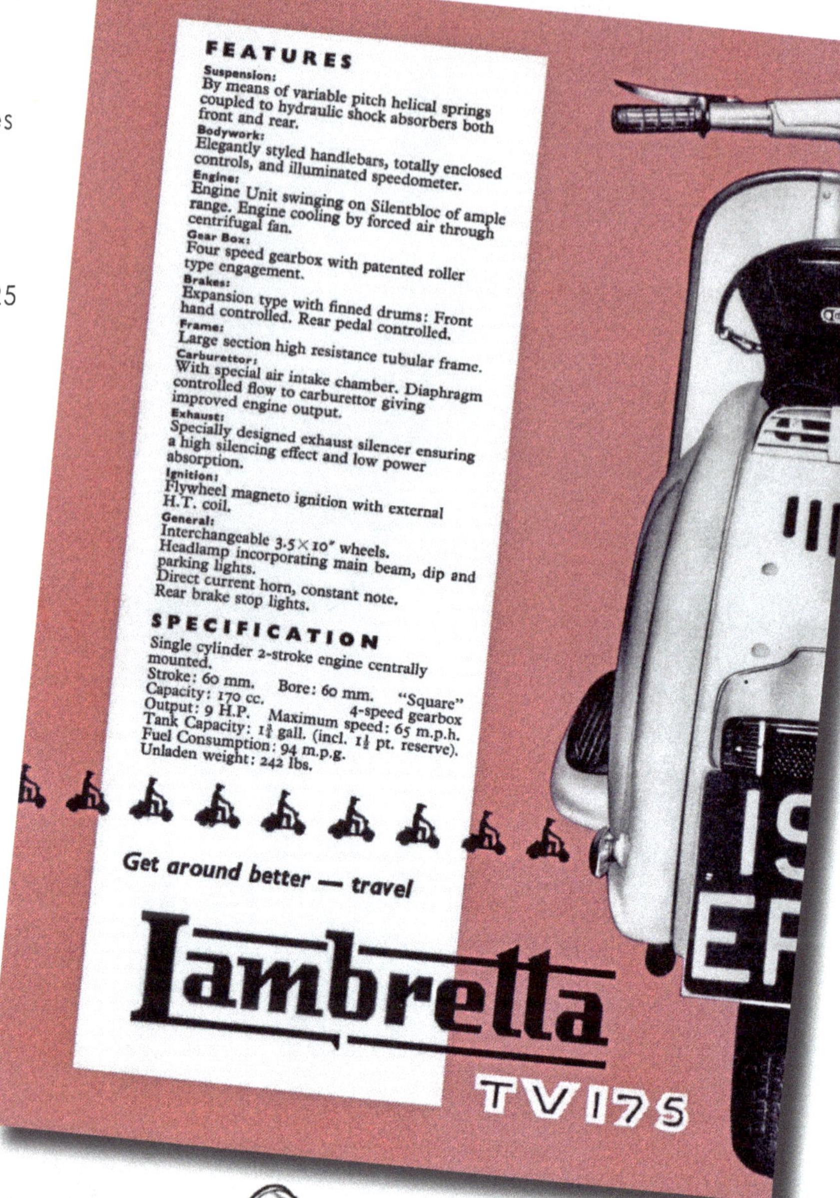

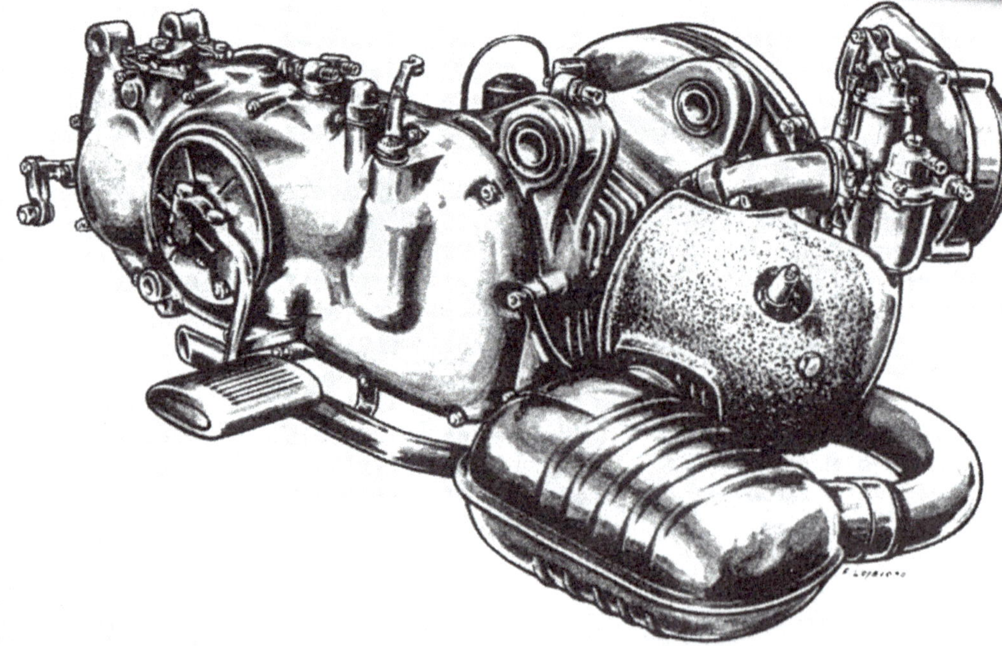

The TV 175 had a chain casing which featured a centrally-mounted kick-start. (Courtesy Innocenti Motor Corporation)

Turismo Veloce 175 Lambretta was demonstrated to an audience in Milan (it wouldn't be introduced to the UK until February 1958). This machine hailed a radical departure for Innocenti from any of the machines that they had previously produced and ushered in a new era, that of the Li-styled scooters. The model demonstrated in April was different to the first production models, in that it had a shorter LD-type kick-start, a horn casting and grille which were cast as one unit and the fuel tap and choke were located under the dual seat, which was featured a cut away for access to them. The production models had a longer kick-start, choke and fuel taps under the toolbox and the horn casting and grille were separate items.

A mere five months later, in September, production of the TV 175 began. Unlike the earlier shaft-driven Lambrettas, the TV 175 used a completely redesigned engine/transmission unit which had a four-speed gearbox gave a top speed of 64mph. Unlike the earlier shaft-driven Lambrettas, the TV 175 used a more modern enclosed duplex chain drive, thus aiding an increase in performance.

The front mudguard on the TV 175 was now a fixed item, unlike that on LD models, and the headlight was incorporated into the horn casting. (Courtesy Roberto & Kimberley Morelli)

The kick-start was in the centre of the chain case and used a large coil spring to return it to the rest position. The TV carried the largest carburettor of any standard Lambretta, at 23mm, and had the longest stroke crank, at 60mm, which combined with a 60mm piston gave the magical 'square' bore and stroke ratio preferred by tuners. Air came to the carburettor via the frame tube. Rear suspension was provided via a helical spring and hydraulic shock absorber, whilst the engine swivelled on silent block bushes. Dampers were fitted to the front suspension and these helped to improve the scooter's handling. The forks were the same as those that would appear on the Li, except that the links are the same as those found on a disc brake model with a solid stud and nut locator for the backplate rather than the peg used on drum brake models.

The curvaceous bodywork had side panels with small slots cut into them to aid engine cooling. The front mudguard was now a fixed item unlike that used on the LD models. The headlight was incorporated into the horn casting and the rear light had a red brake light with orange lenses on each side.

The TV 175's unusual rear light unit with red brake light and orange lenses each side. (Courtesy Roberto & Kimberley Morelli)

Instead of floor strips the TV was fitted with floor mats as standard, though this was to change with later models which had aluminium floor runners fitted. On the headset alloy thumbwheel adjusters for clutch and front brake cables were fitted in order to enable the rider to make adjustments without having to get on their hands and knees. The TV was the only Lambretta to have a slotted bezel around the 70mph speedo.

Although the TV was seen as a luxury scooter, Innocenti chose to offer it in one paint scheme only, this being Ivory. The TV was a hit worldwide and its production run ended in October 1959.

Production changes

1st Version (September 1957 to April 1958): Headlamp cowl with (non-removable) horn grille. Flywheel side ball bearings. No centre stand splash plate. On the first 1800 examples only, brake and clutch control cable thumbwheels did not feature a locking pin.

2nd Version (May 1958 to July 1958): Removable headlamp cowl with integrated horn grille. Flywheel side roller bearings. Centre stand splash plate. Additional locking washer on rear wheel nut.

3rd Version (July 1958 to end of production): The brake and clutch cable adjusters were no longer fitted. Additional rubber protection on the rear brake cable.

Did you know?

Honeymoon Machine. Pauline Moore and Paul Smith were founder members of the Bridlington and District Scooter Club. In 1961 they got married at St Johns Methodist Church in Bridlington and their choice of transport for their honeymoon was their Series 1 TV 175 (registration number 'WWF 231'). Their scooter looks to be either red or blue in colour and looks like it had been re-sprayed as the inner legshields were still ivory in colour.

The curvaceous bodywork of the TV 175: side panels had small slots cut into them to aid engine cooling. (Courtesy Rimini Lambretta Centre)

What the tester said

"The sales motto of the newly introduced 170cc two stroke Lambretta TV 175 scooter is 'Anywhere and Everywhere ... on every occasion ... Comfortable and fast' and it was of particular interest to observe the accuracy of this claim in last week's test. It was found to be fully justified. The newcomer can certainly be taken 'anywhere and everywhere;' the bodywork and front shielding protect the rider and passenger,

Seven months after the introduction of the TV 175, Innocenti introduced the Li 150. (Courtesy Rimini Lambretta Centre)

enabling them to arrive presentable for any social function. The TV 175 was found to be docile enough with adequate power." – Motorcycling February 6th 1958

"Among the most appealing features was the extreme flexibility of the engine. Except when threading through heavy city traffic, the TV 175 was virtually a top and third gear only machine. Minimum non-snatch speed in top gear was 10mph and in normal driving procedure to hold top gear down as low as 18mph in the knowledge that opening the throttle would result in a smooth surge of power. Minimum usable speed in third gear was a shade under 15mph. In bottom gear and with the clutch fully home the machine would trickle along at walking pace." – *Motor Cycle* 3rd April 1958

"There are minor criticisms, although not of handling or performance. The fitting of a dualseat is a retrograde step and lacks the comfort and security of the usual Lambretta arrangement of two proper saddles. The horn would make a reasonable audible warning device for a quiet moped and the rather fussy little ignition/lighting key bent in the lock to cause some trouble. The worst point, however was the near impossibility of starting the machine by kicking. A short push in 2nd gear got it going easily every time so it was not the engine's fault, but the kickstarter has a very short travel and needs modification to make it useful." – *Power & Pedal with the Scooter* April 1958

The Li 150

Cost (when new): £174 17s 6d
Dimensions: Length 1825mm, width 710mm, height 1038mm, weight 105kg
Total production: 110,944
Month of least production: April 1958 – 772 machines
Month of most production: May 1959 – 9607 machines

Seven months after the introduction of the TV 175, Innocenti launched the Li 150. The Li 150 was a great commercial success for Innocenti, and its wide-style bodywork paved the way for later models. As with the TV 175, the Li 150 now had its headlamp contained within the upper part of the horn casting. There was no move away from the new frame-style or bodywork, with the wide front mudguard and curvaceous side panels producing the scooter's curvy look. The frame breather principle that had been used on the early TV 175 machines was retained on early Li 150s, though it was dropped on later models. It should also be noted that, like the Series One TV 175, the early production Li 150 had slots cut into its side panels. To mark this model out as a more luxurious version (as compared to the Li 125 which would follow) aluminium floor runners were fitted with rubbers and alloy end caps. Polished gear change and switch housings also featured. To establish the Li as a different model to the TV, they were fitted with single seats as opposed to the dual seat found on the larger capacity TV. It is interesting to note that the legislation of various countries meant that some Li 150 machines had brake lights fitted, whilst others didn't.

The Li 150's 148cc engine was designed to overcome the problems that had been found with the TV unit. Most noticeable being the relocation of the kick-start to the rear of the chain casing. The Li 150 engine produced 6.5bhp at 5300rpm with a bore/stroke of 57mm x 58mm. Although not as fast as the larger capacity TV, the Li 150 could still reach 50mph. The frame breather (air intake) was initially retained, but was later changed to a small air scoop fitted under the rider's saddle with a separate airbox being fitted underneath.

The Li 150 was produced in a number of paint schemes. Those that were painted in 'River Grey' paint had their side panels painted in the same colour. However, those machines finished in 'Dawn Grey' had their headset, side panels and horn casting painted in a variety of colours including 'Ruby red,' 'Nile green,' 'Coral red,' 'English blue' and 'Flaminia blue.'

Production of the Li 150 ceased in October 1959 and, out of the total production, 1960 machines were built for the Indian market.

Series 1 scooters had a headlight incorporated in the horn casting. (Paul Hissey)

Production changes

1st Version (April 1958 to September 1958): Oval air intakes at the base of the side panels (early examples through to June 1958). Fixed, non adjustable chain tensioner guides. Air filter with metal mesh with air intake beneath the rear saddle. Passenger grab handle on rear seat.
2nd Version (September 1958 to December 1958): Adjustable chain tensioner guides. Cylindrical supplementary air filter with paper element. Passenger grab handle on front seat. Additional dust protection bellows on rear brake cable.
3rd Version (December 1958 to end of production): New air induction system with oval filter and air intake beneath the front seat. Shorter exhaust tailpipe collar. Rear brake pedal with small spray guard.
Final version (to March 1959): Fuel cap with incorporated breather. Double threaded removable wheel hub studs. Front brake cable moved outside the fork (from July 1959 onwards).

Did you know?

Lands End Li. London to Lands End was a popular event in the late 1950s and early 1960s. In 1960, Tony Lucas, from the Scooter Centre in Palmers Green, rode an Li 150 in the event, along with his boss, Roy Cooper, who rode a Vespa GS. Twelve hours before the event Tony's Li was involved in an accident which called for major repairs. Although that was the end of the need for repairs, as the 605 mile required no mechanical attention, not even a sparkplug change. The 16.5 hour trip produced an average fuel consumption of 86mpg with an average speed of 38.4mph.

What the tester said

"Handling was in keeping with a vehicle designed to appeal to the layman – and woman. The machine was manoeuvrable in traffic and easy to handle in the garage. However, the absence of hydraulic damping, so efficacious on its TV 175 stablemate, could make bumpy surface cornering somewhat erratic. Detail points of the Li 150 combine simplicity with effectiveness. The fuel tap and choke are as accessible as they well could be, the filler cap and its shrouding cover do their job, and the lights are sensibly controlled from a handlebar cluster." – *Motorcycling* November 1958

Air reached the carburettor via the frame on early Series 1 machines – hence the 'Frame Breather' name. (Courtesy Lambro Motori)

"There is no startling unorthodoxy in the design; in fact, were the average scooter rider given pencil and paper the result would undoubtedly look very much like the Li. Forgive us for quoting the old adage, but this is an example of 'what looks right is right.' There is a sensible minimum of bright metal parts to please those who do not like polishing and the paintwork seems durable and adequately thick. The LD-type owner will be able to recognize the surroundings from the saddle as distinctly Lambretta." – *Motor Cycling* with Scooter Weekly 5th March 1959

"We first handled the machines in dense London traffic and found them easy and comfortable to ride from the first few yards. On open roads the higher speed of the 150cc model was a distinct advantage but it was noticeable that even when driven continuously at full throttle, both engines stayed cool and ran smoothly. What little vibration was felt at all came in when pulling hard at rather less than 30mph and the units tended to get smoother as the revs mounted." – *Power & Pedal with The Scooter* February 1959

The Li 125

Cost (when new): £115 17s 6d
Dimensions: Length 1825mm, width 710mm, height 1038mm, weight 105kg
Total production: 47,747

Month of least production: October 1959 – 2 machines
Month of most production: September 1959 – 5047 machines

"Lively performance, first class braking and handling and attractive styling; these features combine to make the initial impression of the Lambretta Li 125 a favourable one." That was how The *Motor Cycle* magazine opened its road test of the Li 125 in its February 1959 edition. Innocenti launched the Li 125 in June 1958 two months after the Li 150 and, as with the TV and Li 150, the 125 had the improved Li wide-style bodywork, which proved to be an obvious winner with the scooter buying public. However, as the Li 125 was the base model in the range, Innocenti introduced some cost-cutting features including cast alloy floor runners and painted handlebar gear change and switch housings. The speedometer was an optional item as was a rear seat. As with the early TV and Li 150 machines, the early Li 125 retained the frame breather style bodywork which was dropped on later models.

The Li 125's engine had the same design as the Li 150 with a horizontal cylinder barrel, four-speed gearbox and chain drive. A smaller Dell'Orto MA 18BS5 carburettor was used and this had air fed to it through a grille at the rear of the seat which then went through the frame tube and into the airbox, although, as previously stated, this feature was dropped on later Li 125s. The 123cc engine had a bore/stroke of 52mm x 58mm and produced 5.2bhp @ 5200rpm and gave a respectable top speed of 43mph.

Manufacture of the Series 1 Li 125 ceased in October 1959. As for paint schemes the Li 125 was

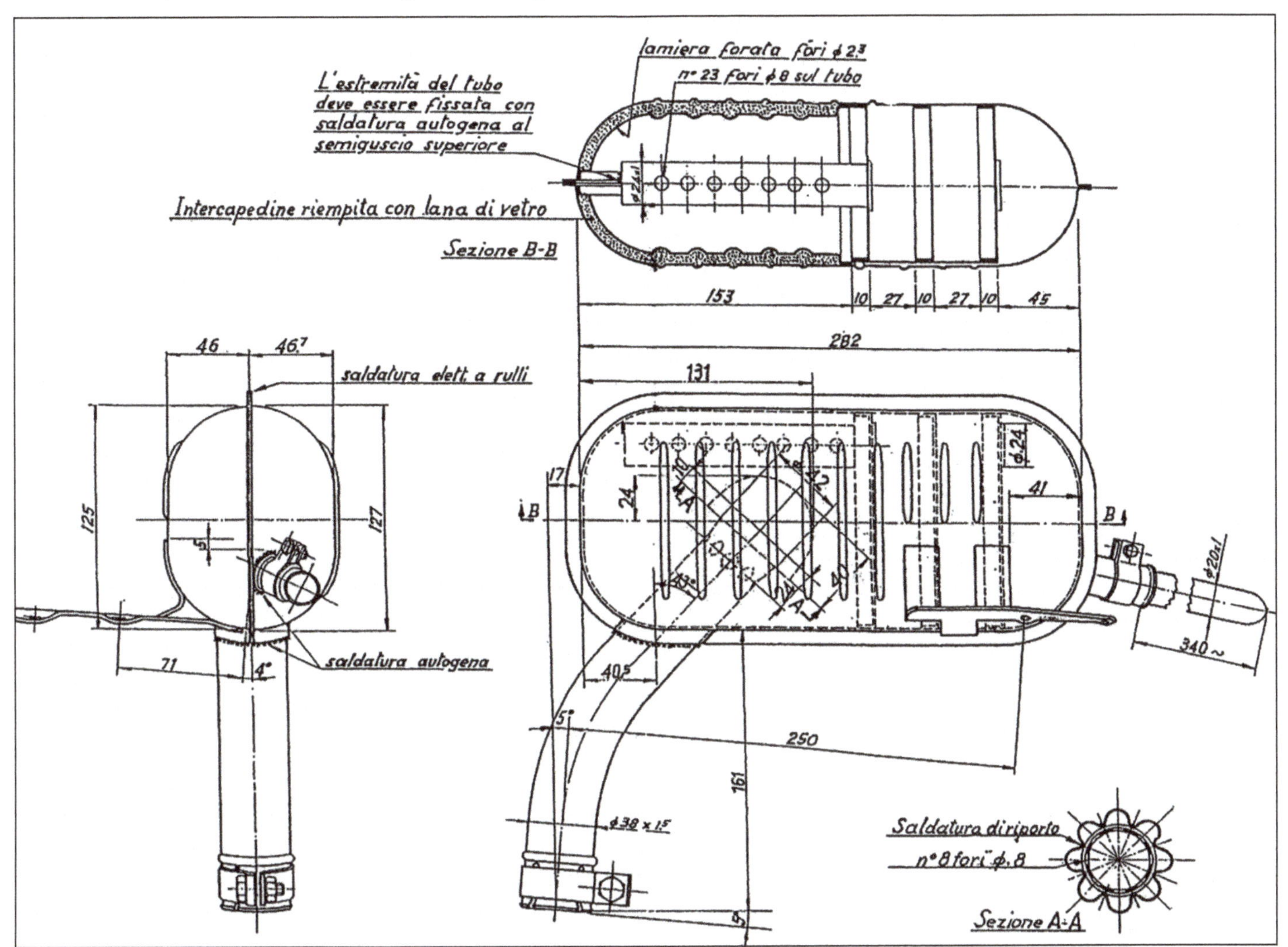

The Series 1 Li 125 & 150 featured a newly-designed exhaust. (Courtesy Innocenti Motor Corporation)

Early Li 150s featured a cylindrical air filter. (Courtesy Rimini Lambretta Centre)

offered in 'Dawn Grey' with the side panels being painted 'Steel Grey.'

Production changes

1st Version (June 1958 to September 1958): Oval air intakes at the base of the side panels (early examples through to June 1958). Fixed non-adjustable chain tensioner guides. Air filter with metal mesh with air intake beneath the rear saddle. Passenger grab handle on rear seat.

2nd Version (September 1958 to December 1958): Adjustable chain tensioner guides. Cylindrical supplementary air filter with paper element. Passenger grab handle on front seat. Additional dust protection bellows on rear brake cable.

3rd Version (December 1958 to end of production): New air induction system with oval filter and air intake beneath the front seat. Shorter exhaust tail pipe collar. Rear brake pedal with small spray guard.

Final version (to March 1959): Fuel cap with incorporated breather. Double-threaded removable wheel hub studs. Front brake cable moved outside the fork (from July 1959 onwards).

What the tester said

"The machine could be placed on the centre stand with ease and the widely spaced legs ensured that there was no chance of its falling over even on a steep camber. Although spring loaded the stand required light pressure to return it to the retracted position. Each side panel could be quickly removed simply by undoing a single catch at the rear; with the panels removed the power unit is well exposed for routine maintenance. At the front of the bodywork there is a useful lockable compartment (measuring about 7 x 8 x 8in) which housed the tool kit and left room for other small items." – *Motor Cycle* 5th February 1959

"Steering has been improved by the slightly larger wheels and the suspensions catered well for all normal roads. On real rough stuff some damping would have been appreciated,

The cover of the Italian 1959 sales brochure for the Series 1 Li 125 and 150 scooters ...

... the inside of the brochure shows the difference in paint schemes for the Li 125, Li 150 and TV175. (Courtesy Innocenti Motor Corporation)

but even on semi-trials going the springs coped at reasonable speeds. Both brakes were smooth and powerful, equally so on all three test machines and the finger adjustment provided makes it easy to maintain the brakes 100 per cent efficiency." – *Power & Pedal with The Scooter* February 1959

sei

6 The Scottish Six Days Trials model

Cost (when new): Not applicable
Dimensions: Length 1825mm, width 710mm, height 1038mm

Built by Lambretta Concessionaires in 1959, the Scottish Six Days Trials scooter was limited to a build run of just three machines. The three scooters having the following registration numbers; '240 GPL' (competitor number 7), '835 GPJ' (competitor number 3) and '171 GPF' (competitor number 8). Starting life as standard Series 1 Li 150s the machines were prepared by Rex White and Tony Sutton, who had to make a number of changes in order to make them ready for the competition. The factory-fitted exhaust was removed and, in its place, an exhaust that swept up and over the engine casing on the kick-start side of the machine was installed. At the front of the scooter a Model D-type mudguard was used and the Li legshields were cut down to Model D-type proportions. Just below the headset a small Model D-style headlight was fitted and bulb horns (like those fitted to bicycles) were fitted under the handlebars. To provide better handling capabilities at the front of the scooter, the Li forks were changed for Series 1 TV items as these had dampers fitted to them.

L-shaped angle-iron brackets were attached to the rear of the floor section to prevent the riders feet slipping off as no footboard strips were fitted to any of the machines. To strengthen the wheels a steel hoop was welded around the wheel rims; the rear wheel was a 4.00 x 10 inch item. Also the bridge piece was not fitted, so allowing access to cables.

So that the riders' weight was shifted forward, the rear seat was bolted in the front seat position and behind this an LD-type grab handle was mounted. A flat rear carrier was fitted for the spare wheel. Each of the three machines was then sprayed white. It is interesting to note that the three machines had their headsets and side panels painted blue – which from footage of the event, would appear to be 'English Blue.' Machines number 3e and 8 had round black discs with their number in yellow on the front and machine number 7 had a square item with the number in yellow. The footage of the event shows machine number 8 minus any sidepanels and with small black squares mounted on the side of the fuel tank with the number on. The other two machines had their event numbers painted in yellow on black squares on the middle of their sidepanels.

As for number plates, 240 GPL and 835 GPJ has their number plates fitted inside their spare wheels, while 171 GPF had its number plate cut down (so that it was no wider than the rear of the frame).

During the Scottish Six Days Trials the three machines were ridden by Lewis Ludo Moore, Geoff Parker and Alan Kimber. In reserve were Jack Hornsby, Mike Karslake and John Bennett. The six day event included sections with rock strewn streams, hairpin bends, narrow tracks and 1:3 gradients: all ably managed by the Lambrettas. None of the riders won any awards during the event, but they all completed it without any major mishap.

Following the event Lambretta Concessionaires were flooded with enquiries for the scooter.

Despite the interest and the demand for the machine, no other machines were built.

The Scottish Six Days event wasn't the end of the line for the scooters with at least one of them being used in other sporting trials in the years following the Scottish Six Days Trials event.

Production changes

No known production changes.

What the tester said

Not applicable as this machine was not available for general sale.

One of the three machines being put through its paces. (Courtesy Lambro Motori)

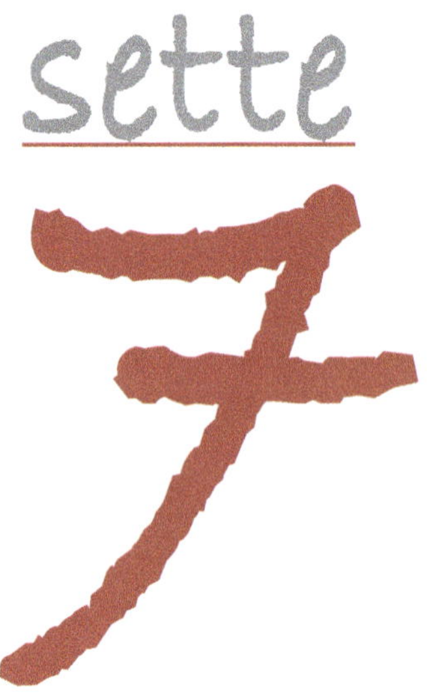

Series 2 machines

"Get out! Get about! See exciting new places. Enjoy new exciting experiences ... make exciting new friends with Lambrettability ... low cost mobility at its safest, speediest and most comfortable." That's how Lambretta Concessionaires marketed the Li 150 using the advertising slogan – "Lambrettability."

1959 had got off to a flying start though, with Innocenti launching the Series 2 TV 175 which was £20 cheaper than its predecessor. Innocenti had now redesigned the front end of the scooter, giving the headlamp a new position as an integral part of the headset, and thus enabling the headlight beam to move with the handlebars: a real advantage at night. From both an aesthetic point of view, and indeed from a road-safety point of view, this change was a winner. As well as modifications already mentioned, Innocenti made many of the mechanical parts interchangeable between models making the scooter easier and cheaper to produce.

Ten months later the Series 2 Li 150 and Li 125 would begin production. By 1960 all three models in the Series 2 range were being tested in a 24-hour county challenge, the Li 125 being ridden by B. Lowrie from the Bromley Innocents club, the Li 150 ridden by M. Evans from the Ace of Herts Lambretta Club and the TV 175 ridden by A. Palmer of the North London (The Braves) Lambretta Club. By the time they'd finished the challenge, they'd covered 600 miles and 27 counties! Members of the ELK Lambretta Club, who were also members of the St John Ambulance Brigade, used their TV 175s for their first-aid work.

Reserve yourself

TWO Ist CLASS SEATS

to *ANYWHERE* by LAMBRETTA

With the trouble-free, super-comfortable LAMBRETTA, you can always be sure of first-class travel—to work or to faraway places—at much less than second-class fares. *And* you can make sure of having a wonderful holiday this year by buying your Lambretta NOW!

You can buy the famous Li 150 for as little as £159.17.6 (incl. PT) or the more powerful TV 175 for £179.17.6 (incl. PT). HP Terms are, of course, available from your local dealer.

GET AROUND BETTER—TRAVEL

Lambretta

AND SMILE AS YOU GO BECAUSE YOU WILL

- be quite independent of public transport
- be able to save on travel time and fares
- be able to park when and where you choose
- save money on week-ends and holidays
- join the happiest band of people on the road today

Open the door to better first-class travel anywhere NOW by filling in and posting this coupon to

LAMBRETTA CONCESSIONAIRES LTD.

Trojan Works : Purley Way : Croydon : Surrey

Please send me full details of the LAMBRETTA Li 150 and TV 175, together with the name and address of my nearest dealer.

NAME ....

ADDRESS ....

.... SMEES

In order to get more people on Lambrettas, adverts stressed the benefits of Lambretta ownership. (Courtesy Smees Advertising Agency)

For some, the Series 2 also became a worthy prize. Female rally drivers Pat Moss and Ann Wisdom were each presented with a Series 2 Li 150 after their success in the Monte Carlo Rally.

It seemed that the new styling of the Series 2 range was a winner all round as the plaudits from road testers rolled in. *Motorcycling* and *Scooter Weekly* summed-up the TV 175 as "... the performance, handling, appearance and finish are all top class," and the *Motor Cycle* said that the Li 125 was "... an attractive scooter with a stout heart, a healthy appetite for hard work and exquisite manners." This popularity was shared worldwide and by November 1961 a total of some 316,827 Series 2 machines had been produced.

The TV 175

Cost (when new) £189 17s 6d
Dimensions: Length 1830mm, width 710mm, height 1060mm, weight 115kg
Total production: 34,928
Month of least production: November 1960 – 386 machines
Month of most production: July 1960 – 3037 machines

Introduced in October 1959 the Series 2 TV 175 was billed by Lambretta Concessionaires as the Sportsman's scooter. Although retaining the now familiar wide-style bodywork, the Series 2 TV 175 was the first machine in this range to feature the reworked headset which contained the headlamp. Unlike its predecessor, the Series 2 TV 175 came equipped with runners on the floorboards. Under the standard dualseat was the air scoop. Early machines had the same rear light as the Series 1 machines, with those produced mid production run having a Series 3 style unit. Also, the horn casting grille on early models was round, whilst later models sported a more pear-shaped item. As for colour schemes, the TV 175 was available in either ivory or pale blue and, on this model, the wheel rims were now painted the same colour as the rest of the scooter. The scooter carried chrome-plated brass Lambretta and TV 175 badges, these being held on by nuts as opposed to the Li Series badges which were riveted on. Behind the curvaceous side panels a rubberised solution was used to reduce engine noise. The front end of the scooter retained the TV 1 set-up of drum hub fitted to disc type links and additional external dampers to aid handling.

As the Series 1 Li machines had been a massive success, Innocenti decided that for the Series 2 TV 175 it would base the new engine unit on the Li design. However, the 175cc version featured a 58mm stroke crankshaft (bore/stroke 62mm x 58mm), a longer conrod and a different piston and barrel. All of this producing 8.6bhp @ 6000rpm. According to sales literature of the time 65mph was the estimated top speed. Early machines were fitted with a Dell'Orto MB 23 BS5 carburettor, whilst later machines had a Dell'Orto MB 21 BS5 fitted. The air filter was a paper element-type – fixed with a screw clamp, subsequently changed to a spring from February 1961. The kick-start, which had been in the middle of the transmission casing on the Series 1 machine, was now to be found at the rear of the casing, in line with that fitted to the Li machines. At the end of 1959 a larger rear light was fitted and the horn enlarged. One last improvement was the fitting of a redesigned exhaust. The Series 2 TV 175 came equipped with a 70mph speedo and had key ignition. Braking was improved by the use of an uprated drum hub fitted to disc type links. External dampers were fitted to the front forks and these gave better handling. Production of the Series 2 TV 175 ceased in November 1961 when the last batch of 977 machines came off of the line.

The scooter carried chrome-plated brass Lambretta and TV 175 badges, held on by nuts, as opposed to the badges of the Li Series which were riveted on. (Courtesy Roberto & Kimberley Morelli)

Production changes

1st version (from January 1959 to October 1959; frame numbers start 100,000): Frame with longitudinal rib welded along centreline of the frame tube. Small rear light. Round horn grille. Paper air filter. Short piston. Dell'Orto MA 23 B5 carburettor. Splash plate fixed by eight 5mm bolts. Flywheel side bearing lubricated by the petroil mixture.

2nd version (October 1959 to mid 1960; frame numbers start 200,000): Frame with normal tube and no welding. Dell'Orto MB 21 BS5 carburettor. Flywheel side bearing lubricated with grease. Long piston. Large rear light. Air filter fixed with screw clamp.

Although retaining the familiar wide style body work, the Series 2 TV 175 was the first machine in this range to feature the reworked headset containing the headlamp. (Courtesy Innocenti Motor Corporation)

3rd version (from mid 1960 to January 1961): Stand mudguard fixed with two 8mm bolts (from October 1960). Round horn grille. Air filter pipe fixed with screw clamp.

4th version (from February 1961 to end of production): Air filter pipe fixed with a spring clip. Larger air filter used.

Did you know?

Dealer Achievement. 1960 saw Harold Rowell from the Salisbury Garage, Isle of Man, leave Croydon at 11am on Monday 10th October. He arrived in Milan the following day at 9.42am, a total time of 22 hours and 42 minutes, completed on a standard TV 175 which had the carburettor, sparkplug and other parts sealed by Ian Hills (Secretary of the National Scooter Association). Rowell's route had been mapped out for him by the RAC, yet, despite this, many of the roads that he crossed were either flooded or mud-covered, making the trip more hazardous. The Simplon Pass provided the biggest test as it was practically a sheet of ice from one end to the other. Outside of Milan Rowell was met by members of the Lambretta Club d'Italia, who escorted him into the city.

What the tester said

"The Lambretta TV 175 Series II cannot be regarded as anything other than really good value for money. In exchange for £189 10s the buyer receives a well-equipped luxury scooter which is built for the enthusiastic sportsman and provides safety and reliability all the way up the range to its top speed in the upper fifties. Some £20 cheaper than the Series I,

The horn casting grille on early Series 2 models was round, whilst later machines sported a more pear-shaped item. (Courtesy British Lambretta Archive)

first introduced early in 1958, this model has a revised headlamp mounting enabling the light to move on the handlebars. This is the only major visible alteration but, underneath the cowlings, attention has been paid to the mechanical side. Five cubic centimetres have been added to the capacity and many mechanical parts are now interchangeable with the Li series, thus the scooter itself is cheaper to produce and spares stocking is simpler."
– *Motorcycling with Scooter Weekly* August 27th 1959

"A pleasant cruising speed seemed to be about 50mph. Then the machine purred along very happily and gave an average fuel consumption of 90mpg. Riding hard we noted consumption dropped to 73mpg while, oddly enough, keeping under 30mph the TV only did 88 miles to the gallon. The explanation; a slightly rich fuel mixture and the fact that the tester felt the machine was happier in third gear rather than top under 30mph." – *Scooter News* June 1960

"The TV 175 Lambretta equivalent to the [Vespa] GS, is a nippy scooter and perhaps extra engine size gives it the edge on the GS on hill-climbing. I didn't ride the one we had for test very far ... far enough to know that the engine had plenty of performance – and quite a lot of vibration. A pity. In every other way the TV was a 'beaut.'" – *Scooter News Mechanics* February 1961

The larger rear light unit used on Series 2 machines from mid 1960. (Courtesy British Lambretta Archive)

The Li 150

Cost (when new): £169 17s 6d
Dimensions: Length 1825mm, width 710mm, height 1060mm, weight 105kg
Total production: 206,020
Month of least production: August 1961 – 828 machines
Month of most production: April 1960 – 9044 machines

The Series 2 Li 150 was by far the most popular scooter produced by Innocenti during a

The Li 150 was available with single seats as standard, though Lambretta Concessionaires offered pillion seats, windscreen, dual seats, and carriers as extras. (Courtesy Paul Hissey)

production run that ran from October 1959 until November 1961. On top of the machines built for the Italian and other markets, a large number of Series 2 Li 150s were exported in kit form to India, Brasil, Chile and Argentina. The parts for India were produced during 1959-1961, with 1630 machines being supplied in kit form in 1959, 11,300 in 1960 and 15,500 in 1961. The machines for Brasil were produced during 1960-1961 with 2600 being manufactured in 1960 and 3000 being manufactured in 1961. Chile received 950 scooters in kit form in 1961 whilst Argentina received 9000 in the same year.

With Kit Kite from *Motorcycle Mechanics* magazine calling it "lively and reliable," the second model in the new Series 2 range again featured the restyled bodywork. The exhaust was of a new design with a slightly shorter neck and a round exhaust body but, unfortunately, it did not increase the engine's performance. The airbox was to be found in its now-familiar slot between the toolbox and the fuel tank. A speedometer was now a standard item on the Li machine.

The 148cc engine was significantly revised with the barrel and piston now being longer items, whilst a less obstructed inlet port shape was utilised. Lubrication for the flywheel side main bearing was changed from the open exposure to petroil mix of the Series 1 machines, to having an extra oil seal and using grease to lubricate the bearing (a system utilised on all later Lambrettas). The engine had a bore/stroke of 57mm x 58mm and produced 6.5bhp at 5300rpm giving a top speed of 50mph, although adverts of the time claimed a cruising speed of 55mph. Stopping power for the scooter was provided by drum brakes at the front and rear.

The Li 150 was available with single seats as standard, although Lambretta Concessionaires offered pillion seats, windscreen, dualseats and carriers as extras for the scooter.

The Lambretta Concessionaires-prepared Series 2 machines were generally two-tone, namely red/grey, blue/grey, coffee/cream, yellow or orange/grey and also in single colours such as 'Mistletoe Green,' 'Winchester Blue,' 'Powder Blue' and 'Red.' As far as badges go, this model carried 'Lambretta' on each side panel and 'Li 150' on the left-hand leg shield.

Production changes

1st version (October 1959 to mid 1960): Small rear light. Round horn grille. Air filter pipe fixed with screw clamp. Splash plate fixed with eight 5mm bolts.

2nd version (mid 1960 to January 1961): Large rear light. Oval horn grille. Air filter pipe fixed with screw clamp. Splash plate fixed with two 8mm bolts (from Oct 1960).

3rd version (February 1961 to end of production): Air filter pipe with spring clip. Larger air filter.

Did you know?

First Scooter On The Motorway. November 1959 saw a Series 2 Li 150 become the first scooter to travel along the London–Birmingham section of the motorway. A request had been received at Concessionaires for some urgent spares by Coventry dealer Chas E. Cope & Sons. In order to gain publicity and to test the scooter, the spares were sent by Li 150, and met at the Birmingham

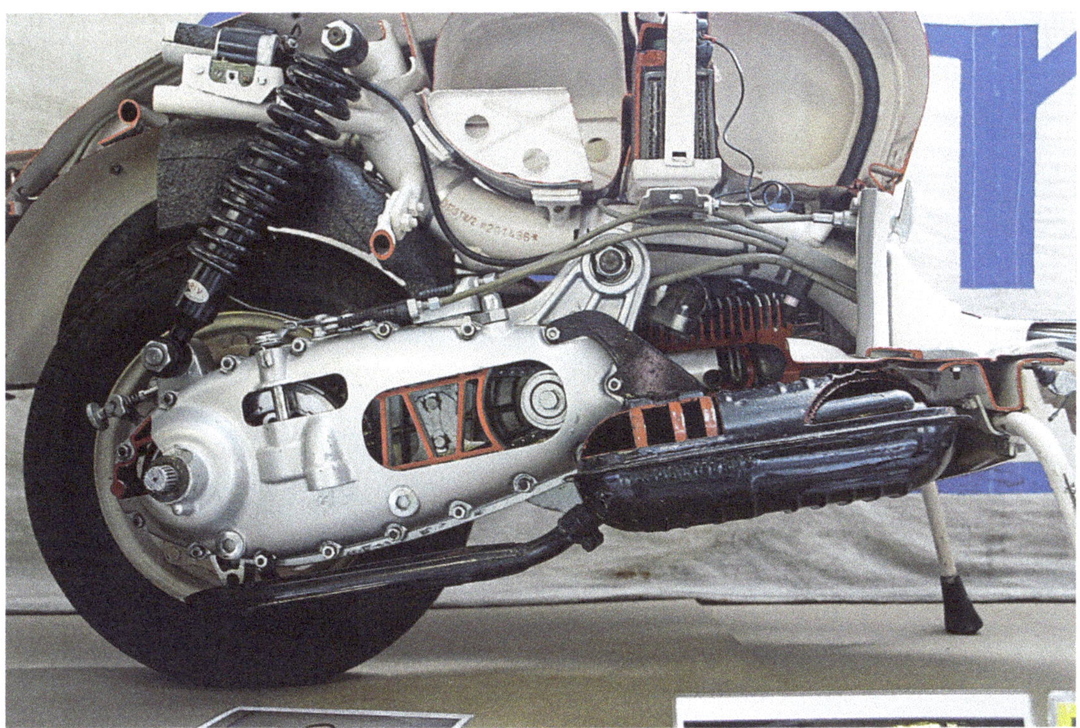

A cutaway model of the Series 2 TV 175 shows the inner workings of the engine and exhaust. (Courtesy Lambro Motori)

end by a van from the dealers. The complete journey of 142 miles was covered in 2 hours and 35 minutes – an average speed of 54.9mph.

What the tester said

"The Li 150 is a full-sized scooter, quite capable of taking a pillion passenger up any of the normal main road hills in the United Kingdom. During the time it was in my possession starting was usually easy and reliable. Only the most clumsy rider could possibly make a noisy gear change provided the clutch was used carefully. The gear positions were positive, and neutral was found quite easily. The only criticism I have concerning this part of the machine was the acute angle of my hand when releasing the clutch in bottom gear." – *Motorcycle Mechanics* August 1961

"Starting the engine was always very easy, even after dewy nights in the open. An easily operated choke control ensured a satisfying roar after only one or two kicks. We found though, that a good hefty kick was necessary – not too easy for light weight ladies – and that one had to get off the scooter to do it properly. At first we found difficulty in using the four close ratio gears. Between each gear there is a neutral and it was all too easy to slip into this. Even after a lot of riding, one occasionally slipped into one of the spaces and it could be extremely frustrating." – *Power & Pedal with The Scooter* October 1960

The Li 125

Cost (when new): £157 19s 6d
Dimensions: Length 1825mm, width 710mm, height 1060mm, weight 105kg
Total production: 111,087
Month of least production: September 1961 – 2356 machines
Month of most production: July 1960 – 6467 machines

Described by *The Motorcycle* magazine in October 1960 as "... having elegant line and top class performance," the Series 2 Li 125 came into production in October 1959. Although not as many of the 125cc machines were produced as the 150cc, the scooter's production run was still an impressive 111,087 units. As with its Series 1 predecessor, the Li 125 was built as

Series 2 Li 150 machines were provided for press use during the 1961 Rome Olympics. (Courtesy Rimini Lambretta Centre)

costruita dalla INNOCENTI divisione motori

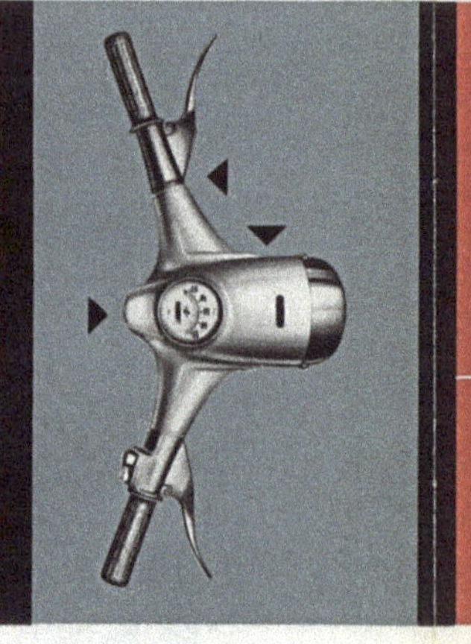

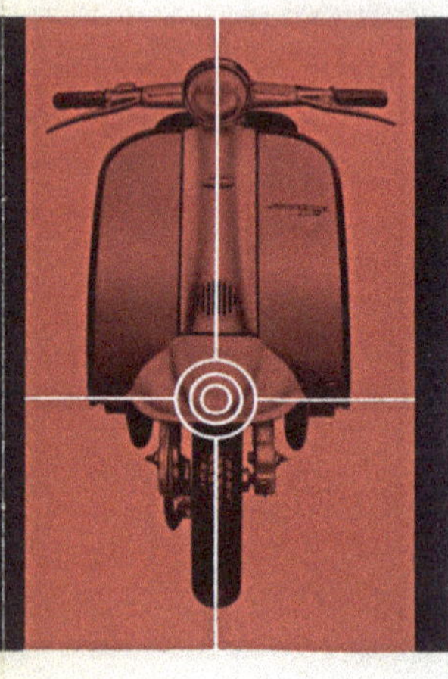

lambretta 125 li
seconda serie

il cambio a 4 velocità

permette un completo sfruttamento della potenza del motore senza affaticarlo
la manovra è facile e permette il passaggio da una marcia all'altra anche senza l'uso della frizione

faro e contachilometri

sono incorporati in un unico blocco posto sul manubrio

Il motore centrale è stabilità

il motore centrale è posto in modo che il centro di gravità si trovi sull'asse di simmetria assicurando una perfetta stabilità

This brochure extols the virtues of the Series 2 Li 125.

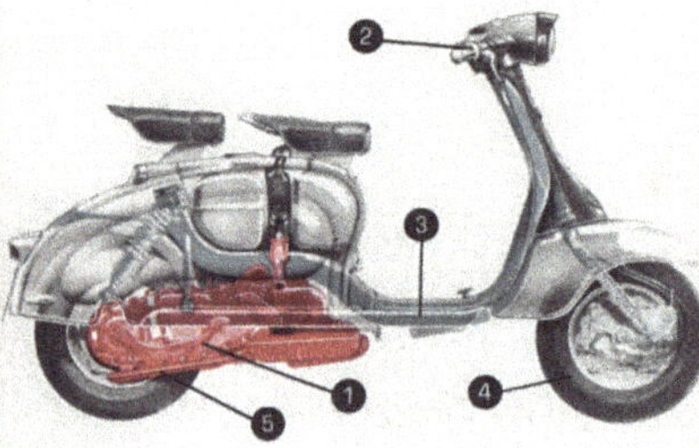

1 il motore è centrale: perfetta stabilità in ogni condizione di guida e di fondo stradale — nessun sbandamento nelle frenate, anche le più brusche; **2 il cambio è a 4 velocità:** completo sfruttamento della potenza senza affaticare il motore — minor consumo — maggiore « spunto » e « morbidezza » di marcia; **3 il telaio è un unico tubo di acciaio:** robustezza e compatezza della macchina — maggior peso che assicura una maggiore tenuta di strada; **4 le ruote sono grandi (3,50 x 10"):** maggior confort — più stabilità; **5 lo scappamento è notevolmente silenzioso (non supera gli 80 phon).**

lambretta 125 li seconda serie

comodità per il passeggero

il posto del passeggero è comodo perchè le fiancate della macchina sono strette e permettono una confortevole posizione a cavalcioni

descrizione

lambretta 125 li seconda serie

motore	centrale, a due tempi, a cilindro orizzontale, raffreddato in corrent d'aria forzata, lubrificato a miscela, con trasmissione a catena doppia maglia completamente guidata, in carter a bagno d'olio e avviamento a pedale. Accensione a volano magnete con bobina alta tensione estern
cambio	a 4 velocità con ingranaggi sempre in presa; permette il pa saggio da una marcia all'altra anche senza l'uso della frizion
telaio	in tubo di acciaio a forte sezione resistente; carenatura in lamier stampata a fiancate smontabili; ampio bauletto.
sospensioni	anteriore a bielle oscillanti; posteriore a carter oscillante ammo tizzato, caricante due molle elicoidali a passo viabile.
freni	ad espansione; mozzi in lega leggera alettati, con ampia superficie di frenatura su anelli in ghisa.
ruote	grandi, dimensioni 3,50×10".
impianto elettrico	con alternatore volano da 6 V che alimenta il faro, il fanalino posteriore, il segnalatore di arresto e l'avvisatore acustico.
scappamento	notevolmente silenzioso, in regola con le prescrizioni del nuovo Codice della Strada.

altezza della pedana da terra mm 290
altezza massima della sella (guidatore) da terra mm 780
larghezza mass. al manubrio mm 720
larghezza mass. alle fiancate mm 420
larghezza pedane laterali appoggiapiedi per secondo passeggero mm 100

L'acquisto di una  125 li dà il diritto all'assistenza tecnica di oltre 3000 stazioni di servizio in Italia e di oltre 3000 stazioni di servizio sparse in tutto il mondo.

PROP. N° 1207 // 10-59

INNOCENTI
SOC. GENERALE PER L'INDUSTRIA METALLURGICA E MECCANICA
MILANO
NEW YORK PARIGI ROMA LONDRA CARACAS

a budget model and again featured painted handlebar switch and gear change housings, alloy floor runners and the 125 was only available in a two-tone grey paint scheme ('Dawn Grey' body work with 'Steel Grey' side panels). During its production run the horn casting was revised (early models had a round horn grille) with later models sporting a pear-shaped item. On early Series 2 Li 125s the Series 1 rear light was used, though this was changed on later models to that of the larger Series 3 light unit.

The 125cc engine had a four-speed gearbox, a bore/stroke of 52mm x 58mm and produced 5.2bhp at 5200rpm giving a top speed of 43mph. A Dell'Orto MA 18 BS5 carburettor was fitted and *Motorcycling and Scooter Weekly* opined that the engine seemed to be quite tireless and a 40mph cruising speed could be held. The 123cc engine had a barrel and piston that were longer than those found on the Series 1 machine. As with the Li 150, the Li 125 featured an exhaust with a new design with a slightly shorter neck and a round exhaust body.

The October 1960 road test of the Series 2 in *The Motor Cycle* magazine saw the tester find that "... comfort was an issue with the single saddles on the Li 125, for long out of town runs the Lambretta was less satisfying. The twin saddles became progressively more uncomfortable as the miles mounted, and since the rider's saddle is set rather far forward the position proved a bit cramped."

Manufacture of the Series 2 Li 125 ceased in November 1961 with 2720 machines leaving the factory in that month.

Production changes

1st version (October 1959 to mid 1960): Small rear light. Round horn grille. Air filter pipe fixed with screw clamp. Splash plate fixed with eight 5mm bolts.

2nd version (mid 1960 to January 1961): Large rear light. Oval horn grille. Air filter pipe fixed with screw clamp. Splash plate fixed with two 8mm bolts (from Oct 1960).

3rd version (February 1961 to end of production): Air filter pipe with spring clip. Larger air filter.

Did you know?

RAC/ACU Scheme. The RAC/ACU training schools were set-up to teach riders who hadn't yet bought a scooter how to ride. The learners had to use machines supplied by the individual school and, since the scheme was run as cheaply as possible, provision of machines was a problem. In 1960 the Lambretta Hire Company of Wimbledon presented an Li 125 to the Wimbledon and District Motorcycle Club, who ran the scheme in the Wimbledon area. The Crystal Palace scheme was given an Li 125 by Gilbert Scooters of South Norwood.

What the tester said

"First impression as a rider straddles the Lambretta is of the tidiness of the control layout. Clutch and front brake levers are well placed (though perhaps a shorter reach would be an advantage particularly for girls) and the horn push, lighting switch and dip switch are neatly grouped in a box on the right of the handlebar. The control cables, electric wiring and pivots of the clutch and front brake levers are all neatly concealed by the main handlebar casting. An ignition cut-out button is mounted at the rear of the headlamp and below it is a steering lock. No shopping bag hook is provided but a small, lockable compartment, suitable for gloves is located in the forward face of the bodywork, below the rider's saddle." – *The Motor Cycle* 21st October 1960

"The kick-starter on the Li is mounted very far back and is highly geared. Experience showed that the trick was to move it half way down, by freeing the clutch, and then to give a swift jab instead of the more normal swing. Starting was instant and a good point, the choke opens the throttle slightly. There was more to it than this because it was easier to start the machine while it was on its stand, since the stands feet do not lift the wheels from the ground, our testers soon developed a little party trick of riding off from the stand down position letting the stand flick up on its own." – *Motor Cycling with Scooter Weekly* March 5 1959

"The 125cc Lambretta unit pulls staunchly so that even though a four-speed gearbox is provided the rider can leave it in top or third for most of the time. For snappy getaways, full use can be made of the intermediate ratios and the unit will produce useful power at high revolutions. A practical limit is set to the rate of turn over by a vibration period which becomes noticeable at the 'full revs and chocks away' point but the rider who wants absolute maximum performance will probably buy one of the larger Lambrettas in any case so this is of no consequence." – *Motor Cycling with Scooter Weekly* 18th August 1960.

The Rallymaster

The Rallymaster
Cost (when new): £183 15s 0d
Dimensions: Length 1825mm, width 710mm, height 1060mm

Lambretta Concessionaires newsletter number 25 of 1961 announced the arrival of the Lambretta Rallymaster – calling it a model designed for the sporting enthusiast. Prior to this a prototype of the scooter had been ridden by Alan Kimber (competitor number 2) in the 1961 Welsh Three Day Trial and in which he had won the scooter award. Lambretta Concessionaires also noted the trend amongst many scooterists towards more serious sporting events, and it was at this group that the Rallymaster was aimed. Initially the scooter had a launch date of 1st June 1961, however, on 30th May 1961 it appeared in the *Financial Times*, *Daily Mirror*, *Daily Mail* and other newspapers.

Intrinsically, the Rallymaster was the tried and tested Series 2 Li 150 scooter but with a number of sporting modifications, to improve performance and road handling. The 150cc engine was Stage 2 tuned and had a bore/stroke of 57mm x 58mm. A 21mm carburettor was fitted as was a different gearbox from that featured on the standard Li 150. To further aid an increase in speed a high performance exhaust was fitted. The chain case had a fitment on it allowing a cable-drive to the rev-counter.

In respect of bodywork the following modifications were made: a Spanish-style turning front mudguard was fitted, but with a stone remover attached to it. On the legshields a spotlight was mounted on the left-hand side, while on the right-hand side, and at the rear of the scooter, rally number plates were fitted. The headset had a small Perspex flyscreen and the handlebars had ball-ended levers. The Perspex fly screen was attached to two arms that were fixed to the inside of the screen and then bolted to the headset top. The second set of mountings were bolted from the front of the screen to the two screws that secured the headlight rim in place. Inside the legshields were fixed a spare wheel carrier and spare wheel. Mounted above this was an instrument panel that housed a rev-counter, stopwatch holder, a separate switch for the spotlight and an illuminated map board. At the rear of the machine, behind the rally number plate, a heaving handle was fitted. Concessionaires supplied the Rallymaster in standard Li 150 colours, but with black striped side panels.

Despite Lambretta Concessionaires attempt to create a sporty machine, sales were not good, as the Rallymaster was priced higher than the Series 2 TV 175. It is not known how many Rallymasters were produced by Lambretta Concessionaires, but it is thought that their production span ended in May 1962

Production changes

No known production changes

Did you know?

The International Six Days Trial in 1961 saw Alan Kimber riding a Rallymaster over the 1200 mile course. The scooter was a standard, but ACU-sealed, production machine that survived a

From the front it's clear to see that the Rallymaster was no ordinary Series 2 machine. (Courtesy Terry Crook)

Although intrinsically the Rallymaster was a tried and tested Series 2 machine, it had a number of sporting modifications to improve performance and road handling. (Courtesy Terry Crook)

Behind the seat a grab handle was fitted so that the scooter could be manoeuvred over difficult ground. (Courtesy Terry Crook)

course that saw 86 other machines fail to finish. Kimber said "The Rallymaster stood up to the rough going extremely well and showed no falling off in performance throughout the six days. The course got progressively worse each day and this was particularly noticeable on those sections which we used again in the reverse direction and were terribly cut up as a result."

What the tester said

"From the type of equipment fitted to the 'Rallymaster' it is obvious that its sporting capabilities can be used in two directions ... for road going rallies or for the scooter trials which are becoming increasingly popular these days. Taking first things first and concentrating on the rallying side, one can see what an advantage the 'Rallymaster' rider would have over the owners of other models. There would be absolutely no need to spend precious time or money in adding special parts. Everything necessary is already fitted! The willing little engine will cruise all day at speeds around the 45mph mark and, if that little extra is needed to make up lost time, then a tweak on the throttle would send the needle flickering into the low 50s." – *Motorcycling* Jan 4th 1962

"Introduced earlier this year, the Rallymaster is basically a 148cc Li model with a 21mm choke carburettor replacing the standard 19mm instrument. Rear tyre section is 4.00 instead of 3.50in. The front mudguard turns with the fork. Special equipment includes a spotlamp, spare wheel, competition number boards fore and aft, nail catcher for the front wheel, abbreviated flyscreen and ball-end control levers. A supplementary instrument panel carries a clear plastic watch holder, a rev meter, a map reading light, and switches for the map light and spotlamp. Price of the model, everything included is £183 15s. Useful stuff, most of it, but whether or not the rev meter is a worthwhile fitting I wouldn't like to say." – *The Motor Cycle* 5th October 1961

"Trying to look at the Rallymaster with the eyes of potential trials riders, we had our doubts about one or two points. The first was the position of the kickstarter, which is as normally fitted on standard machines. This, we felt, is much too close to the footboards and difficult to keep one's foot on, especially under slippery conditions. There were one or two painful occasions spent hopping about with a stinging foot after trying a bit too eagerly to get away to a quick start! Once running, the engine is noticeably noisier than the average scooter, to be expected of course, but the road test machine was fairly difficult to start." – *Power & Pedal with The Scooter* April 1962

Dual-control Lambrettas

Cost (when new): Not available for general sale
Dimensions: Series 2: Length 1825mm, width 710mm, height 1038mm
Dimensions: Series 3: Length 1800mm, width 700mm, height 1035mm

12 noon on Thursday 27th October 1960, at the Waldorf Hotel in London, saw Lambretta Concessionaires introduce the dual-control Lambretta tuition scooter, in the presence of the right Honourable Lord Chesham (Parliamentary Secretary from the Ministry of Transport).

This was a scooter that wasn't for sale to the general public but it was devised in the wake of a public outcry over scooter-riding casualties. Concessionaires confidently claimed that the dual-control Lambretta would do much to reduce the casualty figure. At the Earls Court motorcycle show, both Lambretta and Vespa introduced training versions of their 125cc scooters, as legislation had been changed to allow learner riders to ride with instructors on the back of the scooter.

The idea was essentially that the scooter would be made available to 650 dealers who would buy one of these machines and then, when a potential customer came along, the dealer could take them out on the machine in order to instruct them on how to ride. Unfortunately not many dealers wanted to buy such a machine, so, despite a sound idea not many were purchased. The main reason being the cost of the machine which dealers found hard to recoup.

The machines were used in the main by the Royal Automobile Club (RAC) who ran many

During 1960 Lambretta Concessionaires introduced the dual controlled Lambretta. It wasn't for sale to the public, but was created in response to public outcry about the high number of scooter riding casualties. (Courtesy Lambro Motori)

The dual control Lambretta had an extra set of handlebars mounted between the single seats. (Courtesy Lambro Motori)

instruction schools for learner riders. Though it should be noted that Harrow-based Lambretta dealer Ted Pink did donate one of the Series 2 Li machines to the Harrow Road Safety Council in 1961. So, it was an idea that some dealers liked.

Mallaby & Co., based in York, was the originator of the dual-control idea and Lambretta Concessionaires, having conducted extensive tests, adopted the concept and then arranged to have the modified scooter produced (though it is not known how many machines were actually converted). The scooters were essentially Series 2 Li 150 and Series 3 Li 125 machines which had an extra set of rigid (non-steering) handlebars fitted behind the front seat. The downside of this for the rider was discomfort, as they had to sit bolt upright! However, the hapless instructor faired no better, as when they were sitting on the machine their legs were directly under the bars, meaning they had to lean forward over the hand controls for the clutch and rear brake lever. These controls gave the instructor the ability to override those used by the learner. The instructor also had an ignition kill button in order to be able to shut off the engine; this was mounted on the handlebars. The cables for these controls were fed through two holes that were drilled into the top of the seat arch. It is important to note, that the instructor

From the side it's clear to see how simple the dual controlled set-up was. (Courtesy Lambro Motori)

could not drive the scooter as there was no linkage to the throttle. The instructor could however stop the scooter using the brake lever or the kill button. The brake on the scooter was a very effective item as extra leverage was created by making an extension to the rear brake arm.

The handlebars used by the instructor were mounted onto a metal plate that was bolted under the rear seat. An upright tube was welded to this plate with additional triangular support fillets. The handlebars were then fitted into a bicycle-style handlebar clamp located at the top of the upright tube. A modification was also made to the clutch arm and adjuster block to allow for fitment of a second clutch cable.

In essence the dual-control Lambrettas were a novel idea from Lambretta Concessionaires to try to improve the riding skills of novice riders. However, it wasn't just the cost that put dealers and their staff off of the idea of such machines. Ian Newman (Rafferty Newman) recalls the dual-control Lambretta from his days as a mechanic at Fareham based Lawton & Wilson. He describes it as so frightening that "... neither I, nor any other staff member would use it again."

Production changes

No known production changes for this model

Did you know?

Scooter Donation. In 1961, Harrow-based Lambretta dealer Ted Pink donated a dual-control Series 2 Li 150 to the local road training scheme that was being run by Harrow Council. The scooter bore the registration number '8770 ME.'

What the tester said

Despite extensive searching no known road tests have been found for either the Series 2 or Series 3 dual-control Lambrettas.

dieci

10

Series 3 machines (Li 125 to TV 200)

Lambretta Concessionaires advertised the launch of 1961's newly-designed Slimstyle range by announcing "Lambretta do things in style!" Adverts of the time state "This is the most beautiful scooter in the world! For three years, Lambretta's top designers have been aiming towards a single target – to match performance with perfect appearance. Now success is theirs – and it can be yours too, the moment you put your hands on this slim, sleek, superb new machine. Revolutionary styling has resulted in a scooter par excellence – a scooter that makes its rider instantly aware that he is the proud owner of a thoroughbred new 'Slimstyle' Lambretta."

Sales brochures described the Li 125 as a beautiful, aerodynamically designed scooter that would be the envy of all those not fortunate enough to have one (and overleaf). (Courtesy Innocenti Motor Corporation)

See how Lambretta do things in style . . .

readily accessible foot and hand controls

higher speed and greater economy due to smaller frontal area and aerodynamic styling

improved handling and manoeuvrability due to lower weight and reduced size

a complete new range of matching accessories

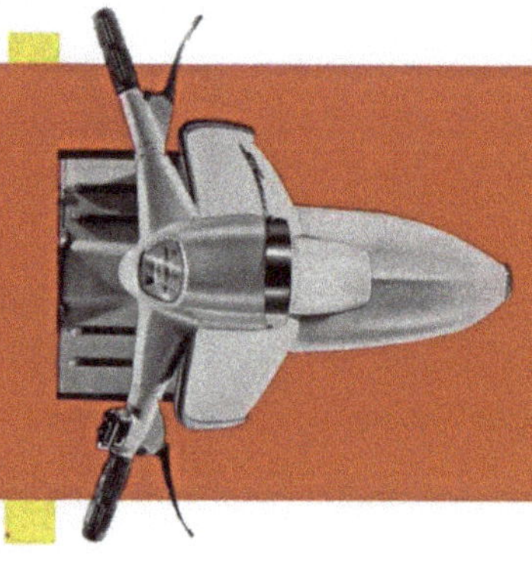

. . . with these additional SLIMSTYLE refinements

beautiful new illuminated speedometer

improved lighting switch

gracefully styled horn enclosure

rear number plate accommodated in body pressings

tank cap in internal weather proof compartment

accessible, large-capacity tool box

NEW, COMPLETELY AUTOMATIC CARBURETTOR WITH A NEEDLE-LESS CENTRAL FLOAT CHAMBER GIVING YOU UP TO 124 MPG

Have you experienced all the thrills and advantages of owning a Lambretta

In the first place, it gives you an independence such as you have never known before, enabling you to travel to and from work unhampered by such snags as queues and time-tables, allowing you to explore the countryside and far-distant places in your spare time. Secondly, the LAMBRETTA provides you with by far the most economical means of getting around on the roads today, costing you considerably less than a penny a mile to run. With a new ***125*** 'SLIMSTYLE' LAMBRETTA you can really be somebody. This beautiful, aerodynamically designed scooter will be the envy of all those less fortunate than yourself. And it is backed by a second-to-none after sales service network throughout the UK and Europe – a service that has been praised over and over again by 2,500,000 satisfied owners of LAMBRETTA, the world's best selling scooter.

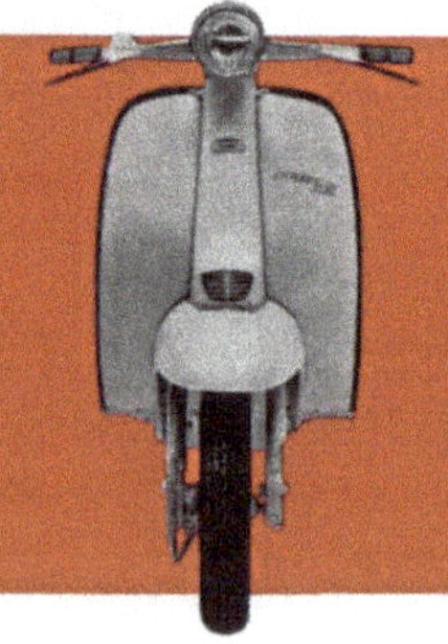

SLIMSTYLE *125*—technical data that will be of interest to you

HP at 5,200 rpm	5.5
Compression ratio	7.5 : 1
Maximum speed	48 mph
Overall length	70¾"
Overall width	27½"
Overall height	39¾"
Width at footboards	20¾"

There could be no doubt that the new machines were different to their predecessors. The Series 3 machines featured an entirely new frame and bodywork. The seat arch was now more angular, slimmer panels were used along with slimmer leg shields. The front forks were modified and a hub with different fining was used, though the TV 175 and TV 200 machines were fitted with, as the leaflets stated, for the first time ever in scooter history powerful disc brake on the front wheel. *Scooter & Three Wheeler* magazine went as far as to say "lower, lighter and faster than previous models".

In this series both the Li 125 and Li 150 were popular machines with a combined total of 289,825 being made, especially the Li 125 which in a change for Innocenti was the first series 3 model to be launched, followed by the Li 150 and then the TV 175 and TV 200 machines.

The TV machines had the same bodywork as the Li machines except that the mudguard was restyled, now being more angular and made of fibreglass. The machines also had a new design of horn casting, an octagonal headset and came with a front disk brake as standard. With the series 3 machines came the introduction of rear frame badges which carrying the machine's designation. Another innovation was the use of carburettors with a needle-less central float chamber which simplified maintenance. Another major change, in May 1965, concerned the frame: up to that point a chrome ring had been fitted underneath the headset, this was now dropped and, therefore, newly designed headsets and leg shields had to be introduced. Machines imported into the UK were painted in the usual Innocenti 'New White' but in road tests of the time this colour is often described as being grey, which it wasn't. Both the Li 125 and TV 175 were shown at the 1962 Italian Trade exhibition in Moscow. The Li 125 had its horn casting and sidepanels painted in a contrast colour to the rest of the scooter. The TV 175 had its sidepanels, horn casting and mudguard in a contrast colour. Whereas the Li had two single saddles fitted, the TV at this show had a black dualseat, and both scooters were fitted with flat spare wheel carriers fitted to the rear. To confuse matters, the May 1963 advert for the Li 150 shows the machine finished in white with its horn casting and sidepanels in contrast colours. 1963 would also see Alan Kimber offering lower gear ratios for the Li 150 and TV 175 machines. The TV 175 gearing that was offered came with the 1st and 2nd gears from the Li 125 and the 3rd and 4th from the Li 150. The Li 150 was modified by using the 1st and 2nd gear from the Li 125. These modified gearboxes were offered in the main for the sporting scooterist. Fitting these modified gearboxes also meant that certain layshaft gears had to be changed as wells. For the TV 175 this meant changing 1st, 2nd and 4th and for the Li 150 both 1st and 2nd layshaft gears had to be changed.

Both the Li 125 and the Li 150 had production runs that ran well into 1967, though production of the TV machines ended in 1965 with them eventually being superseded by the SX 150 and 200 machines.

The Li 125

Cost (when new): £139 19s 6d
Dimensions: Length 1800mm, width 700mm, height 1035mm, weight 104kg
Total production: 146,734
Month of least production: December 1965 – 0 machines
Month of most production: July 1963 – 5687 machines

The Series 3 Li 125 was the best-selling 125cc Lambretta that Innocenti ever produced, production began in December 1961 and continued until November 1967. The first month of manufacture saw 3125 machines being made. This was a significant increase over the production figures of the Series 1 and Series 2 Li 125s, these being 47,747 and 111,087 respectively. Sales material stated "... that this beautiful, aerodynamically-designed scooter will be the envy of all those less fortunate than yourself." As previously stated the Li 125 now came with the new Slimstyle bodywork which made the scooter slimmer than the Series 2 machine (700mm in width as opposed to 710mm) and shorter in length (1800mm as opposed to 1825mm). The redesigned headset also featured a newly-designed trapezoid shaped speedometer. Fitted as standard to the scooter were two single seats, the front seat having a passenger grab handle fitted: a dualseat was offered as an optional extra.

Early Series 3 Li 125s were produced with a four-pole generator, though this was changed to six-pole in September 1962. The 123cc engine had a bore/stroke of 52mm x 58mm and utilized a new style Dell'Orto SH 1/18 carburettor with a needle-less float chamber. With its four-speed gearbox the scooter produced 5.5bhp at 5200rpm and had a claimed top speed of 48mph. It's worth noting that the gearbox on the Li 125 was subject to changes in specification and therefore varies between early and late models of this scooter. Another point worth mentioning is that the Li 125 had its handlebar control covers painted the same colour as the rest of the scooter.

For the UK market, the colours listed for the Li 125 at the time of its launch were: two-tone grey/red or grey/blue, but it's worth pointing out that the test model in the *Scooter & Three Wheeler* road tests was a single colour (white). The scooter had the registration mark '778 RK.' However, the same scooter was to appear on the cover of the August 1962 edition of *Scooter & Three Wheeler* and, at that time, was white with red side panels, showing how concessionaires changed the colour of the machines they imported. Coupled with this, the test scooter used by Mike Evans, who road tested the Li 125 in 1963, was white with red side panels.

Production changes

1st version (December 1961 to December 1962): Series 2 type floor board tunnel. Side panel anti-vibration buffers without springs. Speedo with small square dial (Li Series 2 type). Single wire to the engine kill button.

2nd version (December 1961 to mid-1965): Larger footboard tunnel. Speedo with large dial. No battery. Side panel anti-vibration buffers fitted with two small metal springs (from mid 1964).

3rd version (mid 1965 to May 1967): Chrome ring eliminated from beneath headset. Side panel clamps simplified (from Jan 66).

Did you know?

Li 125's for the RAC. 1964 saw Peter Agg presenting 25 new Series 3 Li 125s to RAC Chairman Wilfred Andrews. These machines were to be part of the RAC/ACU training scheme which was used to teach new scooterists road skills so that they would become better riders. Interestingly enough, the 25 scooters lined up side by side only filled two car parking spaces. Also of note is that all of the machines that were presented to the RAC came fitted with a single seat.

What the tester said

"The tool roll is housed in a useful luggage locker below the front saddle and there is provision on the rear cowling for fitting a spare wheel and carrier. If preferred, a dualseat may be specified instead of the twin saddles. However, on the test machine the saddles were found to be very comfortable. Starting was simplicity itself; a twist of the fuel knob (and when cold, the choke knob), a couple of light prods on the starter pedal and the little engine buzzed merrily. At tickover it two-stroked with the reliability of a grandfather clock. A cut out button for stopping the engine is provided on the handlebar. Lighting was good and permitted the full cruising speed to be used on dark roads." – *Motor Cycle* 25th April 1963

"Braking tests revealed the smoothness and efficiency usually found with Lambretta models. The front brake on the model tested would squeal at a very high pitch under certain conditions, but it was felt that this would disappear later with increased mileage. Braking tests produced the figures of 51 feet to stop from 30mph, for the front brake, 58 feet for the rear brake, and 40 feet when both brakes are used together. The rear brake has a stoplight switch connected, and the stoplight itself is good and bright even in the daytime." – *Scooter & Three Wheeler* July 1962

The Li 150

Cost (when new): £159 17s 6d
Dimensions: Length 1800mm, width 700mm, height 1035mm, weight 104kg
Total production: 143,091
Month of least production: August 1966 – 0 machines
Month of most production: February 1962 – 5835 machines

Introduced by Innocenti in January 1962, the Series 3 Li 150 had a production run a mere 3643 machines behind that of the Li 125. Although it's worth noting that production of the Li 150 did finish six months before that of the Li 125 in May 1967. May 1967 also saw 274 machines being built for export to the United States of America. The Li 150 proved that the new Slimstyle Lambrettas were a hit with scooter riders worldwide. The 150cc machine shared the bodywork changes that had appeared on the 125cc scooter, though it was slightly more powerful, producing 6.6bhp @ 5300rpm. As with the 125cc machine, the electrics on the Li 150 were changed in September 1962 from four-pole to six-pole generation, giving the machines a more powerful electrical system. Dependent on which market the scooter was made for, it could be supplied with, or without, a battery to power the scooter's parking lights, horn and brake light without the engine running. The 148cc engine had a bore/stroke of 57mm x 58mm with a claimed top speed of 55-58mph.

Innocenti offered the Li 150 in three paint schemes with the main bodywork being white (although grey was used on very early models) while the side panels and horn casting were offered in either 'New Blue,' 'Ruby Red' or 'Nile Green.' Whereas the Li 125 had the handlebar control housings painted, they were chromed on the Li 150. UK models were listed in 1962 as being offered in the following colour schemes: grey/turquoise, grey/red and grey/blue. 'MGH 68D,' the test model used by *Power and Pedal* for their road testing in 1966 was a blue and white machine,

Gerry & The Pacemakers with Series 3 Li 150s in the film *Ferry Cross the Mersey*. (Courtesy Lambro Motori)

Left & overleaf, top: A month after the introduction of the Series 3 Li 125, Innocenti presented the world with the Series 3 Li 150. (Courtesy Innocenti Motor Corporation)

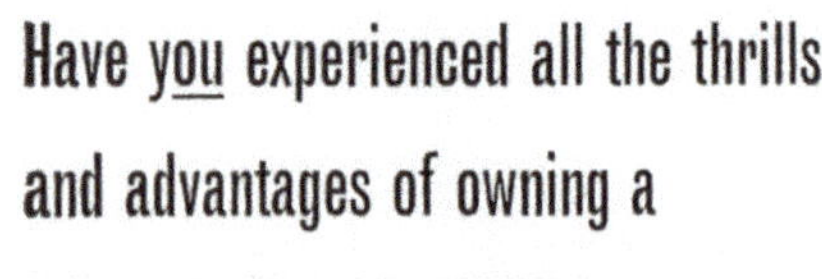

The 150cc machine replicated the bodywork changes that had appeared on the 125cc scooter, although, engine-wise, it was slightly up on power, producing 6.6bhp at 5300rpm. (Courtesy Rimini Lambretta Centre)

with the horn casting and sidepanels being white, whilst the rest of the scooter was blue. It's also worth noting that in the UK, as with the Series 2 Li, a Slimstyle Gran Luxe model was offered, this being the standard model with chromed side panels. York City Police used the Li 150 for patrol work within the city boundaries, with machines being delivered initially in 1963 and then two more in 1967. Between 1963 and 1967 these scooters covered 25,000 miles each.

Production changes

1st version (January 1962 to December 1962): Series 2 type floor board tunnel. Side panel anti-vibration buffers without springs. Speedo with small square dial (Li Series 2 type). Battery.

2nd version (December 1962 to mid 1965): Larger footboard tunnel. Speedo with large dial. No battery. Side panel anti-vibration buffers fitted with two small metal springs (from mid 1964).

3rd version (mid 1965 to May 1967): Chrome ring eliminated from beneath headset. Side panel clamps simplified (from January 1966).

Did you know?

Trading Stamps for a Scooter. 1964 saw the pupils at St Gregory School, Kirby, Liverpool saving trading stamps. The reason they did this was because they had heard that a missionary in India needed a scooter for his work. All 1400 pupils collected trading stamps and, in only eight weeks, they had filled 155 books with 195,000 stamps – enough to exchange for an Li 150. The scooter was handed over to the school by Mr J. Whittaker of Green Shield Stamps.

Offered by Lambretta Concessionaires was the Gran Luxe model, essentially the standard Series 3 Li 150 with chrome sidepanels. (Courtesy Power & Pedal)

What the tester said

"Adaptable? We actually started off in top gear, and the Lambretta managed it without fuss. Its true top gear range is from 15mph to 58mph. Innocenti, the makers, have dutifully provided marks on the speedometer, giving their recommended speeds in each gear. Respectively, and quite accurately, these are: 20mph in first, 33 in second, 44 in third and 55 to 57mph in top. Exhaust noise is well muffled by the big capacity silencer. Any touring speed can be held on this bike: around 40mph being most acceptable." – *The Scooter with Power and Pedal* April 1966

"Overall impression of the Li 150 was that it is completely fuss-free, will start readily and tickover reliably. A very creditable maximum speed is coupled with 100mpg fuel economy. The headlamp of the test model was well up to its job and night riding was a pleasure. Above all, the rider gets the feeling that here is a machine that is not so much a bepanelled miniature motorcycle as a two wheel car. The greater part of the test mileage was done with no more protection than a helmet, a scarf and a pair of gloves. And there was never any danger of oil soiling my trousers." – *The Motor Cycle* 5th September 1963

The TV 175

Cost (when new): £189 17s 6d
Dimensions: Length 1800mm, width 700mm, height 1035mm, weight 110kg
Production: 37,794
Months of Least Production: August 1964, February 1965, August 1965, September 1965 – 0 machines
Month of most production: March 1963 – 2221 machines

Scoring 101 points (out of a maximum of 150) in the *Motorcycle Mechanics* January 1963 road test, the Series 3 TV 175 was described as follows: "What a wonderful improvement! There is simply no comparison between the early unstable, feeble run about scooters and the latest Slimstyle TV 175. Since its introduction in early 1962, the Slimstyle TV has created terrific interest with its unique disc-type front brake."

The TV was an obvious winner and was introduced by Innocenti in March 1962, in a reversal of their previous protocol of launching the TV models first. During its 44 month production run, a total of 37,794 machines left the Milan plant to be exported worldwide. The TV featured the now familiar Slimstyle bodywork, however it had an octagonal headset and fibreglass front mudguard. Early models had the same side panels as those fitted to the Li Series machines, though this was changed in December 1963, when the TV machines received reworked side panels which featured three fingered chrome flashes (a large one at the front of the panel with a smaller one fitted to the rear). Unlike the Li series machines the TV 175 came equipped with a dualseat as standard. A drum brake at the rear and a disc brake at the front provided stopping power. Extra front shock absorbers were fitted to aid damping.

The 175cc engine had extended front engine mounts, which were white rubber on early models. The engine had a bore/stroke of 62mm x 58mm and produced 8.7bhp @ 5300rpm with a claimed top speed of 62.5mph. A 20mm Dell'Orto carburettor was fitted and Innocenti also made improvements to airflow, porting and the exhaust. The crankcase was different to that found on other models as it was made to accommodate a larger cylinder.

During its production run, the TV 175 was available in a variety of paint schemes: plain white, white with yellow or red panels, horn casting and mudguard, light grey with dark grey panels, and metallic blue (these models had a metallic blue rear frame badge). The UK market machines were listed as being available in grey/red, grey/yellow and grey/charcoal. The test model in *Scooter & Three Wheeler* in August 1962 (registration number '777 RK') was white with red side panels, horn casting and mudguard, and fitted with a tan Pegasus dualseat.

Production changes

1st version (March 1962 to December 1963):

Early models had the same side panels as those fitted to Li Series machines, though this changed in December 1963. (Courtesy Rimini Lambretta Centre)

disk brake without white plastic grilles. Earliest examples had Li side panels. Side panel anti-vibration buffer in rubber, 'TV 175' badge with white background. Speedo cable with small dial until December 1962, then large dial fitted, four pole flywheel magneto (changed to six pole in September 1962.

2nd version (December 1963 until end of production): Side panels now Special-type, side panel anti vibration rubbers now fitted with small metal springs. Rear frame badge with 'TV 175' on blue background.

Did you know?

California Horsepower Law. In September 1961 California introduced a horsepower law that effectively banned scooters from Californian freeways. The law basically said that if a vehicle produced less than 15 gross brake horsepower then it wasn't allowed on the freeway. Innocenti carried out tests on the TV 175 and showed that it produced 15.4 gross horse power. A certificate was submitted to the California Highway Patrol which saw the 175 lawfully back on the freeway.

What the tester said

"The new disc brake on the Lambretta is very good. It is almost impossible to lock on, but you can hear the tyre squealing in protest as you gradually apply the unit. The only time the front wheel slid was when one of the testers was pulling up at the kerb and he hit a patch of gravel. The rear brake, which is the normal drum pattern, also proved quite adequate for the performance of the new TV 175. Vibration was one of the points from which this particular road test machine suffered. At tickover, which was very quiet, the machine seemed to shake like a jelly."
– *Motorcycle Mechanics* January 1963

The Series 3 TV 175 was another Lambretta that was popular with sporting Lambretta riders. (Courtesy Lambro Motori)

"Starting was immediate upon depressing the kick-start pedal, and the extra power was appreciated the moment the machine was accelerated away from rest. This extra power could be felt even when accelerating to overtake at quite a high speed in top gear, and no particular 'nobbliness' due to the increased compression ratio was noticed when pottering along at fairly low revs in slow traffic. The engine was as smooth and sweet to use as Lambretta units usually are."
– *Scooter & Three Wheeler* June 1962

"Disc braking ... that's the talking point about the new Lambrettas. No motor cycle has disc braking and no other scooter. The disc brake is fitted to the new 175cc model, the Slimstyle 175, as Lambrettas have called it – but not on the other scooter, the Slimstyle 125. The revised body styling is clear; slimmer than it used to be, slightly lower, slightly shorter, and there is a sharpness about the styling too. And as well as these changes, there

A one-off chrome-plated TV 175 was produced by Innocenti for promotional purposes. (Courtesy Innocenti Motor Corporation)

are others, not so apparent ... a new rear number plate as part of the main body, horn mounting as part of the steering head column at the bottom, anti-dazzle speedometer face ... more positive lighting switch ... enclosed fuel cap." – *Scooter News Mechanics* May 1962

"On the road the new engine seems to have the best of both worlds. It is really smooth and quiet, easy to start and free from all vices but at the same time it has speed and acceleration comparable with true sports motorcycles and if driven that way, with full use being made of the clutch and gearbox and plenty of twistgrip the machine is really exciting to handle. On the other hand it is possible to keep the engine turning over smoothly down to 20mph in top gear, two-stroking evenly all the time and so quiet that the exhaust cannot be heard from the saddle in normal traffic." – *Power and Pedal with the Scooter* June 1962

The TV/GT 200

Cost (when new): £199 17s 6d
Dimensions: Length 1800mm, width 700mm, height 1035mm, weight 110kg
Total production: 14,982
Months of Least Production: January 1964, September 1964 – 0 machines
Month of most production: April 1965 – 1648 machines

The TV 200, or GT 200 as it was known in the UK, was introduced in April 1963, with adverts of the time proclaiming: "Join the Jetset get a GT 200." *Motorcycle*

The brochure for the TV 175, showing new colour schemes and all the new features (and overleaf). (Courtesy Innocenti Motor Corporation)

Contachilometri e tachimetro sono illuminati ed incorporati in un elegante faro a ghiera poligonale. Ampio bauletto situato in posizione facilmente accessibile anche durante la guida.

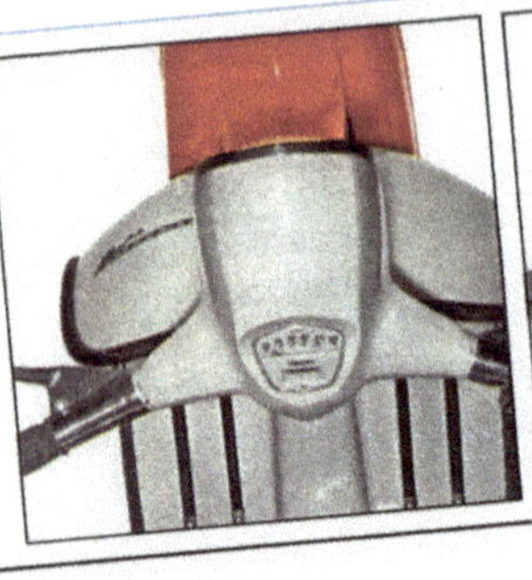

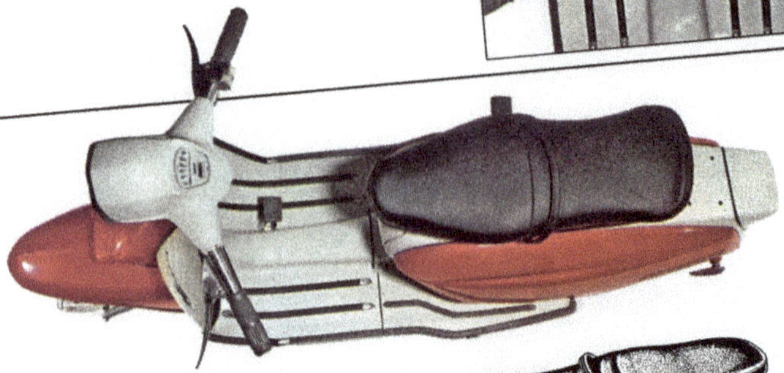

La nuova carrozzeria, dalle specifiche caratteristiche aerodinamiche, compendia quanto di più elegante e funzionale esiste attualmente sul mercato, permettendo una maggiore velocità ed un superiore comfort di marcia anche per il secondo passeggero che può disporre di fiancate strette e di un'ampia pedana avvolgente, senza incomodi ed antiestetici ingombri laterali.

La Lambretta scooterlinea mantiene inalterata la classica disposizione centrale del motore sostenuto da un telaio a forte sezione resistente, sul quale poggia tutta la carrozzeria in lamiera stampata.

Un ampio scudo avvolgente, un parafango anteriore di linea penetrante, fiancate facilmente e rapidamente smontabili ed un portatarga incorporato nel costolone centrale della carrozzeria sono altrettanti particolari che concorrono a rendere più pratico ed elegante questo scooter.

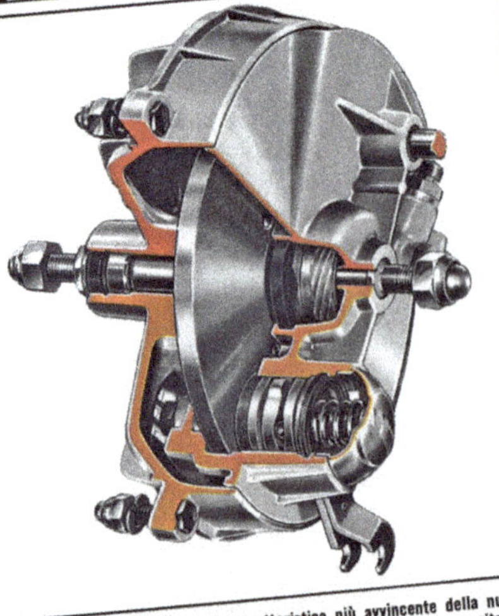

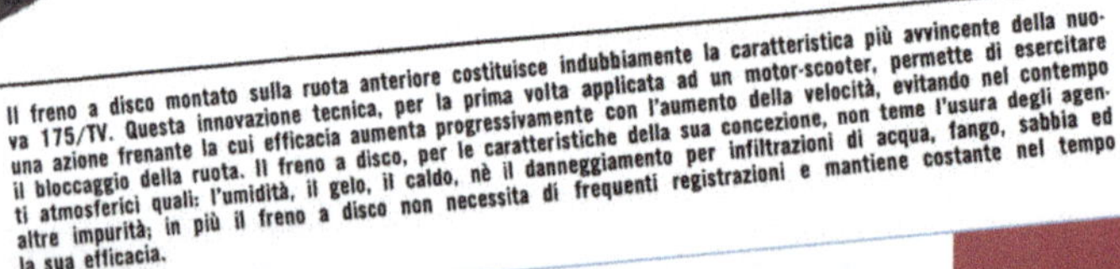
Il freno a disco montato sulla ruota anteriore costituisce indubbiamente la caratteristica più avvincente della nuova 175/TV. Questa innovazione tecnica, per la prima volta applicata ad un motor-scooter, permette di esercitare una azione frenante la cui efficacia aumenta progressivamente con l'aumento della velocità, evitando nel contempo il bloccaggio della ruota. Il freno a disco, per le caratteristiche della sua concezione, non teme l'usura degli agenti atmosferici quali: l'umidità, il gelo, il caldo, nè il danneggiamento per infiltrazioni di acqua, fango, sabbia ed altre impurità; in più il freno a disco non necessita di frequenti registrazioni e mantiene costante nel tempo la sua efficacia.

Mechanics magazine stated: "Built for the enthusiastic British scooter market, the TV 200 is the latest and greatest scooter in the Lambretta range of machines. With a top speed of almost 70 miles an hour and acceleration to match the 198cc Lambretta not only provides first-class about town transport, but is ideal for long-distance touring."

The TV 200 was launched in the UK at the Blackpool Show, where it was listed as being designed "exclusively for the UK market".

Innocenti had a policy of not building a scooter with any bigger engine capacity than 175cc, as they the company felt that this was the best capacity for all round performance, giving good top speed coupled with good fuel consumption. However, British riders felt that the 175 did not give them the performance that they wanted for them to compete in events like the Isle of Man races. Peter Agg (Managing Director of Lambretta Concessionaires) went to Innocenti in order to ask for a bigger capacity machine to be built. However, Innocenti refused stating that should the British require larger capacity then they should buy motorbikes. Undeterred Peter Agg persisted with the Italians and they eventually relented but imposed certain conditions. The conditions were that the barrel would be a normal 175cc item bored out to 198cc. The gearing and everything else was to be left as per the TV 175, although the legshield badge would be changed to a TV 200 item. The downside of the deal was that the machines would come with no guarantees. The British had asked for the machine and the Italians would provide it, but nothing more.

The TV 200 retained the same frame and bodywork as that found on the TV 175. Early TV 200s came equipped with Li-style side panels, although from December 1963 they were fitted with the same side panels found on the later TV 175 and the Li 150 Special. The 198cc engine had a new crankcase with a larger crankcase mouth, a new gearbox was fitted (with the highest fourth gear ratio ever used by Innocenti) and it had a bore/stroke of 66mm x 58mm, which produced 10.75bhp @ 5700rpm, giving a top speed of 70mph. Due to there being no proper development conducted on the machine it suffered from excessive vibration and new owners found that the exhaust frequently fell off. The engine mounts simply couldn't cope with the amount of vibration that the engine generated. Lambretta Concessionaires found a solution by fitting two sets of engine mounts side by side, and an extra bracket was added to the exhaust, thus curing previous problems.

The TV 200 or GT 200 as it was known in the UK was introduced in April 1963. Machines left the factory finished only in white. (Courtesy Innocenti Motor Corporation)

Demand for the TV 200 proved to be huge both in the UK and worldwide, forcing Innocenti to produce the scooter to meet the demand. The machine now featured modified gears, an upgraded carburettor and the modifications that Peter Agg had utilised now found their way onto the latest machine. Even British Police Forces got in on the act with Surrey police having twelve TV 200s for use in traffic control and patrol duties. The Surrey machines being equipped with two-way radio and an electrical system converted from 6 to 12 volts to cope with the extra equipment.

Lambretta Concessionaires marketed the TV 200 as the GT 200. (Courtesy Lambretta Concessionaires)

It is interesting to note a paragraph from the Italian Lambretta Club magazine *Notizario* from April-June 1963. The writer Roberto Patrignani states: "The 200cc Lambretta has been especially developed at the request of British Lambretta fans. The British, who have always been particularly critical of motor scooters (and also motor bicycles of any nationality) have taken to Lambrettas in a big way – so much so that there are more Lambrettas than any other type of scooter on the road in the UK. Critical clients bring improvements to industry and the Innocenti company of Milan decided to please their critical clients of Great Britain by building the Lambretta they seemed to particularly favour. Basically the 200cc Lambretta is a development of the 175TV and has a high degree of flexibility with a maximum speed of 115kph. It has that intense acceleration which British Lambretta fans rate so highly when it comes to judging scooter performance. It is not unlikely that this model will be made available to other Lambretta fans elsewhere."

The TV 200 was supplied in white and Lambretta Concessionaires then offered the machine with striped sidepanels in polychromatic red, green, mauve or blue. Interestingly, in the February 1964 edition of *Scooter & Three Wheeler* the TV 200 is shown with hits headset top and bottom, the horn casting (except the V section), mudguard and top and bottom of the Li sidepanels all sprayed in a contrast colour. Production of the TV 200 ended in October 1965 when the last 200 TV 200's were manufactured.

Production changes

1st version (April 1963 to December 1963): Li-style side panels with anti-vibration buffers all in rubber.

2nd version (December 1963 to October 1965): Special style side panels. Now without chrome ring beneath headset. Side panel anti-vibration buffers fitted with small metal springs.

Did you know?

Record Attempt TV 200. Don Noys, the south London scooter dealer established record times for the standing-start kilometre, flying-start kilometre, standing-start quarter mile and flying-start quarter mile. The TV 200 that Noys rode had to be equipped with sidepanels, horn, lights etc. The ACU monitored the event, and Noys minimal seat didn't conform to the standard so had to be extended. The TV covered its first run in just over 29 seconds at a speed of 77.02mph. The return run was

Pictured in Southend is Bob Wilkinson of the Lambretta Club GB, aboard a TV 200. (Courtesy Bob Wilkinson)

reduced to 27.75 seconds at a speed of 80.584mph. The average of both runs being 78.764mph. Don completed four runs over the standing-start kilometre with his fastest run being at 66mph. Following a change of gear cluster and new clutch plate and springs the attempts started again. The TV used by Noys had been slightly tuned with a raised compression ratio, two sparkplugs fitted to the cylinder head and two ignition coils fitted. The final speeds were: standing-start kilometre – 64.547mph, flying-start kilometre = 78.764mph, standing-start quarter mile – 51.8mph and flying-start quarter mile – 77.892mph.

What the tester said

"First impressions of a machine are always important from the sales point of view and this latest Lambretta with its slim lines and dual tone colour scheme, is one of the smartest models on the market. A dualseat is fitted as standard and the riding position proved comfortable for both the rider and passenger. The performance of the 198cc motor is quite surprising and compares very favourably with any motorcycle of equal capacity. The gear ratios of the four-speed box are well chosen with maximum speeds through the gears of approximately 32mph in first, 47 in second, 56 in third and 69 in top."
– *Motorcycle Mechanics* December 1963

With Miss Lambretta aboard, this TV 200 has its sidepanels finished in one of the contrast colour options offered in the UK. (Courtesy Lambro Motori)

Throughout its production, many records had been attempted on the Lambretta. This TV 200 set a record for the trip from London to Milan. (Courtesy Smees Advertising Agency)

"What about performance? As implied the GT has acceleration to match most vehicles on the road. Over the 600-mile test only larger capacity two-wheelers seemed to have any advantage from a standing start. The GT would buzz easily to 36 in second and a very useful 50 in third, and in top a mean 66mph was recorded. Best one-way speed was 68mph with the help of a slight tail wind. However, it would cruise all day in the fifties and used in this way, fuel consumption was 70mpg. It would, of course, be much better at the 40mph average speed of less sporting scooters."
– *Motor Cycle* 16th May 1963

"In bottom and second gear, under fairly firm acceleration, exhaust noise was considered tinny and rather louder than expected. Wider throttle openings produced more noise, but a much more pleasant note under acceleration. It was only [when] cruising on the open road that the exhaust note was at its lowest and pleasantest. Some loss of smoothness was detected at low speeds, but this was only to be expected from a machine which likes to be revved."
– *Scooter & Three Wheeler* December 1963.

Later TV 200s had the same sidepanels as the Li 150 Special and Li 125 Special. (Courtesy Lambro Motori)

Li 150 & 125 Specials

"Top of the IT parade" was the advertising slogan used by Smee's advertising agency when it put together the advert for the newly introduced Li 150 Special in 1963. The advert went on to proclaim: "You're certainly IT – you're the star of a streamlined, dream-lined hit – when you ride the new LAMBRETTA PACEMAKER. Hop on the top of the scooter pops-pull out the stops and W-H-O-O-M! You're really swinging-on a real scooter with real performance." It certainly seemed to be an advertisers dream. Concessionaires informed Lambretta dealers and the scootering press that the Li 150 Special was "the ideal mount for the more sporting type club member," but the Li 150 Special was more than that.

As a scooter the Li 150 Special was a redesign of the successful Li range. It slotted in nicely between the Li 150 and the TV 175 which had both been introduced in the previous year. However, the scooter wasn't simply a rehash. Innocenti had thought about the scooter and the upping of the compression ratio from the 7.1 of the Li 150 to 7.5:1 on the Li 150 Special was only the start. Coupled with this were the use of lower gear ratios which increased the overall flexibility of the engine, described as having "turbine smoothness." Outwardly, the scooter shared the now-familiar Series 3 styling cues: horn casting, mudguard, headset and the later TV-style side panels complete with their chrome flashes. *The Scooter and Three Wheeler* road test from June 1964 saw the magazine hailing it as a worthy successor to the 175. This, despite the fact that both machines would be built

Introduced as "that fine Lambretta" in this advert, the Li 150 Special was offered in silver and gold. (Courtesy Innocenti Motor Corporation)

alongside each other, though the Li 150 Special production carried on past that of the TV 175. Then a year before the cessation of the Li 150 Special's production, Innocenti launched a 125cc variant of the scooter – the Li 125 Special. A machine that was never to be sold in the United Kingdom, although some models did find their way here and three of them saw success on the Isle of Man in 1968 (see below). Both Special machines were popular and this is reflected in the combined production figures which show that a total of 99,370 Specials were built between 1963 and 1969.

Produced during 1965, the Golden Special came with a green-coloured seat. (Courtesy Rimini Lambretta Centre)

The Li 150 Special

Cost (when new): £191 11s 3d
Dimensions: Length 1800mm, width 700mm, height 1035mm, weight 109kg
Total production: 68,829
Month of least production: February 1966 – 0 machines
Month of most production: July 1964 – 5634 machines

Introduced in September of 1963 the Li 150 Special neatly filled a gap between the Li 150 and the TV 175. Though in its first month of production the assembly line only built 12 machines. The 148cc engine unit benefited from the use of a close ratio gearbox which, allied to the use of a Dell'Orto SH 1/18 carburettor and a new cylinder head and barrel, produced 8.25bhp at 5590rpm: a vast increase over the standard Li 150 which was producing 6.6bhp at 5300rpm. The engine's bore/stroke being 57mm x 58mm. Alongside these improvements, Innocenti introduced larger engine mounts to reduce engine vibration. This set-up made the scooter a hit with racing scooterists, though early models suffered from a thin 3rd gear which was prone to breaking. This thin third gear was believed to have been due to a programmer feeding incorrect information into the gear making machine. This gear was subsequently changed on later models to a thicker type.

The Li 150 Special used the now familiar TV style bodywork with the octagonal headlight rim, more pointed mudguard, redesigned horn casting with its wider horn grille and the later TV-style side panels with their almost gullwing-style top half and a recessed lower half that featured three fingered chrome flashes at the front and rear. Although using the TV-style bodywork, Innocenti decided to offer the scooter in only two paint schemes, these being either all silver or all gold. The rear frame badge on each model simply proclaiming the word 'Special' on either a silver or gold background to match the colour of the machine. By 1965 a chrome badge stating either 'Golden' or 'Silver' was to be found mounted above the large 'Special' badge which was fitted to the legshield. The Silver and Golden Specials were launched onto the UK market in the autumn of 1965.

Within the United Kingdom the Li 150 Special was known as the 'Pacemaker,' a name taken from the Mersey beat group Gerry & the Pacemakers who had ridden Series 3 Li 150s in the 1964 film, *Ferry Cross the Mersey*. The Pacemaker seemingly only being imported in a silver paint scheme (though this was described by *Scooter & Three Wheeler* magazine as being polychromatic grey). Initially, Lambretta Concessionaires put a gold 'Pacemaker' sticker under the 'Special' badge on the legshields and this appeared in the adverts of the time. Although, interestingly enough, the test model ridden by Ian Speller in a 1965 road test for *Motorcycle Mechanics* has no 'Pacemaker' sticker on the legshield, but does have one fitted on the top part of each side panel. As with most things Lambretta, there didn't seem to be too many hard and fast rules and details changed during the production run. Lambretta Concessionaires did offer the Pacemaker with the flash on the horn casting being painted either red or blue along with the gullwing on the side panels. Later they offered the model repainted in white with the gullwing on the side panels being painted in a contrast colour of blue (it is not known if other colours were offered). Production of the Li 150 Special ceased in October 1966 with the final batch of 1142 machines leaving the Milan plant.

Production changes

1st version: (September 1963 to April 1965): Side

Lambretta
INNOCENTI

150s

Kapacitet	148 cc	Motor	Monteret i geometrisk tyngdepunkt, 1-cyl., 2-takt, blæserkølet
Boring	57 mm		
Slaglængde	58 mm	Gearbox	4-gear, skifte i styrhåndtag
Kompressionsforhold	7:1	Transmission	Duplex-kæde i lukket oliebad
Max. effekt	8,25 HK	Kobling	Flerpladet i oliebad
Max. speed	90-95 km/t	Affjedring	For: svingarmsled med spiralfjedre Bag: motoren danner svingarm, dobbelt spiralfjeder og hydraulisk støddæmper
Brændstofforbrug	2,8 l/100 km		
Tanken rummer	8,1 l	Bremser	For: expanderende, aktivering ved håndgreb Bag: expanderende, aktivering ved fodpedal
Olie/benzinblanding	2% olie		
Siddepladser	2 (twinsæde)	Stel	Central-stålrørsstel
Vægt	120 kg	Karrosseri	Stålplade, let aftagelige sideskjold

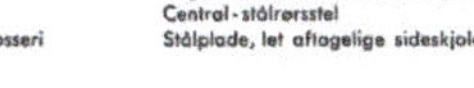

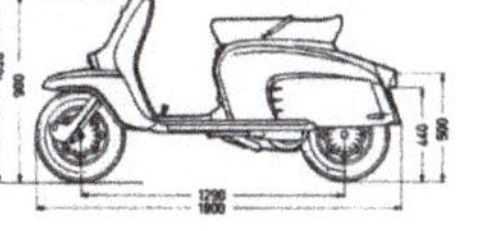

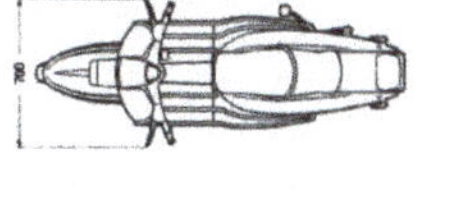

PG 2/L 55-65 Printed in Italy

panel anti-vibration buffers all rubber until mid 1964, then buffers with metal spring. Single 'Special' badge on right legshield.

2nd version: (May 1965 to September 1965): 'Golden' or 'Silver' badge fitted above the Special badge.

3rd version: (October 1965 until October 1966): Frame now no longer fitted with a chrome ring beneath the headset. Side panel handles now without plastic wheels (these being used from January 1966).

A specification sheet for the Li 150 Special showing the scooter in its traditional all-silver paint scheme. (Courtesy Innocenti Motor Corporation)

Did you know?

'JMT 36B' was a Pacemaker owned by Australian teacher Peter Townsend. In 1965 he took the scooter on the 92ft schooner *New Endeavour*, which was undergoing a trip from the UK to Sydney, Australia. Townsend was going to use the scooter as his mode of shore transport when the schooner docked in ports along the way.

What the tester said

"Acceleration was equally satisfactory on hills. In the early stages of the test there was a normal tendency to change down from top to third when accelerating gently up a moderate hill, but it was soon found that this precaution was unnecessary. Cruising speeds in top could virtually be chosen according to the rider's mood and the traffic conditions. Except when idling there was little vibration from the engine, no doubt to a large extent due to the anti-vibration units which are also a feature of the GT 200."
– *Scooter & Three Wheeler* June 1964

"Everything works so easily – no effort is needed for any of the controls and this creates the impression that you are on a conducted tour and all that is necessary is to sit back and admire the scenery. Don't get the idea that this bike is slow though. Its 148cc motor turns out a claimed 7.6bhp at the rear wheel which is enough to give a top speed of 58mph. The motor is only turning over 5590rpm even at this speed."
– *Motorcycle Mechanics* April 1965

"Easily recognised by its polychromatic grey

The internals on both Silver and Golden Specials were painted white. (Courtesy Rimini Lambretta Centre)

finish and by the depressions and chrome flashes on the side panels, the newcomer is decidedly made for two. Not only is the well-shaped and firmly sprung dualseat standard, but the two-rate rear springing is man enough for the heaviest load it is likely to have to bear. Early in the running-in period the test model was called upon to carry a two up weight of 26 stones; and even at that stage the engine and brakes, besides the suspension were more than a match for the job." – *Motor Cycle* 2nd April 1964

"There is no question that this new Lambretta 150 is a Special machine. At first glance you might mistake it for a 175/TV for it has adopted the dualseat, handle bars and the headlight with the octagonal rim of its bigger brother. A second glance, however, will quickly disperse any such thought for it sports a strikingly different coat of metallic grey paint and newly designed sidepanels with two vertical flashes in polished aluminium. Under those new sidepanels lies the secret of the 150 Special. Brake horsepower has been upped from 6.6bhp at 5300rpm to 7.4 at 5600 and, more important, the gear ratios have been changed so that the Special has much greater acceleration and a higher speed than the standard 150." – *Scootourist* May-June 1964

The Li 125 Special

Cost (when new): 155,000 lira
Dimensions: Length 1800mm, width 700mm, height 1035mm, weight 118kg
Total production: 29,841
Month of least production: August 1967 – 0 machines
Month of most production: July 1966 – 2741 machines

A year before the end of production of the Li 150 Special, Innocenti introduced the Li 125 Special in October 1965, a scooter that was hugely popular in Italy. In its first month of production, a total of 1438 machines left the Innocenti plant. As with its larger capacity brother, the Li 125 Special was a more highly tuned Li 125 model but

Innocenti chose to offer the Li 125 Special in one colour – metallic blue – though, in 1968-69, a small batch of the very last models were painted white. (Courtesy Lambro Motori)

was never really imported into the UK. The 123cc engine had a bore/stroke of 52mm x 58mm and produced 7.12bhp at 5500rpm (making it more highly tuned than the standard Li 150) and the scooter was capable of a top speed of 54mph. Although having a smaller cubic capacity than the 150, the Li 125 Special was fitted with a larger Dell'Orto SH 1/20 carburettor.

The Li 125 Special had the same bodywork as the Li 150 Special – except for a large '125' badge that was fitted above the 'Special' badge on the legshield. Innocenti chose to offer the scooter in one colour, metallic blue, although a small batch of the very last models in late 1968/69 were painted white. Unlike earlier 125cc machines the Li 125 Special did not follow the tradition of painted switch housings and cast floor runners, instead being fitted with chrome switch housings and floor runners with rubber inserts. No Li 125 Specials were fitted with a chrome ring beneath the headset as the scooter was introduced after Innocenti's decision to cease using them in May 1965.

During its production run subtle changes were made to the bodywork, early models featured: white light switches, side panels with handles, a metal toolbox, bolt in fork buffers and a horn casting with the shield-type badge. Later models had black light switches, clip on side panels, a grey plastic toolbox, clip in fork buffers and a horn casting with a rectangular badge. The final month of production for the Li 125 Special came in January 1969, during which month only fifteen machines left the production line.

Production changes

1st version (October 1965 to early 1968): Horn casting featuring shield-type Innocenti badge. Painted metal toolbox. Bolt in fork buffers. Side panels with handles (though from January 1966 these were the later type with no wheel).

2nd version (early 1968 to late 1968): Horn casting featuring rectangular Innocenti badge. Grey plastic toolbox. Clip in fork buffers.

3rd version (late 1968 until January 1969): Side panels now clip on items with no handles. 8mm bolts with 13mm heads. Different paint scheme.

Did you know?

Isle of Man 1967. The Druidale event at the Isle of Man Scooter Week is a timed event that saw the dice loaded in favour of the Italian team in 1967. Li 125 Specials (a machine not available in the UK) dealt well with the strict time keeping of the event. The laps were timed and the timing strip was just below the hairpin at Brandywell. Since the Li 125 Specials had a time well within their capacity class, their riders arrived well ahead and they halted on the far side, with one eye on the stop watch. They then started their engines and crossed the line dead on time.

What the tester said

Despite extensive searching no road tests have been found for this model.

The Li 125 Special had the same bodywork as the Li 150 Special – except for a large 125 badge sited above the Special badge on the legshield. (Courtesy British Lambretta Archive)

Like its larger capacity brother, the Li 125 Special also had white painted internals. (Courtesy Rimini Lambretta Centre)

dodici

12

Series 4 machines (Li 125)

Cost (when new): Not known
Dimensions: Length 1800mm, width 700mm, height 1035mm, weight 110kg

The Series 3 Li machines weren't the end of the Li story, as September 1967 saw Innocenti build a number of Li 125s which had frames stamped 125Li4. Looking outwardly like its Series 3 predecessor the Series 4 Li 125 had a relatively short production run of some 1400 machines. Innocenti built a scooter that utilised existing stock and which also incorporated some new items that would feature on other machines. It is not known why Innocenti chose to build these scooters between 1967-68 and no factory paperwork, road tests or adverts appear for this machine.

At the time of the Series 4 being built, the SX 150, SX 200 and (for the Italian home market) the Li 125 Special were all in production. The fact that this scooter was a standard 123cc model lends itself to a possible theory that this scooter was built as an order for an organisation, dealer or government who wanted a simple utilitarian scooter (but the order never seems to be have been fulfilled). Machines have been seen that have the remnants of dealer stickers affixed to the horn casting or the rear light unit which lends some credence to the dealer order theory, but an order of some 1400 machines – highly unlikely to be an order for one individual dealer.

Innocenti chose to use a similar paint scheme to that used on the Series 3 Li 125, though the paint used on the Series 4 was more blue in nature than green. Internals on the scooter were painted white (eg: fuel tank, toolbox [where a metal one was fitted], airbox and flywheel cowling). The handlebar controls were also painted the same colour as the body, as were the wheel rims and hubs.

The horn casting used on the Series 4 was the same item as used on the Series 3, except that it had the oblong 'Innocenti' badge fitted. The badge had the usual blue background but had ridges running length ways on it. Innocenti also took the step of using the same 'Lambretta' 'Innocenti' rear frame badge as found on the SX range and the Li 125 Special. All other badges on the Series 4 machine were the same as used on the Series 3 machine.

Innocenti chose to use clip on type sidepanels on the Series 4, these pre-dating the ones used on the later SX machines. Behind the panels the set-up was the same as on the Series 3 Li 125.

The initial batches of Series 4 machines had metal toolboxes and bolt in type fork buffers. This was changed on later machines to push in fork buffers and a grey plastic tool box. This would appear to simply be Innocenti using up old stock before moving on to new items. As was common with all later built Lambrettas the Series 4 machine did not have a chrome ring fitted beneath the headset.

Dark blue dualseats were fitted to the Series 4, although an original model has been seen that was fitted with single seats (though this could be a change made by a dealer and not the factory).

The engine on the Series 4 Li 125 had the same cylinder barrel as that found on the Li 125 Special and shared the same gearbox set-up utilising the 15 tooth sprocket and 46 tooth crownwheel.

Production changes

No known changes during the production period.

What the tester said

Despite extensive searching no known road tests have been found for this model.

Built as a special order? No one now knows why the Series 4 was built. (Courtesy Lambro Motori)

The Series 4 had an oblong ridged badge fitted on its horncast. (Courtesy Lambro Motori)

The internals on the Series 4 were painted white. (Courtesy Lambro Motori)

As with the later SX machines, the Series 4 Li had a rear frame badge that simply said 'Lambretta Innocenti.' (Courtesy Lambro Motori)

tredici

13

J range

Although Innocenti had produced a 48cc moped, it wasn't the commercial success it had hoped for, so the company's designers and engineers then looked at producing a 50cc scooter, which eventually was shown in the Salone di Milano in 1961. This project didn't gain much public approval and so was put on hold. Innocenti's rivals, Piaggio, saw their chance to produce a smaller capacity scooter and came up with the 'Vespino.' In response to this Innocenti looked at itssmall scooter prototype and reworked it to become the 'Cento,' and part of a new series of models called the Junior range. It's worth noting that the range wasn't known as the J Range in Italy because the Italian alphabet doesn't contain the letter J. However, the Innocenti I had a small curve at its base and to some it looked like a J, hence the reference to 'J Range.'

All of these machines shared the same characteristics and instead of the tubular steel frame found on the Li-style models, the J range machines used a lightweight monocoque frame. This frame was made from pressed steel sections welded together in exactly the same way that the Vespa was built. The frames had no horn casting (though a fake item did feature on the 'Super Starstream') and items such as the mudguard and rear light unit were simply bolted on. Suspension came in the form of a separate damper and spring at the rear of the scooter and an undamped trailing-link fork at the front. Between 1964 and 1970 the J range underwent

Introduced to the UK consumer as the exciting new Lambretta the Cento arrived in 1964 (Courtesy Lambretta Concessionaires)

It wasn't long before sporting Lambretta riders discovered that the Cento was lightweight and quick. (Courtesy Scooter & Three Wheeler)

Early Centos came equipped with single seats. (Courtesy Lambro Motori)

numerous changes, modifications and saw the introduction of a number of different machines in an attempt to appeal to new markets. With a combined production run from March 1964 until May 1971 a total of 167,784 J Range machines left the Innocenti plant.

The Cento/J98

Cost (when new): £109 17s 6d
Dimensions: Length: 1690mm, width 630mm, height 1030mm, weight 80kg
Total production: 17,642
Months of least production: January, July, August and September 1965 – 0 machines
Month of most production: September 1964 – 3014 machines

The Cento was Innocenti's original J range machine, and was first shown in the Spring of 1963, beating the J50 into production. This being despite the fact that a J50 had first been shown in 1961. At 98cc, the Cento was the smallest capacity Lambretta manufactured by Innocenti when it was introduced. Lambretta Concessionaires introduced the machine with advertisements stating: "Lambretta breaks the fares barrier with the amazing Cento."

Production of the Cento began in March 1964 and carried on until November 1965, the first month of production saw 199 Centos being made, while the last month of production saw 1000 machines leave the factory. The Cento featured the light, pressed steel monocoque J frame which made it an extremely lightweight machine. Under the seat was a storage space for tools and oil. Early Cento's had two single seats, although later models featured a dualseat (a point to note here is that the May 1964 advert for the Cento shows it with two single seats and by August 1964 it was shown in an advert with a dualseat). It must be pointed out that the seat pressing for the

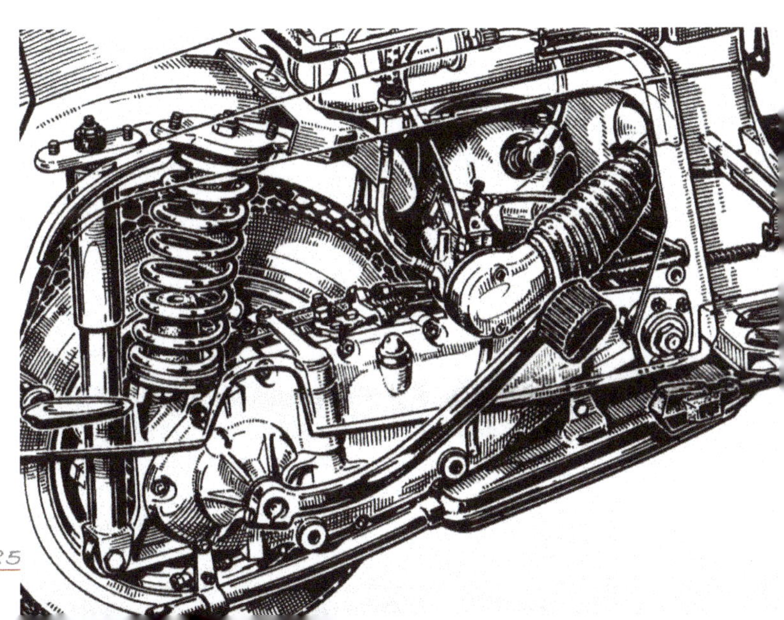
In 1966 Innocenti revised the Cento and offered it with a stronger frame and a 4-speed gearbox.

dualseat was not an integral part of the frame pressing, instead it was a separate bolt on item. As a point of note, the test Cento supplied by Concessionaires (registration '100 COY') came with a dualseat fitted for the 1964 road tests.

The Cento was fitted with grey rubber trim throughout and on the front right-hand side of the legshields a large 'Cento' badge was fitted. On the left-hand side of the legshields 'Lambretta' and '100' badges were fitted. The engine was much the same as that found on the Li machines, except that the barrel was now upright and the engine mountings were at the front. The 3-speed 98cc engine ran with a Dell'Orto SHB 18/16 carburettor and produced 4.7bhp @ 5300rpm, giving a reasonable top speed of 46mph. The front wheel had three bolt fixings on the rims and the front forks had bolt in rubber buffers. The wheels on the Cento having 3.00 x 10 inch tyres.

The UK market were informed that the Cento was available in 'Ivory' when it was launched on the market in 1964. By 1966 Lambretta Concessionaires were offering the Cento with a choice of five different side panel colours.

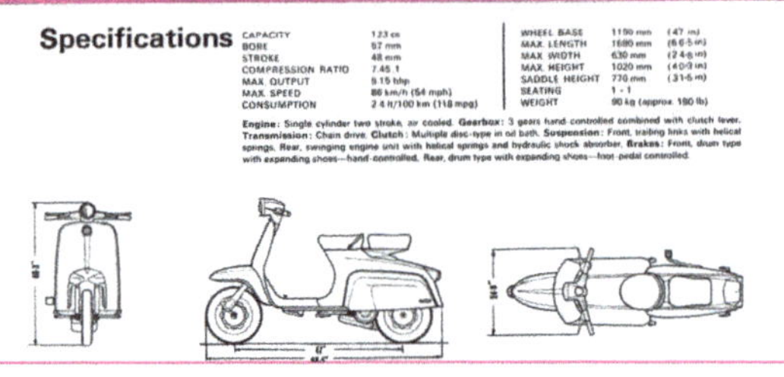

The specification sheet for the J125 shows it with a dual seat, though early models came with single seats. (Courtesy Innocenti Motor Corporation)

Production changes

No major modifications during production. A rectangular steering lock was introduced from December 1964.

Did you know?

Works Centos. The 1964 Cambrian Two Day Scoot saw Lambretta Concessionaires entering two Centos. The scooters were ridden by Colin Campbell and Tony Tessier (both from the Greenford Lambretta Club). Both scooters did well on Day one but on Day two Colin's machine developed carburettor trouble and had to be withdrawn. Tony's machine completed the course on time.

What the tester said

"Although the styling is so obviously Lambretta the engine panels with their crisp, angular treatment give this latest Lambretta a distinctive appearance. Sleekness is further emphasized by stopping the footboards at the front edge of the engine panels instead of continuing them towards the rear as is the practice with other Lambretta models. Twin saddles are included as basic equipment. They are of more substantial section than the normal run of twin saddles and add to the overall neat appearance of the machine." – *Scooter & Three Wheeler* May 1964

"The dualseat proved comfortable even on long runs. During the test period the Cento was driven by a number of people and not even the six-footers were cramped by the fact that the footboards are more restricted than other models in the Lambretta range. Pillion passengers did, however, have to sit well forward for maximum comfort." – *Scooter & Three Wheeler* August 1964

"However much thought Lambretta give to styling, their scooters are not mere ornaments. They go – and well, with the minimum of fuss. The Cento, by virtue of its small size, its 120mpg economy and its agility epitomises the whole range. This is the sort of vehicle that requires only petroil and the regular rejuvenating kick (on the starter, of course). It is the nearest thing to complete mobility that the frustrated car commuter can get – without sacrificing too much of his weather protection." – *Motor Cycle* 16th April 1964

"Latest Lambretta startlingly departs from tradition. Long wedded to tubular notions, Innocenti designers took a deep breath and for their 98cc lightweight Cento plumped for sleek spot welded steel sheet style first set by scooter pioneer Vespa in 1946. Long established, the Lambretta tubular steel chassis has no place in Cento." – *Scooter World* May 1964

"The toolkit contained the barest essentials for very simple adjustments on the road and we feel would need to be supplemented for owner maintenance. A more fitting description of the screwdriver would be a smokers pipe scraper. The brakes, when both applied together, would cope quite well with the capabilities of the machine. The back was a stopper having just that little more bite than the front which required the full span of the brake lever. This in all probability could have been corrected by adjustment." – *The Scooter with Power & Pedal* July 1964

The J125 (3-speed)

Cost (when new): £139 18s 9d
Dimensions: Length 1690mm, width 630mm, height 1030mm, weight: 88kg
Total production: 21,651
Months of least production: January 1966, June, July and August 1966 – 0 machines
Month of most production: October 1964 – 2838 machines

September 1964 saw Innocenti launch the three-speed J125, though it didn't hit the UK market until 1965. Again utilising the pressed steel monocoque frame it was introduced with single saddles as standard, although later models were built with a dualseat. The 122.48cc engine produced 5.8bhp @ 5300rpm which gave the rider a top speed of 54mph, equal to the top speed of some Li series machines, Innocenti were also keen to mention the improved power to weight ratio which helped the performance. Innocenti claimed a cruising speed of 50mph and fuel consumption of 118mpg. However, Innocenti used small engine mounts on this machine and, because of this, it vibrated quite badly.

The legshields had seven grey plastic runners fitted and grey rubber trim was used elsewhere on the scooter. Suspension and brakes and the main running gear of the J125 were exactly the same as that found on the Cento. The UK market was offered the J125 in one colour scheme which was listed as grey but which was actually silver.

Production of the three-speed J125 ceased in September 1966 when the final batch of 23 machines left the factory.

Production changes

1st Version (September 1964 to December 1964): Steering lock housing was cylindrical. Bolt in front dampers fitted.

2nd Version (built between 1965 to 1966): Steering lock now a rectangular item. Press in front dampers fitted. The sidepanels had handles without cogs from January 1966.

Did you know?

Acrobatic J125. 1965 saw Dr Guido Candelo (General Secretary of the Lambretta Club

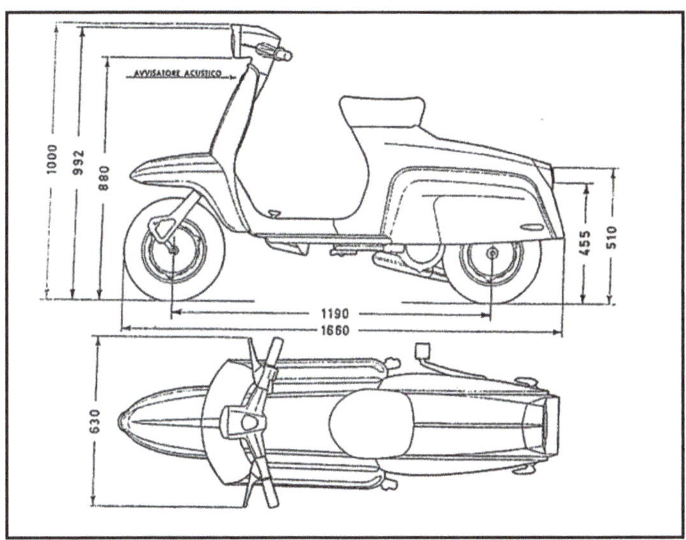

Dimensions of the proposed J50, showing the single seat configuration. (Courtesy Rimini Lambretta Centre)

Not the keys to the house ... but these make you grown-up: the keys to Lambretta J 50 (Courtesy Innocenti Motor Corporation)

International) present the Bromley Innocents Lambretta Club with a J125. The presentation was in appreciation of the Bromley Innocents acrobatic teams display at the Southend International Lambretta Rally.

What the tester said

"Ridden over a variety of surfaces, many of them very slippery, the J125 could be handled easily and confidently at all times. Some pitching on faster corners with uneven surfaces was evident, but the model remained directionally stable. Direct lighting is provided; it is adequate but no more. The horn could, with benefit give a louder note. The Veglia 60mph speedometer is easily read either by day or night; it was substantially accurate, being only 1mph fast at 30mph. With the usual excellent fan and cowl cooling of Lambrettas the J125 showed no ill-effects of hard driving,

A 1968 Italian advert for the J50. (Courtesy Innocenti Motor Corporation)

whether in top or the intermediate gears." – *Motorcycle* 21st January 1965

"Collecting the machine from the works, our first impressions were of cleanliness of line and easy starting. Both choke and fuel taps, below the seat nose, turn inwards and downwards. One push on the long starter primes the engine, the second starts it. After de-clutching and selecting the easy to see gear position, the J moves away smoothly. Reaching down, the choke is easily flicked open whilst riding. The 125cc engine takes the bike anywhere in top gear where accelerating from 15mph to a maximum of 48mph is possible: up hills, or in town there's always plenty of power." – *The Scooter with Power & Pedal* February 1965

"First impression on the road, despite the stiff engine, was one of ready willingness. A tweak at the throttle brought an immediate response and it required a lot of determination to maintain the recommended running-in speeds in the gears. Even at this early stage one would have been excused mistaking the mount for a 150. Later these early impressions were amply confirmed. In the road test report on the Cento (August 1964) every manoeuvre – cornering, braking, slow riding and tight figure of eights – was described as showing that the weight distribution and dimensions guaranteed a stable machine, completely without vice. Because the general layout is similar, all these remarks apply to the J125, but there is the additional advantage of the extra power." – *Scooter & Three Wheeler* February 1965

The J50 (3-speed & 4-speed)

Cost (when new): 109,700 lira
Dimensions (3-Speed): Length 1660mm, width 630mm, height 1000mm, weight: 78kg
Total production: 31,021
Month of least production: October 1964 – 21 machines
Month of most production: July 1965 – 3279 machines

Dimensions (4-Speed): Length 1660mm, width 630mm, height 1000mm, weight: 78kg
Total production: 38,967
Month of least production: August 1967 – 494 machines
Month of most production: September 1967 – 3528 machines

The J50 was an economy model introduced by Innocenti in October 1964, almost three years after it had first been shown. The first time it had made an appearance was at the Milan Show in 1962 where the show model featured some parts that weren't on the final production model. The show model was a two-speed machine that had sidepanels with a slot cut into them – pretty much like on the early TV 175 (Series 1) machines, these panels had no panel handles but used a panel fastener that was fitted in the top centre of the side panel. The kick-start also wasn't the same as used on the production machine, as it had a thin, cylindrical kick-start rubber, similar to that used on the later Luna line machines. The seat fitted was a small single seat with a pressed metal carrying rack behind it. The Earls Court show of 1964 saw a J50 on the Lambretta Concessionaires stand but there was no price tag on the machine and the only details provided were that it would be available in the Spring of 1965.

Again utilizing the pressed steel monocoque frame, the J50 came with a dualseat as standard. However, as the J50 was an economy model, Innocenti cut back in certain areas: no legshield trim was fitted, the rear light was a small item, the headset did not have a speedometer, no steering lock was fitted and the footboards featured four plastic runners with none being fitted in the centre. In place of the speedometer and the steering lock, plastic plugs were fitted. Also on this model, Innocenti used smaller wheels with 2.75 x 9 inch tyres being fitted, though ten inch wheels had been fitted to the prototype.

The three-speed engine had been given an overhaul and produced 1.47bhp @ 4500rpm, giving the rider a top speed of 25mph. As with its predecessors the J50 had the same suspension and brake set-up.

Launched in 1966 as the new star in Lambrettas galaxy. (Courtesy Lambretta Concessionaires)

It is interesting to note that no J50s were ever officially imported into the UK, though three did arrive for evaluation purposes. The final month of manufacture of the 3-speed J50 came in August 1966 when the final 204 machines were built.

In September 1966 Innocenti introduced a four-speed version of the J50 which was a slightly upgraded version in relation to the three-speed model. Gone was the weak frame of the three-speed to be replaced by a stronger body that had a longer area for the dualseat to be bolted to. As with the three-speed model, a small rear light was used and again no speedometer or steering lock were fitted.

However, the four-speed model had better acceleration and fuel consumption and its 49.8cc engine produced 1.47hp @ 4500rpm. Though the top speed for the J50 was still around the 25mph mark. Production of the four-speed model continued until January 1968 with a final batch of 1985 machines leaving the Innocenti plant.

Production changes

1st version (1964 model): 9 inch wheels. Wide legshields. Aluminium kick-start. No rubber trim fitted round the legshield. Bolt in fork dampers and a smooth area below the rear light unit.

2nd version (1965 to 1966 models): Again fitted with 9 inch wheels. Rubber trim now fitted to the legshields. Chromed kick-start. Push in front dampers. Stamped area below rear light unit and J50 badge fitted.

3rd version (1966 to 1967 model): Side panel handles with plastic cog. Newly designed frame, as found on the four-speed J125. Narrow legshields. 9 inch wheels retained. Engine silent blocks reinforced. Stamped area below rear light unit and J50 badge fitted.

4th version (1967 to 1968 models): The last batch of J50s were fitted with clip-on side panels similar to those found on the DL (GP) range.

Did you know?

Earls Court 1965. Although the J50 didn't officially hit the UK, one was shown at the 1965 Earls Court Show and an advert from Concessionaires (also in 1965) showed the J50 but no price was listed. The machine featured on the stand at the Earls Court Show, was a two-tone model with the main body being white and the sidepanels being in a contrast colour.

The Starstream engine was like all the other J range machines and featured an upright barrel. (Courtesy Lambro Motori)

Later Starstreams came equipped with clip-on panels. (Courtesy Lambro Motori)

Trailing-link suspension was featured at the front of the Starstream. (Courtesy Lambro Motori)

The Starstream was even used during tests to measure engine noise. (Courtesy Lambro Motori)

WHAT THE TESTER SAID

"Engine starting is extremely easy, the J50 we tested was left outside, without cover overnight in near zero temperatures, but this did not prevent the engine starting on the first kick of the pedal, without the need for choke and with the throttle closed.

"Other very noticeable characteristics of the engine are the absence of vibrations, even when the motor was highly revved, and remarkable absence of noise during operation. Finally consumption - we averaged 100kms on 2 litres, but one could easily obtain better results. As with other Lambrettas, the J50 has the usual 4% oil mix during the running in period – reducing to 2% thereafter, with all the advantages that this oil percentage brings, less production of smoke, oily residues and expense in usage, and the appreciable consequence of a better output from the motor."
– *MotoCyclisme* 1966

The J125M (4 Speed)

Cost (when new): £129 17s 6d
Dimensions: Length 1690mm, width 630mm, height 1030mm, weight 90kg
Total production: 16,052 (includes Super Starstream)
Months of least production: December 1966, May 1967, July, August and September 1967, December 1967, August 1968, January 1969, February and March 1969 – 0 machines
Month of most production: July 1966 – 2996 machines

In May 1966, four months before the introduction of the four-speed J50, Innocenti launched the 'J125M' or 'Starstream,' with 21 machines being built that month. This model featured the newly-designed and stronger J range frame with a new seat mounting and narrower legshields. As with the previous J range models, the Starstream retained the separate spring and damper rear suspension and trailing-link front suspension. Early four-speed J125s came with side panels that utilized the usual panel handle set-up, though this was to change on later models to clip-on items. Upgrades were not simply limited to the bodywork, as early machines had bolt in fork dampers which changed to push in items on the later machines. Badging on the Starstream was simply a plastic 'Innocenti' badge above the horn and a 'Lambretta' badge complete with a star (and '125' inside it) fixed on the left-hand side of the legshields. The Starstream came finished in pale blue only.

However, Innocenti had now added a fourth-gear which gave the scooter good acceleration and the 57mm x 48mm bore/stroke gave 5.8bhp @ 5300rpm and a top speed of 55mph. The UK market was introduced to the new four-speed machine in the Autumn of 1966, when the new gear set-up was explained as providing a "low" 2nd gear and a "high" 3rd gear. In fact the UK advert started with the following: "Another Lambretta designed for the jet-age. A sporty, speedy, easy to handle 125 that's as smooth to ride as a glide in space."

PRODUCTION CHANGES

No major modifications during production.

WHAT THE TESTER SAID

"Everything about the Starstream is new – it has a restyled streamlined monocoque body, the centre piece being the 4-speed engine unit with an improved bottom end. Overall height of the scooter has been reduced, rear suspension modified and with ample use of fibre glass it has been transformed into a lively lightweight no longer frowned upon by the GT or GS enthusiasts. Top speed is 54mph, which is about 11mph slower than the new SX 200, with 4th gear acting as an overdrive, which means flat out driving with fuel consumption only a few miles less than careful town driving. Maximum speeds in other gears on a flat run were, 1st – 25mph, 2nd – 35mph and 3rd – 45mph, which gave a 0-50mph time of 20 seconds, and a standing quarter mile in 25 seconds."
– *Practical Scooter & Moped* October 1966

"Over nearly 1000 miles of test riding, the Starstream needed no attention whatsoever. The simple tool kit is adequate for removing the sparking plug and carburettor jets and for other

J Range frames during the production process. (Courtesy Innocenti Motor Corporation)

Innocenti marketed the J 50 Deluxe as an upmarket addition to the J Range. (Courtesy Innocenti Motor Corporation)

Again, the Deluxe retained a pressed steel monocoque frame, though this one was slightly extended under the single seat, which had a carrier fitted behind. (Courtesy Marco Frosio)

small jobs, though it is a pity none of the spanners fits the nut of the front brake cable adjuster. To sum up, the Lambretta Starstream is a highly accomplished, reliable and well-engineered scooter for ride-to-work journeys. It also willingly copes with country runs. Smoother braking would do most to make this attractive machine even better." – *Motor Cycle* 29th September 1966

"The Starstream that we borrowed from the Lambretta works had been prepared for rallying and had twelve volt electrics and a spare wheel fitted. Neither of these affected the performance however, but we were glad of the fantastic headlamp when the bike was ridden up to Snetterton at night. The light was far better than

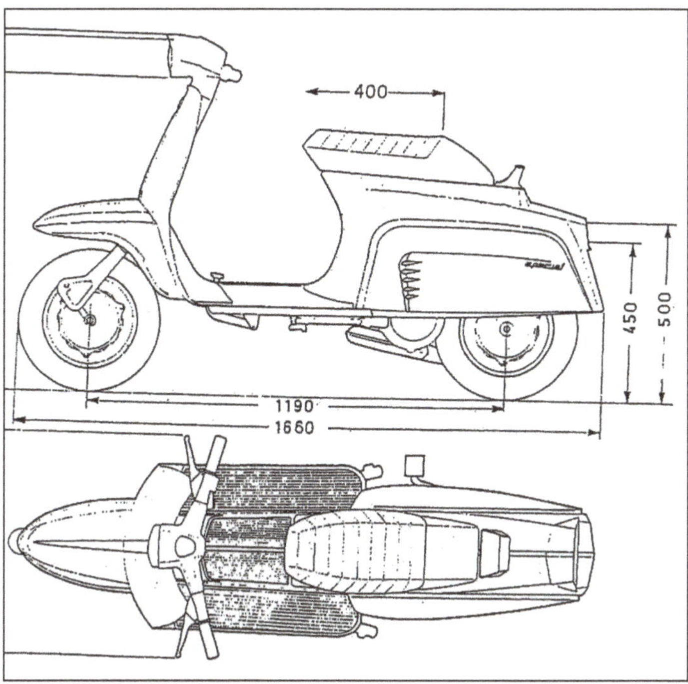

Original specification drawing for the J 50 Special. (Courtesy Rimini Lambretta Centre)

The final J range machine, the J 50 Special, was introduced in April 1970. (Courtesy Rimini Lambretta Centre)

the rather dim six volt beam of the SX and the larger scooter ended up following the Starstream. Once warm the little 'tooter' could be cruised flat out without any trouble. The only bother with cruising on full throttle is that the engines become very thirsty." - *Motorcycle Mechanics* Nov 1966

The Super Starstream

Cost (when new): £139 17s 6d
Dimensions: Length 1690mm, width 630mm, height 1030mm, weight: 90kg

Alongside the Starstream, Innocenti launched the 'Super Starstream' in May 1966. Although it shared the same frame and bodywork as the Starstream it was identifiable by its turning front mudguard, fake horn casting and clip-on side panels.

As with the Starstream, the Super Starstream had a four-speed transmission and enlarged engine mounts to reduce vibration. Rear suspension remained the tried and tested form of a single spring and damper set-up.

It is not known how many Super Starstreams were produced, but the number is considerably less than that of the Starstream.

Production changes

No major changes during production.

Did you know?

In 1968, Peter Lumley, the editor of *Scootering and Lightweights* rode a Super Starstream to Milan for the 21st Lambretta Birthday Rally. During the trip he accompanied Ken Peters who was riding a Model A. Peter's Starstream being loaned to him by Lambretta Concessionaires. The scooter (bearing the registration 'UYE 66F') covered 1500 miles during the five day trip.

What the tester said

"Economywise this is also a pleasing machine, when I first brought it home from Lambretta Concessionaires I had a bare 143 miles for the first two gallons, then as the running in period was completed this improved considerably to an average of 90mpg with reasonably fast traveling. I found that the mid-80s was a fair figure for in-town work and then on that run to Italy and back the consumption worked out at five litres for every 110 or 120 miles with an overall consumption of 8 gallons for the 740 miles from Milan to Ostend.

Bear in mind, though, that I was carrying most of the luggage – equal to more than two up – and that occasionally I went ahead to film Ken and then had to catch him up again." – *Scootering and Lightweights* July 1968

The J50 De luxe

Cost (when new): 120,000 lira
Dimensions: Length 1660mm, width 630mm, height 1000mm, weight 80kg
Total production: 28,852
Months of least production: June 1969, June, July and August 1970 – 0 machines
Month of most production: February 1968 – 3040 machines

Ostensibly a re-working of the J50 machine, the 'J50 De luxe' was launched in January 1968 with the first 366 machines being built. Innocenti marketed the Deluxe as an up-market addition to the J range. Again the De luxe retained the pressed steel monocoque frame, although this one was slightly extended under the single seat which had a carrier fitted behind it. The single seat was finished in dark blue fake leather.

The J50 Deluxe had clip-on side panels which had Li-style flashes fitted along with a 'De luxe' badge. Around the legshields Innocenti fitted chrome legshield trim in place of the more usual grey rubber item. However, although this was marketed as an up-market machine as a 50cc model it still had no speedometer. It should be noted that with this model, Innocenti went back to painting the wheel rims and hubs in silver.

The 49.8cc engine had a bore/stroke of 38mm x 44mm and produced 1.47bhp @ 4500rpm which gave a top speed of 24mph. To aid handling the J50 De luxe had 3.00 x 10 inch wheels fitted. Production of the J50 De luxe ceased with a final batch of 50 machines in October 1970. In fact the final six months of production saw only 67 machines being built.

Production changes

No major production changes.

What the tester said

Despite extensive searching no road tests have been found for this model.

The J50 Special

Cost (when new): 120,000 lira
Dimensions: Length 1660mm, width 630mm, height 1000mm, weight 78kg
Total production: 13,599
Month of least production: March 1971 – 1 machine
Month of most production: July 1970 – 1796 machines

The final J range machine to be introduced by Innocenti was the 'J50 Special' which was launched in April 1970, alongside the J50 De luxe. Unlike the J50 De luxe, the J50 Specials first batch of machines numbered some 963. Though the production run for this machine was relatively short, ending just over 12 months later in May 1971. As with all of its predecessors the J50 Special again used the pressed steel monocoque frame and, like the J50 De luxe, came equipped with clip-on side panels. However, these had panel flashes with five 'fingers' on them along with a 'Special' badge.

A two-tone slope back seat was fitted, behind which was a plastic grab handle. Instead of the usual floor runners, a rubber mat was fitted and in place of the usual rubber legshield trim aluminium trim was used. As with the J50 De luxe, the J50 Special came equipped with 3.00 x 10 inch wheels.

The engine had a bore/stroke of 38mm x 44mm, however it received no modifications and again produced 1.47bhp @ 4500rpm, with the machine's top speed being 24mph. May 1971 saw the final batch of 162 J50 Specials leave the factory.

Production changes

No changes during production.

What the tester said

Despite extensive searching no road tests could be found for this model.

quattordici

14 Lambretta Amphi-scooter

Cost (when new): Not for general sale
Dimensions: Not known

The Lambretta amphi-scooter started life as a three-speed J125 which bore the registration number '52 DOY' (with this scooter being featured in a road test by Peter Fraser, when it was still land based, in the January 1965 edition of *Motorcycle*).

So just how did 52 DOY become a floating Lambretta? The story started back in 1965 when Philip Keeler (PR Manager at Lambretta Concessionaires) had the idea of creating an amphibious Lambretta for an exhibition in Brighton. The idea gathered pace and Rex White (one of Lambretta Concessionaires technical representatives) was asked if he would ride the scooter out of the sea at Brighton and onto the beach. Rex wasn't up for that, but did say that he would ride the scooter along the Brighton shoreline so that people could see that the scooter worked and didn't sink. So the wheels (or should that be floats?) were now in motion.

Jack Hornsby and pillion on the Thames. (Courtesy Power and Pedal)

Work started on the Lambretta amphi-scooter, which essentially was the three-speed J125 with two surfboards attached on either side – the surfboards being attached to the scooter with struts made mainly out of exhaust tubing. The tubing was fitted lengthways underneath the scooter, firstly in the area of the main stand and at the rear of the machine near to the rear wheel. Sections of tubing also went up by the sides of the sidepanels and were bolted behind the dual seat. To test the scooter's waterborne capabilities out, Rex White and another technical rep, Dougie Bedford, took it down to Portsmouth for some sea trials. All was going well, Rex was riding the scooter around the harbour while Dougie watched from a jetty. Rex then realised that his feet were getting

Dougie Bedford with the Amphi-scooter. (Courtesy *Power and Pedal*)

wet and that the scooter was effectively sinking. As he rode it round the jetty, Dougie had the bright idea of jumping off the jetty and onto the scooter. Now it did sink!

Having retrieved the scooter and still keen to carry on with the idea of an amphibious scooter, Rex realised that the surfboards were too heavy and it was their weight that had caused the scooter to sink. The solution? Simple, the surfboards were cut in half along their length, thus reducing the weight, and they were reattached. Further tests showed that the scooter now floated and there were no problems. Well, not at this time anyway. The surfboards had the name 'Lambretta Amphi-scooter' written on them and were positioned in an upright position when the scooter was out of the water and, obviously, placed in a downwards position when on water.

It's interesting to note that during the early days of the Amphi-scooter it had nothing over the flywheel cowling. This was later changed when a section of metal was made to cover the cowling and this metal section went up the side of the sidepanel and the top section faced rearwards, thus allowing air to flow in.

The January 1966 edition of *Scooter with Power and Pedal* carried a photograph of a bowler-hatted gent riding along the River Thames with a female pillion passenger (the bowler-hatted gent being Jack Hornsby, a West London Lambretta dealer, and the pillion his daughter Stella). *Power and Pedal* stated that the idea of an Amphi-scooter had no possibility of being a commercial proposition, though they did concede that the idea in essence was a good one.

The Lambretta Amphi-scooter managed to be ridden on a number of waterways, not just the early sea trials in Portsmouth harbour. These were followed by it being ridden along the seafront at Brighton, along the River Thames, along the Manchester Ship canal, in the Solent at the 1966 Portsmouth Rally (with Dougie Bedford dressed as Jack Tar), on the lake at Southend (when it was ridden by Bob Wilkinson), on the lake at Mallory Park and on Lake Windermere by Donald Campbell. The scooter also had its 15 minutes of television fame in September 1966 when it appeared on the BBC programme *Blue Peter*. Presenters Christopher Trace and Valerie Singleton tried it out on the River Thames at Putney.

Overall, a novel idea by Lambretta Concessionaires and one which would have been interesting had it been put into full production.

Production changes

No production changes as this was not a factory produced model.

Did you know?

Amphi-scooter sinks. In May 1968 Doug and Marion Saunders of the Bromley Innocents Lambretta Club took the Amphi-scooter onto the lake at Mallory Park. Up to that point the scooter had been used on various waterways and was now showing signs of fatigue due to its contact with salt water. Doug and Marion completed a couple of laps of the lake when one of the float supports snapped and the scooter disappeared under the water, although it was later recovered.

What the tester said

As this was not a production model no road tests exist for it.

quindici 15

SX 200 & 150

Although the TV 200 had not been available on the Italian home market, the Italians didn't have to wait long for a 200cc machine to be built that would be available to them. So, in January 1966 the 'SX 200' was launched, with 50 machines rolling off of the production line in the first month, the slow start soon speeded-up with 1468 being made in February 1966 and 2181 in March 1966.

Styling-wise the SX 200 retained the TV 200 and Li Special-style headset, horn casting and mudguard. However, the side panels were redesigned, and except for different gearing, the engine retained the same bore/stroke and carburettor as the TV 200. Interestingly, the April 1966 edition of *Scooter World* refers to the SX 200 as the "SX Grand Prix 200" and quotes Lambretta Concessionaires' Sales Manager Maurice Knight as saying "I have just ridden one of the new models, which although it had only one mile on the clock, impressed me with the smoothness of its acceleration, its latent zest and power, and its quite exceptional road holding qualities."

Lambretta Concessionaires adverts for the SX 200 proclaimed "Silk smooth acceleration ... at your finger-tip reserves of zest and power ... up to 90mph speedometer shows the performance potential. It wasn't long before the sporting Lambretta fans discovered this potential. The SX 200 became one of the most popular scooters

(Right & overleaf) Adverts for the SX 200 proclaimed: "silk-smooth acceleration ... at your finger-tip reserves of zest and power ... up to 90mph speedometer shows the performance potential." (Courtesy Innocenti Motor Corporation)

200 X SPECIAL

Capacity 198 cc • Bore 66 mm • Stroke 58 mm • Compression ratio 7 : 1 • Maximum power 11 HP at 5500 r.p.m. • Maximum speed 107 km/h (66 mph) • Consumption 3.0 l/100 km • Maximum length 1800 mm • Maximum width 700 mm • Maximum height 1030 mm • Wheel base 1290 mm • Weight 123 kg (270 lbs). ENGINE: Centrally mounted single cylinder two stroke, forced air cooled • GEAR BOX: Four speed constant mesh in oil bath • CLUTCH: Multi disc in oil bath • SUSPENSION: Front: twin trailing links with helical springs - Rear: swinging engine unit with helical spring and hydraulic shock absorber • BRAKES: Front: disc - Rear: drum • FUEL: Petroil mixture • CHASSIS: High tensile steel tube.

The information and illustrations on this leaflet are indicative and not binding.

INNOCENTI

SOC. GENERALE PER L'INDUSTRIA METALLURGICA E MECCANICA

MILANO ROMA NEW YORK PARIGI LONDRA CARACAS DÜSSELDORF

built by Innocenti, though its selling price in Italy of 190,000 lira put many people off buying one. In the UK, however, it was a popular choice for many Lambretta fans and it was used in many promotional events. The 1968 opening of Lambretta House in Croydon saw Bruce McLaren breaking a bottle of champagne over the side panel of an SX 200. That same year the Hepworths store in London's Regent Street had an SX 200 on display as the first prize in the Lambretta Club of Great Britain Championship. The scooter even had Hepworths logos on each side panel and the left-hand legshield.

Innocenti wanted a replacement for the Li 150 Special and, in October 1966, it launched the SX 200's smaller brother, the SX 150. Again, a slow start to production: 134 machines in the first month, followed by 2180 in November 1966. Aesthetically the SX 150 was different from the Li 150 Special as it sported a chrome horn grille, a chrome flash on the front mudguard and a change in paint schemes from the silver and gold of the Special to 'Spring Grey' and 'Apple Green' of the SX. Innocenti's engineers had also worked on the engine unit, which produced 9.38bhp at 5600rpm, as opposed to 8.25bhp at 5590rpm that was produced by the Li 150 Special. Again, the new scooter's name wasn't lost on the advertisers with adverts of the time proclaiming "Lambretta gives you SX appeal" and then, following outright wins for the SX machines on the Isle of Man, "Success is SX shaped." As with its larger capacity brother, the SX 150 was a hit with sporting scooterists, and 1968's Isle of Man scooter week saw John Ronald (Nottingham & District Lambretta Club) win the Manx 400 event on his SX 150.

By 1968 Innocenti was looking to replace both the SX 200 and the SX 150, their popularity resulting in a combined total of 52,021 machines leaving the Milan plant. Even with the eventual updating of the Lambretta by Bertone, the SX models remained first choice for many *Lambretisti*.

The SX 200

Cost (when new): £219 11s 5d

Dimensions: Length 1800mm, width 700mm, height

1035mm, weight 110kg
Total production: 20,783
Months of least production: August 1967, July 1968 – 0 machines
Month of most production: March 1967 – 2184 machines

Due to positive response to the TV 200 overseas, Innocenti decided to launch a new 200cc Lambretta in 1966 on the home market, this being the SX 200. This new model was allegedly designed by Pininfarina, but there weren't many changes over the style or shape of the TV 200. The SX 200 retained the slimstyle bodywork but had the familiar octagonal headset and redesigned side panels which carried large three finger arrowhead style flashes, with the number '200' on the middle finger. The design of the side panels accentuating the forward movement of the new scooter. However the changes did not stop there. The front mudguard was now a steel item as opposed to the TV's fibreglass one and the speedometer was now a 90mph version. The rear frame badge no longer stated the model variant but simply had a white background that had 'Lambretta' 'Innocenti' on it.

Italian home market machines were finished in white and came with a cardinal red seat.

Front suspension was greatly aided by the use of external dampers, while stopping power came via a disk brake. (Courtesy Lambro Motori)

The SX 200 retained the Slimstyle bodywork but had the familiar hexagonal headset and redesigned sidepanels which carried large, three finger arrowhead-style flashes with the number 200 on the middle finger. (Courtesy Lambro Motori)

The SX 200's legshield badge was the familiar Special with the addition of a smaller X200 badge. (Courtesy Lambro Motori)

Interestingly, Lambretta Concessionaires in the UK offered the scooter in a number of colour options. In 1966 the SX 200 was offered in white with a choice of 8 other colours. By 1968 the colour combinations being offered were: lemon/black, orange, lemon, black, royal blue and British racing green. These formed the Carnaby range meaning that Lambretta Concessionaires could offer 16 colour combinations at that time for the SX 200.

Throughout the SX 200's production run there were a number of changes to the scooter. Early models came equipped with a white-faced 90mph speedometer, white plastic switches, a horn grille that was painted the same colour as the scooter, the usual shield type Innocenti badge, painted metal tool box, grey rubbers and white-painted wheel rims. Later models came equipped with black switches, a rectangular 'Innocenti' horn casting badge, a polished horn grille, a grey plastic toolbox, black rubbers and the wheel rims were painted silver. A feature that changed on the scooter was the use of side panel handles: early machines used side panels that came equipped with panel handles, later models had clip-on side panels – a nod in the direction of the soon to be introduced DL/GP range of machines.

If all of this was not enough, the SX 200's engine had its piston, cylinder and exhaust reworked. With a bore/stroke of 66mm x 58mm the 198cc unit produced 10.3bhp @ 5500rpm. Top speed was quoted as 66mph but a *Motorcycle Mechanics* road test of November 1966 quoted 61mph. The reworking of the engine meant that the power characteristics of the scooter were changed and there was a reduction in vibration. Lower port timings and compression ratio gave peak power that was slightly down on that of the previous TV 200 model, but power at low revs was dramatically increased. Innocenti also looked at the scooter's gearing and they abandoned the high ratios of the TV 200 in favour of the ones used on the Series 3 TV 175. This resulted in a machine that produced 10.3bhp, that accelerated better than a TV 200 but had a marginally reduced top speed. To facilitate easier starting of the scooter an extra long kick-start was fitted.

In 1967 Hepworths, the tailors, donated a golden SX 200 to the Lambretta Club of Great Britain as the top award for the 1966/67 LCGB Championship.

Production of the SX 200 stopped in January 1969, with the final batch of 10 machines being built.

Production changes

1st version: (January 1966 to early 1968): Horn casting with shield badge. Painted metal toolbox. Bolt in fork buffers.

2nd version: (early 1968 to Autumn 1968): Horn casting now featured a rectangular badge. Grey plastic toolbox. Push in fork buffers.

Final batch: the final SX 200 models came with clip-on side panels, a chrome flash on the mudguard and a polished horn grille.

Pictured here is Eddie Hine of the South Devon LC, competing on the Isle of Man. (Courtesy Eddie Hine)

Did you know?

Win on First Appearance. The SX 200 model hadn't been out long before it was being put into use in the 12th Lambretta Club of Great Britain Reliability Trial at Snetterton. The scooter, ridden by Andy Bailie and Dougie Bedford, was the only SX 200 entered in the event. The event was marred by diabolical weather conditions and only 25 of the original 59 starting machines finished. Despite the weather, the SX 200 finished first, providing a huge publicity boost for the model. In total the scooter covered 406.5 miles during the 12 hour test.

What the tester said

"The SX 200 has the usual Lambretta control layout. The choke and fuel tap are found on the front of the engine compartment just under the seat, while lights and sparks are controlled from the central switch and key mounted in the rear of the steering column. The fuel tap has a reserve position which is just as well, as the bikes proved thirsty when ridden hard. The choke is necessary from cold but it can be turned off after only a couple of minutes. Gears and clutch are in the classic Lambretta style with the left-hand lever working both. Four gears are fitted to the SX with neutral in the normal place between first and second. To be able to change quickly and without fluffing the whole thing takes a little practice. The gears are not provided with a positive stop and it is possible to change from first to third without bothering about second – but this does not give very good acceleration times.
– *Motorcycle Mechanics* November 1966

"Acceleration is truly remarkable. By opening the throttle, you have to keep tight because it seems that your upper body is pulled backwards by a mysterious force. The maximum speed indicated by the speedometer is 107km/h which actually is usual under ideal conditions."
– *Motociclismo* May 1966

The SX 150

Cost (when new): £184 19s 6d
Dimensions: Length 1800mm, width 700mm, height 1030mm, weight 110kg
Total production: 17,642
Month of least production: October 1966 – 134 machines
Month of most production: November 1966 – 2180 machines

Launched ten months after the larger capacity SX 200, the SX 150 came into production in October 1966. The SX 150 was brought in as a small capacity sporting scooter to take over from both the Li 150 Special and the TV 175. Marketed as "The scooter with SX Appeal," the SX 150 had the now-familiar Slimstyle bodywork, the same side panels as the TV 175 (Series 3) and a redesigned headset. As with the SX 200, the SX 150 was to see a number of production changes during its 23 months of production. Early machines came with white switches, a horn casting grille that was painted the same colour as the scooter, side panels with handles, white wheel rims and hubs, grey rubber trim and the familiar 'Innocenti' shield badge on the horn casting. Later models, however, had black switches, polished alloy horn casting grilles, clip-on side panels, silver wheel rims and hubs, black rubber trim and a rectangular horn casting badge. However, familiar to all SX 150s was the use of a chrome flash fitted onto the front mudguard.

Modifications had been made to the scooter's 148cc engine which gave it a useful power increase to 9.38bhp at 5600rpm, with a bore/stroke of 57mm x 58mm. This was achieved by using revised cylinder porting and a new free-flowing exhaust system. The engine unit was treated to new gearbox ratios which had lowered first, second and third gears for good acceleration round town, and a larger than normal gap to fourth gear. A new type crankshaft, with extra big end side float, was also used which gave greater flexibility in all gears. This meant, overall, that a top speed of 56mph was achievable. The last batch of SX 150s (all 167 of them) rolled off of the Innocenti production line in January 1969.

Production changes

1st version (October 1966 to early 1968): Horn casting with shield-style Innocenti badge. Metal toolbox. Forks with bolt in buffers.

2nd version (early 1968 to Autumn 1968): Horn

US specification machines were fitted with Lucas Stinger rear light units. (Courtesy Lambro Motori)

Give yourself SX APPEAL

SX APPEAL is built every Lambretta - that's why they are the world's finest scooters
SX APPEAL is power to spare (at 40 m.p.h. the engine is reving at only half its maximum
SX APPEAL is comfort and economy
SX APPEAL is rocket-like acceleration
SX APPEAL is ease of handing (powerfull brakes and ultra smooth suspension)
SX APPEAL is to enjoy guaranteed Lambretta service throughout the world

Vi da il SX APPEAL

SX APPEAL è in ogni Lambretta - questo perché sono i più bel scooter al mondo
SX APPEAL è potenza di scorta - perché a 65 Km/h il motor gira al 50% dello sua potenza massima
SX APPEAL è comodità ed economia
SX APPEAL è un razzo per accelerazione
SX APPEAL è facile da guidare (freni potenti e sospensioni supe morbide)
SX APPEAL è il piacere di disporre di una assistenza Lambrett in tutto il mondo

Give yourself SX APPEAL with the latest LAMBRETTA the SX 150

Lambretta Concessionaires enthusiastically marketed the SX 150 as the scooter with 'SX' appeal. (Courtesy Innocenti Motor Corporation)

casting now with a rectangular Innocenti badge. Grey plastic toolbox. Push in fork buffers.

Final batch 1968: Side panels with no handles,

Did you know?

Isle of Man Success. The 1970 Isle of Man Scooter Week saw Anne Weir (riding for the Manchester Lyons Scooter Club) riding an SX 150 (bearing the registration 'XML 26G' – competitor number 43). The scooter had only 571 miles on the clock at the start of the event, but had done considerably more by the finish. Anne won a Gold medal in the Full Day Trial. The scooter developed problems on the Hillclimb meaning the clutch plates had to be changed.

What the tester said

"The SX 150 is a machine which has been developed (along with the SX 200) from the GT 200 design. The main modification is a new crankshaft assembly. This has spacing washers on either side of the small end between the rod and the piston bosses which gives more flexibility in performance. The con-rod is aligned from the small end eye instead of from the big end which is the usual way. Alterations have also been made to the porting, cylinder barrel and piston. The gearbox is the same design as that in previous models but the ratios have been altered. The ratios from the TV 175 are being used in the SX 200 while a completely new set have been made for the SX 150."
– *Motorcycle Mechanics* February 1968

"The dual seat was comfortable, but for the

annoying position of the seat strap which is about the only part on the bike which could well be lost. Starting was always first time and the rest of the electrics were all adequate but for the horn. Even with the six volt battery to supply a constant voltage the noise was no more use than a bicycle bell. The toolkit was very well stocked even down to a small file for cleaning the plug and the like, though on the one occasion I needed to use the kit, the only thing missing was the tool I needed. This was a small screwdriver to undo the screws around the headlight rim."
– *Practical Scooter & Moped* April 1967

"I collected the SX from Croydon on a cold, January day and with the predominance of ice and snow must admit that it was with some misgivings for what worse way to start a road test than with a view to the heavens from underneath 265 pounds weight and 190 pounds of borrowed machinery. As it was the bike behaved well, even across rutted ice, and I experienced no bother. Very early on I discovered the very ample acceleration – with in town traffic, single decker Green Lines and North Circular road lorries getting the brush off before I needed to change into fourth." – *Scootering & Lightweights* March 1968

"Only one or two scooters have impressed me as much as the SX 150. The only aspect I did not like was a very minor one. I feel very sore about the dualseat strap! The only reason I can think that makes the manufacturers continue to fit this item is because it can be so easily removed. I did not because I felt the test should be carried out on the machine as it was handed to me. The type of dualseat fitted is identical to that on the SX 200. The colour of the Lambretta we tested was plain white and as yet we have no information of the colours that will be available when the SX 150s reach the shops." – *Scooter & Three Wheeler* April 1967

"The SX 150 is decidedly quick off of the mark and it will more than hold its own in average company. Third gear, even at the lower 7.97 to 1 ratio, is good for 50mph. It is necessary to use cog to the full to minimise the effect of the jump to top gear (5.56 to 1) which is greater than the old model. Nevertheless, top gear is a flexible gear and frequent changes down to third are not necessary unless every ounce of performance is to be squeezed from the willing engine. A steady 50mph can be maintained in top and when needed up to 60mph is on tap. Mean maximum speed of the test machine was 58mph." – *Motor Cycle* 23rd March 1967

UK machines had their side panels and horn casting painted a contrast colour, as on this 1967 machine. (Courtesy Peter McNally)

sedici 16

Luna line

For 1967 Innocenti wanted a new scooter aimed at the teenage market. To this end, the design of the scooter was handed to the renowned Italian designer Nuccio Bertone and the result of Bertone's work was named 'Lui,' a scooter that even to the untrained eye could be seen to be radically different to any other Lambretta. With an appearance harking back to earlier Lambrettas like the Model C and D, the front half of the Lui's frame was tubular steel with the legshields bolted onto it, while the rear section was a pressed steel monocoque design. The wheel rims and hubs were designed to give a sporty look, with the hubs made out of a single piece of cast alloy.

The introduction of the Lui saw Innocenti's

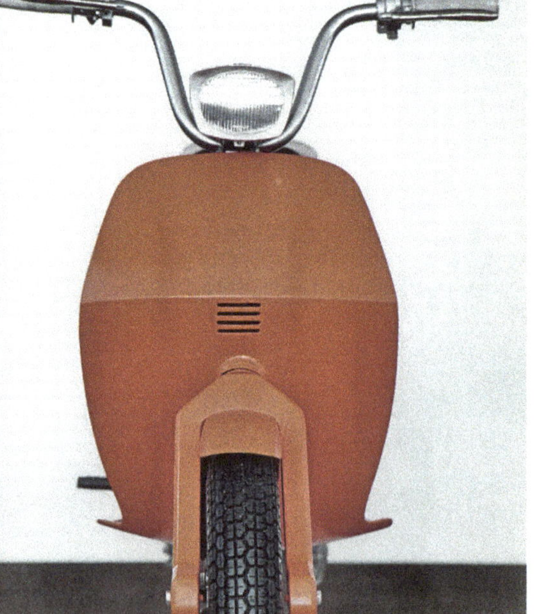

These photographs of two Luna line prototypes are stamped on the back by Innocenti and dated 1967. (Courtesy British Lambretta Archive)

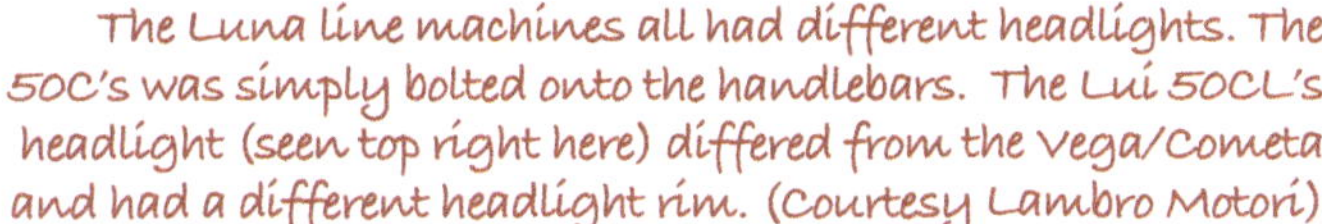
The Luna line machines all had different headlights. The 50C's was simply bolted onto the handlebars. The Lui 50CL's headlight (seen top right here) differed from the Vega/Cometa and had a different headlight rim. (Courtesy Lambro Motori)

advertising machine swing into action and a huge marketing campaign was undertaken with the slogan "All for Lui and Lui for all." Innocenti even advertised in school books in their attempt to capture the youth market. Adverts also appeared in many of the major Italian magazines of the time.

The first month of production of the Lui 50 saw just 150 scooters being made, while the ten months of production during 1968 saw a total of 20,665 50cc machines being built. The following 6 months of manufacture in 1969 would see a further 7147 50cc Lui's leaving the Innocenti plant.

The Luna line machines landed in the UK at a launch hosted by Lambretta Concessionaires at the London Planetarium (on Tuesday November 26th 1969). The Lambretta Concessionaires explained that the scooters had been identified with the space age by their futuristic styling and the use of lightweight metals and miniaturised components. However, despite the scooter's space age looks, an economic crisis hit the Italian motorcycle and scooter industry with many companies going bust and the Lui was not the commercial success that it should have been. Innocenti were not put off by this and introduced 75cc versions of the scooter called 'Vega' (75S) and 'Cometa' (75SL). The Cometa was another first for the Italian motorcycle and scooter industry as it featured an automatic oil injection system which received plenty of praise in the Italian press. However, the scooter buying public were not as impressed and preferred the Vega.

Although production of the Vega and Cometa didn't start until August of 1968, production numbers were small with only 4542 being built. Production of the Vega and Cometas only took place during January to June in 1969 and this period saw a further 4329 machines being built. February, April, September and December 1970 were the only months of production for the Vega and Cometa and a lowly 531 were made before production of the Luna line ceased in 1970, by which time a combined total of 37,214 machines had been built.

The Lui 50C

Cost (when new): 89,500 lira

Dimensions: Length 1700mm, width 660mm, height 966mm, weight 68kg

Of all of the Bertone-designed Luna line machines, the Lui 50C was the most basic and was introduced by Innocenti in March 1968. This machine had a small seat which was shorter in length and different in style to that fitted to the Vega. As the 50C was a base model, tubular bicycle style handlebars were fitted, onto which was bolted a small headlamp that had no dip beam, while a blanking plate was fitted in the space for a speedometer. The three-

A late 1960s Italian advert for the Lui 50CL: the differences between it and the Lui 50C are immediately obvious. (Courtesy Innocenti Motor Corporation)

speed 49.8cc engine had a 12mm Dell'Orto SHA 14/12 carburettor fitted and featured a narrow transmission casing (due to the small gearbox used). With a bore/stroke of 38mm x 44mm, the engine produced 1.48bhp at 4600rpm, and gave a top speed of 25mph. The 50C's exhaust was similar in style to that found on the J range machines. As far as the UK was concerned, the 50C was never officially imported into this country.

Production changes

1st version (March 1968 to early 1969): Standard levers. 'Lambretta' badge on left-hand side above '50C' badge.

2nd version (early 1969 to end of production): Ball end levers. 'Lui' badge in centre of legshields and, sometimes, a 'Lambretta' badge found above it ('Luna' badge used on export machines).

Did you know?

Racing Lui. In 1968 a Lui 50C was imported into the UK by Arthur Francis who then set about converting the scooter for use in grass track and field events. The 50cc engine was dispensed with and a 125cc unit used in its place. The scooter stayed in Arthur's possession until 1970 when it was passed to John and Norman Ronald who tuned it further for use on the track.

All for Lui and Lui for all; this 1970 advert shows the Vega and the Lui 50 CL. (Courtesy Innocenti Motor Corporation)

The Lui 50CL

Cost (when new): 95,000 lira

Dimensions: Length 1700mm, width 660mm, height 1028mm, weight: 68kg

Produced alongside the Lui 50C was a more luxurious model, the 'Lui 50CL' which had a proper integrated headset and used the slotted handlebars that were also found on the Vega and Cometa. However, although the 50CL's headset was the same as that found on the Vega and Cometa, it had no dip beam facility and no speedometer was fitted, just a blanking plate. Also, whereas the 50C had a black rear light unit,

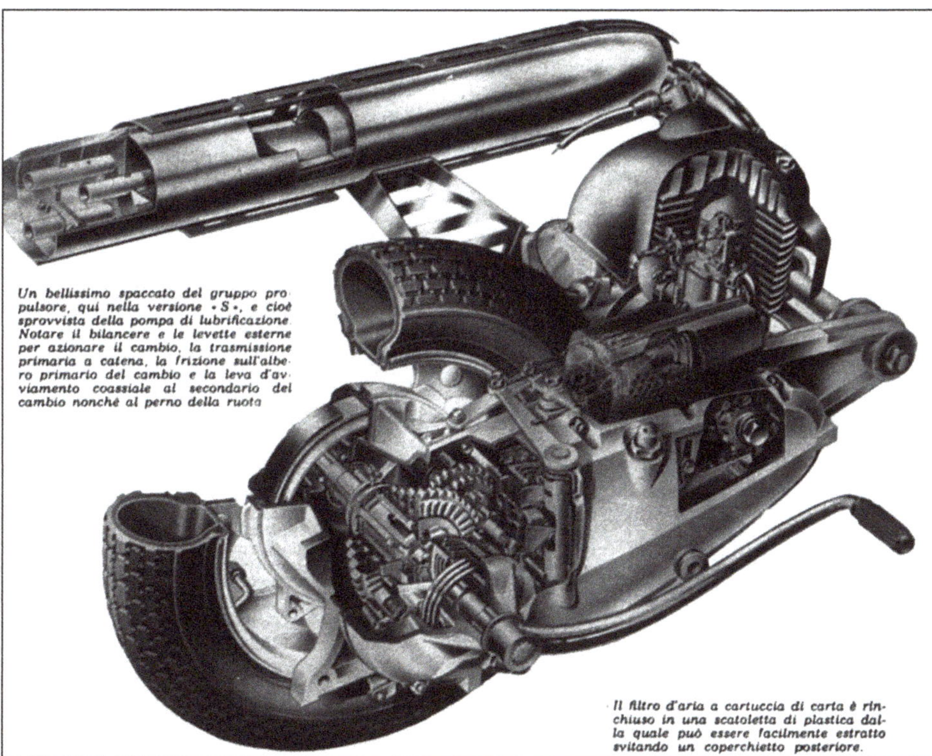

The Vega engine featured a radical exhaust and a new type of air filter. (Courtesy Lambro Motori)

the 50CL had a chrome item fitted. Behind the headset a plain grille could be found on early models, although this was changed from early 1969 when a grille bearing the 'Lambretta' name was used. As regards the engine this was exactly the same as that fitted to the Lui 50C. Three Lui 50CLs were brought into the UK for evaluation purposes though the decision was taken not to import them for sale.

Production changes

1st version (March 1968 to early 1969): Standard levers. Chrome grille behind headlight with no script. 'Lambretta' badge on left above '50CL' badge.

2nd version (early 1969 to end of production): Ball end levers. Grille behind headset with 'Lambretta' script. 'Lui' badge in centre of legshields and, sometimes, a 'Lambretta' badge above it ('Luna' badge used on export machines).

Unlike the smaller 50cc machines which had an exhaust under the footboards, the Vega and Cometa had an upswept chrome exhaust with matt black heat shields on the outside. (Courtesy Lambro Motori)

The Lui 50S

Cost (when new): not known
Dimensions: Length 1700mm, width 660mm, height 1028mm, weight: 68kg

This machine was produced by Innocenti for export only. As with all Luna line machines it had the same bodywork as the other 50cc models, though in a departure from their design it came with the longer Vega-style seat. The engine was the same 50cc unit, but was fitted with the upswept exhaust that featured on the larger 75cc machines. Coupled with this was the use of the same rear light and number plate holder that was also featured on the Vega and Cometa models. It is interesting to note that a longer front mudguard was fitted to some of these models, especially those that were exported to Scandinavia.

Production changes

1st version (March 1968 to early 1969): Standard levers. Chrome grille behind headlight with no script. 'Lambretta' badge on left.

2nd version (early 1969 to end of production):

Luna line models built for export markets like Australia had indicators fitted at the headset and by the rear numberplate. (Courtesy Johnny Lambrettista)

Ball end levers. Grille behind headset with Lambretta script. 'Luna' badge in centre of legshields and, sometimes, a 'Lambretta' badge above it.

The 75S (Vega)

Cost (when new): £115 19s 6d
Dimensions: Length 1700mm, width 660mm, height 1028mm, weight: 76kg

A few months after the introduction of the Lui, Innocenti used the Tokyo Motor Show to launch the Vega and Cometa, with production starting during August 1968 (although only 4 machines were made that month). These scooters were aimed firmly at people who wanted a small lightweight machine that had good performance. It was here that the main changes had been made and both machines were equipped with a four-speed, 74.4cc engine that had a bore/stroke of 46.4mm x 44mm and produced 5.2bhp @ 6000rpm. This coupled with the fact that the Vega had a 20mm carburettor fitted and a close ratio gearbox meant that a top speed of 51mph was now attainable.

Unlike the smaller 50cc machines which had their exhaust under the footboards, the Vega now had an upswept chrome exhaust with matt black heatshields on the outside. The bodywork remained as the 50C and 50CL machines, but the electrics received an upgrade and the headlight was now equipped with both dip and main beam. A rear brake light was also introduced. Another improvement was the introduction of a replaceable paper element filter that was used in the airbox.

In the UK neither machine was popular initially. It was not until Lambretta Concessionaires dropped the price of the machines to less than £100 that they started to sell, and then supply could not keep up with the demand. Many people realised that the machines were quite potent and good for competitions, provided a few modifications were made.

Production changes

1st version (August 1968 to early 1969): Standard levers. Chrome grille behind headlight with no script. 'Lambretta' badge on left above '75S' badge.

2nd version (early 1969 to end of production): Ball end levers. Grille behind headset with 'Lambretta' script. 'Lui badge' in centre of legshields and, sometimes, a 'Lambretta' badge found above it.

Did you know?

Welsh Two Days. The 1970 Welsh Two Days Trial included a competing Lambretta Vega ridden by John Davies of Alta Motorcycles. The Vega was the only scooter entered in the event. In fact the Vega's light weight, high ground clearance, low centre of gravity and easy handling made it an ideal choice for this event. That wasn't enough though, so this Vega's engine capacity was increased to give a higher maximum speed (near to 70mph) and the machine's acceleration was also improved. As the event involved 150 miles a day across the Welsh countryside, a sump shield and front dampers were fitted, the wheels were strengthened and knobbly tyres fitted. The electrics received attention to protect them from the elements and the cables were routed so that they couldn't be snagged.

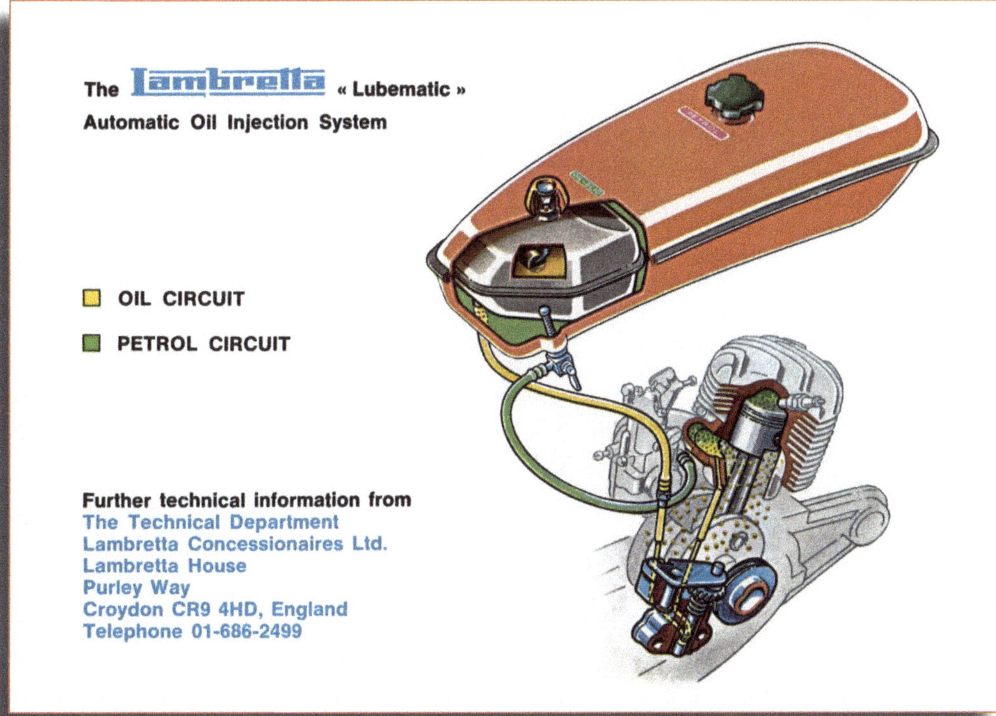

Prior to the Cometa's introduction, no other manufacturer had offered a machine that allowed the fuel and oil to be mixed automatically. (Courtesy Innocenti Motor Corporation)

What the tester said

"The exhaust system is unique on production scooters, the line is much as many motor cycle trials machines and has a grill over the pipe; there was never any great amount of heat built up to worry about and a pillion – if carried – would not have any problems. The fact that the exhaust is fitted does help handling when cornering the whole appearance too is enhanced. The noise emission is quieter than any other Lambretta I have heard, it also has a note which is better described as a warble – due possible to the two small bore pipes which leave the main 'box.' There are no sharp angles or bends, brackets or projections which might suffer after prolonged use." – *Scootering & Lightweights* December 1969

"Apart from looking very stylish the lights do work and they're well up to the standard required for the speeds available. The headlamp has a main and dipped beam with 6 volt 25/25 watt bulb and a 6 volt 5 watt 5 watt pilot light. Sparks come from a Ducati 6 pole magneto with a 33 watt output. Standard fittings include a steering lock and centre stand, which was well positioned and showed no signs of weakness though it looked rather flimsy. To sum up, the latest from the Lambretta factory is great fun to ride and should give very good service to those with low running costs in mind." – *Motorcycle Mechanics* January 1969

"Everyone was impressed with the power this fussy little two stroke produced. Careful use of the gears gave nippy acceleration up to about 40mph when it started to run out of steam, The long kick start is a joy to use, and never failed to start the machine on second prod, in fact first kick usually got the engine running. In the usual scooter manner the engine cooling is catered for by a ducted fan system, simple and at the same time extremely efficient." – *Meccano Magazine* September 1969

"The riding position, as on all large and small scooters was excellent. Both in town as well as out, without making you tired. The saddle was 77cm off of the ground but given the limited width of the seat even young people have no difficulty in placing both feet on the ground. The best comfort was at the end of the seat, but we preferred that the platform itself was flat instead of being slightly concave." – *Motociclismo* October 1969

The 75SL (Cometa)

Cost (when new): £125 19s 6d
Dimensions: Length 1700mm, width 660mm, height 1028mm, weight 76kg

Innocenti's advertising said that "... the Cometa has the space age sophistication of an oil-injection system which operates automatically from two separate tanks, one pure petrol [gasoline] – one pure oil." It was this 'Lubematic' oil-injection system that gave Innocenti another first within the Italian motorcycle and scooter industry. Prior to this no manufacturer had offered a machine that allowed both the fuel and oil to be mixed automatically. The system featured a pump which was driven from the engine's crankshaft, and this delivered oil direct to the inlet port in relation to the amount of throttle applied. This strictly controlled metering system ensured that the engine received the correct amount of oil at all times. Bodywork-wise and engine-wise the Cometa was exactly the same as the Vega, though 'Lubematic' stickers were affixed to each side of the frame.

Production changes

1st version (August 1968 to early 1969): Standard levers. Chrome grille behind headlight with no script. 'Lambretta' badge on left above '75SL' badge.

2nd version (early 1969 to end of production): Ball end levers. Grille behind headset with 'Lambretta script.' 'Lui' badge in centre of legshields and, sometimes, a 'Lambretta' badge above it.

What the tester said

"It impressed first of all for the tight turning circle – little over a machine's length – the lightness in handling and overall weight. All so very important for about town use but it didn't drop a point when hurried along and cornered hard. With this machine gone must be the tales of scooters not being any good on corners. The inherent qualities make it ideal for rough riding and I found endless pleasure in doing just that over all sorts of terrain without too much bother. In this sort of going its easy handling outweighs the disadvantages of a low capacity engine."
– *Scootering & Lightweights* June 1969

"During the past few years great advances have been made in two stroke design, notably by Yamaha and Suzuki with their breakaway from the traditional two-stroke mixture which was expensive to buy as well as being inconvenient to mix if you happened upon a garage without the right equipment. Now, with the Luna, Lambretta have followed suit and separate oiling is no longer an expensive luxury, but within the reach of Mr Average in the street. There are two separate tanks on the 75SL, one for a gallon of petrol and the other for two pints of oil. Oil is driven by a crankshaft operated pump in direct ratio to the demands of the engine at any given time."
– *Motorcycle Mechanics* January 1969

"The Cometa is a scooter which you like the more you ride it. The high perched handlebars allowed a comfortable driving position. The cut down legshield proved to give good protection. The tiny, almost non existent footboard was quite adequate and although the open engine gave a fairly high noise level at least the kickstart could be used without getting out of the saddle. On the other hand the saddle, which looked nice, was not exactly the best choice for a long journey. Most of our test riding was done in severe cold weather. The Cometa was left out overnight and started easily next morning. It seemed to thrive on icy winds, of which we met plenty, and it stuck to its line, and was almost unaffected by strong gusts – a very pleasing feature. The choke was always used for first start of the day."
– *Scooter World* April 1969

diciassette

17

DL/GP range

The talents of designer Nuccio Bertone were again employed by Innocenti in 1968 as it wanted to update the Li & SX scooter ranges that had essentially remained the same for ten years.

Engines had been modified over that time and the bodywork had received various facelifts, so could any improvements be made? Bertone rose to the challenge and came up with the DL/GP: a completely new design, but utilising the same power unit. Bertone determined that all DLs were to be one standard colour, whether it be red, blue, yellow, white or turquoise, but common to all the machines would be parts that were chromed or polished, such as the headlight rim, kick-start lever fuel and choke taps, while brake and clutch levers were to be matt black. This regimentation did not go down too well with Innocenti, had it refused to accept Bertone's ideas.

Bertone subtly changed aspects of the bodywork to set apart this new range. The bodywork redesign wasn't purely aesthetic. New forks with a shorter headstock featured clip-in buffers, rather than bolt-in items for the links, and a new spring and rod arrangement so that the forks could be disassembled without the need for a specialist tool. The headset was redesigned to make use of a more powerful rectangular headlight, and the handlebars were altered and raised to achieve almost the same ride height as previous models, despite the shorter headstock. The mudguard was restyled, as were the legshields, side panels and the rear light unit. The legshields were slimmer, the side panels had louvres and no badges, and a plastic rear light unit was used.

Performance-wise these were the best of any Lambretta models. It should be noted that, in the UK, these models were known as the 'Grand Prix' ('GP') range and they came with a chequered flag sticker on the legshield. In Italy and other countries these models were known as the 'DL' range and it came with an ink splat sticker on the legshield. The model identification badges are also different, for example, the UK machines had 'Grand Prix 125' badges, whereas the Italian machines had 'DL 125' badges.

The DL/GP 125

Cost (when new): £184 19s 6d
Dimensions: Length 1800mm, width 680mm, height 1012mm, weight 118kg
Total production: 15,300
Month of least production: February 1969 – 0 machines
Month of most production: September 1969 – 1026 machines

January 1969 saw the introduction of the DL/GP 125 which made an impression within the UK, by winning at the Isle of Man scooter week, even before it was actually available. In the first month of production, Innocenti built 836 DL 125s. The 125cc machine shared a new crankshaft with the 150cc machine, which featured a thicker flywheel taper and big end with more endfloat to cope with the higher revs that the DL engines were designed to run at. A new wider flywheel bearing also gave more support to the crank. A new, close-ratio, gear set was designed for this model and this was shared with the DL 200. Unlike the

The talents of Nuccio Bertone were again employed by Innocenti in 1968, resulting in a new design for the DL/GP range. (Courtesy Rimini Lambretta Centre)

other DLs, the DL 125 had a 20mm carburettor. The engine had a bore/stroke of 52mm x 58mm and produced 7.3bhp at 6200rpm giving a good turn of speed and good fuel consumption.

Inside the chaincase was a redesigned bronze clutch thrust bush and a plain phosphor bush replacing the twin roller bearings supporting the rear sprocket. The ramp which releases the kick-start plunger was now no longer a separate item that bolted onto the chaincase casting but was cast integrally with the gearbox endplate. Early production machines had an alloy rear frame grille that was painted the same colour as the scooter. However, on later models this was changed for a black plastic item. Likewise the horn casting grille on early models was metal and painted like the scooter, this was changed for a black plastic one on later models. But the changes did not stop there; early machines had metal fuel cap covers and a grey plastic toolbox, however, on later machines these were both black plastic. The DL 125 was available in only white or turquoise, with the wheels, hubs, splash plate and stand all being painted silver. Manufacture of the DL 125 ceased in April 1971 when the final batch of 40 machines left the factory.

Production changes

1st version (1969 to mid 1970): Cast aluminium horn grille. Dummy rear air intake. Fuel filler flap painted.

2nd version (mid 1970 to end of production): Plastic horn grille, plastic rear air intake and plastic fuel flap.

Did you know?

Oil Refinery Scooters. Southampton dealer Alec Bennett Ltd secured a contract with Esso to supply Lambretta scooters to its oil refinery at Fawley. This included an order for 22 turquoise GP 125s (taking the total of machines on the site to 150 in 1969).

What the tester said

"The footboards appear to have been slimmed, but are still adequate. The rear light unit is handsomely built into the bodywork. The headlamp unit is flat topped, integral with the handlebar cowling. Although the position of the exhaust system has been altered, there have been some radical styling changes since the Slimstyle Lambrettas were introduced. The main difference seems to be slimming amidships, with a gently drooping line. The front mudguard – always an awkward problem – has also been slimmed somewhat." – *Scooter World* April 1970

"Braking was adequate for the performance, but care has to be taken when applying the rear unit as the footboard mounted pedal can easily be 'stamped on' too hard to lock the rear wheel. Acceleration for a machine of this capacity was average, while fuel consumption must be described as excellent. Average was between 70 and 80mpg and with careful use 90mpg was possible. Electrics were also adequate for the performance, although the horn, like most two wheelers was not really loud enough."
– *Motorcycle Mechanics* August 1970

The DL/GP 150

Cost (when new): £212 19s 6d
Dimensions: Length 1800mm, width 680mm, height 1012mm, weight 120kg
Total production: 20,048
Month of least production: March 1971 – 107 machines
Month of most production: July 1969 – 2016 machines

Alongside the launch of the DL/GP 125 in January 1969 was that of the DL/GP 150 machine. The bodywork and frame were the same as its smaller capacity sibling, with the DL/GP 150 having the same minor production changes as the 125cc machine (eg: alloy rear frame grille on early models, etc.) Modifications were however made to the engine on the 150cc machine. The gear set was the same as that used on the SX 150, although the porting on the engine was now revised to make use of a 22mm carburettor. These changes to

Bertone explained that all DLs were to be a standard colour, whether it was red, blue, yellow, white, orange, or turquoise. (Courtesy Rimini Lambretta Centre)

When produced for export markets, the DL/GP 150 was available in white with ocean blue horn casting and side panels. (Courtesy Innocenti Motor Corporation)

the engine gave the DL 150 the same peak power as its predecessor but more power was produced through the rev range at both lower and higher revs. Power now peaked at 9.4bhp at 6300rpm. Machines built for the UK market had white bodywork with either blue or red horn casting and panels. However, in Italy the DL 150 was either white, red, orange or yellow ochre. Manufacture of the DL 150 also saw months of production where 'knock down' kits were made. These being supplied to other countries to be built in-situ. Total production of the 'knock down' kits was 1402, with their being made in March 1970 (300), May 1970 (100), June 1970 (352), September 1970 (250), November 1970 (250), December 1970 (50) and January 1971 (100). The final batch of 200 DL 150s left the Innocenti factory in April 1971.

Production changes

1st version (1969 to mid 1970): Cast aluminium horn grille. Dummy rear air intake. Fuel filler flap painted.

2nd version (mid 1970 to end of production): Plastic horn grille, plastic rear air intake and plastic fuel flap.

Did you know?

Best Seller. *Scooter World* magazine visited the Purley Way premises of Lambretta Concessionaires in March 1971. It noted that the main selling lines for Lambretta Concessionaires were the GP 125, 150 and 200 machines. Best seller out of them all being the GP 150.

What the tester said

"The 150 Grand Prix received from Lambretta for test was almost straight 'off the boat' with barely 200 miles on the speedometer. We covered over 400 miles during our test, and during that time we encountered no mechanical trouble whatsoever and we could find no faults in reliability. Starting from cold in the morning was always a first or second kick affair, providing the choke was fully closed. Then after 30 seconds, the choke could be fully opened and the machine ridden without further use of the choke. Starting was equally easy

Like its 125 and 150 counterparts, the DL 200 featured all of the Bertone-designed refinements such as slimmer legshields, narrower handlebars, a shortened horn casting, clip-on side panels, and a powerful rectangular headlight. The brochure builds excitement about Lambretta's Grand Prix models. (Courtesy Lambretta Concessionaires/Rimini Lambretta Centre)

when warm although no choke was needed."
– *Motorcycle Mechanics* June 1969

"The makers are claiming 9.42bhp at 6,300rpm and students of form will notice that they have quoted what is a quite high rev rate for Lambretta engines. From the road testing I did I can confirm that the engine does rev high and at the same time is running far smoother than any Lambretta I have been on before. It definitely gets smoother as it gets quicker. The electrics are powered by Ducati 6-pole flywheel magnetos and there is a battery. The main beam and dip are excellent, even at low revs, but I would appreciate a more strident horn. The headlamp design is unique on Lambrettas and the speedo dial is more easily read with more use being made of black."
– *Scootering & Lightweights* April 1969

The DL/GP 200

Cost (when new): £249 19s 6d
Dimensions: Length 1800mm, width 680mm, height 1012mm, weight 123kg
Total production: 9350 (this figure includes the DL 200 Electronic)
Month of least production: January 1969 – 1 machine
Month of most production: July 1969 – 997 machines

Production of the DL/GP 200 began, like its 125 and 150 cc counterparts, in January 1969 when a solitary machine was built. The paperwork listing the dimensions and details of the scooter were lodged with the Ministry of Transport on the 14th December 1968. Like the 125 and 150 machines, the DL 200 carried all of the Bertone-designed refinements such as slimmer leg shields, narrower handlebars, a shortened horn casting, clip-on side panels and a powerful rectangular headlight. Early models had a black metal horn grille while this was changed to plastic on later models. The DL 200's toolbox was grey plastic on early models and black plastic on later models. The rear light unit was redesigned and was a black plastic item on all models. The DL 200 had a disc brake fitted at the front along with external dampers. The 198cc engine had a longer chain, 22mm carburettor and the same gearbox as the DL 125, although on the DL 200 it featured 18-47 sprockets. This unit had a bore/stroke of 66mm x 58mm and produced 11.7bhp @ 6200rpm. The DL/GP 200 was available in three colours: white, red and yellow ochre.

The last 500 or so DL/GP 200s were supplied with electronic ignition, and wore a legshield sticker proclaiming the fact. (Courtesy Roberto & Kimberley Morelli)

Production of the DL 200 in 1969 was some 4777 machines, In the months up to June 1970 another 2111 DL 200s were made. The figures then becoming complicated because of the introduction of a new machine, the 'DL 200 Electronic' which had been tested by Italian magazine *Motociclismo* in June 1970. This model had a different seat fitted and an 'Electronic' badge on the legshield as a Ducati electronic ignition system was fitted which gave the advantage of a more powerful, maintenance-free ignition system for improved reliability and starting.

Italian home market machines were designated DL, whereas overseas they were known as GP. (Courtesy Roberto & Kimberley Morelli)

PRODUCTION CHANGES

1st Version (1969 to mid 1970): Cast aluminium horn grille. Dummy rear air intake. Fuel filler flap painted.

2nd Version (mid 1970 to end of production): Plastic horn grille, plastic rear air intake and plastic fuel flap.

DID YOU KNOW?

Diabolical Disc. The December 1971 edition of *Scooter World* magazine saw Miss J. Ellis from Leeds, writing in about her GP 200. She praised the scooter's performance, claiming 85mpg and on the odd occasion 100mpg. Her only complaint was the "so called first class stopper, the front disc brake, its absolutely diabolical." In fact she took the scooter back to her dealer to complain about the disc brake and was simply told to use it more firmly!

WHAT THE TESTER SAID

"At a time when people are talking about scooter racing being the next step in scootersport, along comes a standard machine which has speed and acceleration which has up to now only been attainable from tuned scooters. Aptly it is called Grand Prix and comes in Formula 150 and Formula 200 capacities, although I have test ridden the Formula 150 previously, and the report appeared in the April issue of *Scootering*, my first outing on the bigger version came at the Press Preview to the Brighton Motorcycle Show at the Brands Hatch Racing Circuit. Those first dozen laps were followed by over five hundred miles of test driving when I found the Grand Prix gives more than the makes claim." – *Scootering & Lightweights* May 1969

"For the enthusiast with long journeys at the back of his mind and £243 to spare this machine would take a bit of beating and is certainly worthy of serious consideration. Without exception our four test riders were impressed with the looks and terrific performance of this, the largest engine capacity scooter on the market. The horn was constantly criticised for its poor output, especially on such a quick machine, as indeed was the front disc brake which was rather below the standard we would expect from a system generally accepted to be more efficient than a drum brake." – *Meccano Magazine* January 1970

"We took over the GP 200 when it had less than 100 miles on the clock and we had therefore to wait patiently before opening the throttle wide. We therefore did more than the usual amount of riding in city streets since this is the best kind of riding for a new scooter. In crowded traffic the advantages of the GP 200 gearbox were very plain. Also very plain was the fact that the engine note is far from being subdued and third gear running in city traffic lets people know there is

The red rectifier box found on the DL/GP 200 electronic model. (Courtesy Roberto & Kimberley Morelli)

The DL 200's toolbox was of grey plastic on early models and black plastic on later models. (Courtesy Rimini Lambretta Centre)

Early DL/GP machines were supplied with horn grilles and rear frame grilles painted the same colour as the scooter, though later versions were supplied with horn grilles and rear frame grilles that were coloured black. (Courtesy British Lambretta Archive)

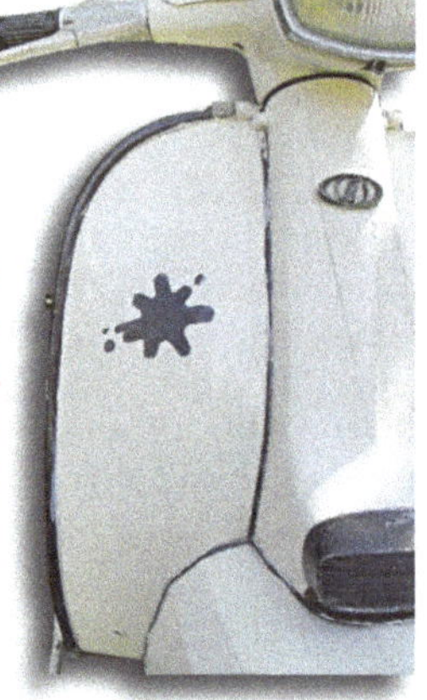

Italian home market DL machines had an ink splat sticker, and export models featured a chequered flag. Some ink splat versions were exported on demand. (Courtesy British Lambretta Archive)

something approaching them. It also showed how docile, flexible and safe the GP 200 was and how nicely the gears – rather low and close together – have been arranged.".
– *Scooter World* November 1969

"At first the much vaunted front disc brake seemed very disappointing. There was no bite and the rear brake seemed much the better of the two. However, after examining the front brake, it was found that only one pad was operating and in fact we were getting under half braking efficiency. With both pads working properly the front disc proved to be a first class stopper. Both units had plenty of 'feel' and although both wheels could be locked in an emergency stop very delicate application was possible when conditions warranted it." – *Motorcycle Mechanics* April 1970

"In performance, both GP models provide better acceleration and a higher maximum speed: this is obtained by engines having a bigger carburettor and a higher maximum output at higher revs than the SX series. The 200 engine gives a higher bhp and is geared lower to take advantage of the wider rev range. Internally both engines have modified crankshafts and other details to cope with the bigger output."
– *Motorcycle and Cycle Trader* August 1969

"The GP 200 is a reliable and easy starter. Petrol and choke on, ignition on and a couple of prods on the kickstarter and immediate response is guaranteed. In no time the engine settles to a perfect tickover – quite the best I have found on a single-cylinder two-stroke. Acceleration is brisk, to say the least, and it is more than ample to keep ahead of most cars and even a few motor cycles of equal power. Some vibration was evident in the lower rev range of the test machine but once the motor was singing it was as sweet as could be right up to top speed. This was claimed to be 68mph but to achieve it I had to use flat on the tank methods – something that most scooterists will not relish, particularly since it adversely affects the control of the machine." – *Two Wheeler Dealer* May 1970

The Companions SC from Essex, showing how popular the DL/GP range was. (Courtesy British Lambretta Archive)

The DL/GP 200 Electronic

Cost (when new): £249 19s 6d
Dimensions: Length 1800mm, width 680mm, height 1012mm, weight 120kg
Total production: Not Known

Around June 1970 Innocenti launched the last of their Bertone-designed DL/GP models, the 'DL/GP 200 Electronic.' Like the other DLs it had all of the Bertone-designed refinements: slimmer leg shields, narrower handlebars, clip-on side panels, a powerful rectangular headlight and shorter forks. The DL/GP 200 Electronic also came equipped with a sloped back seat that had waffle sides. As with the other later DLs the Electronic version had a black plastic horn grille and rear frame grille. The toolbox and fuel cap cover were also black plastic. As for the engine, gone were the traditional points and condenser to be replaced by electronic ignition. On original models the electronic box has a red rubber cover and a red HT lead. The original CDI units were Ducati made. The engine had a different crankshaft to that of the 125 and 150 models, a 22mm carburettor, the same gearbox as the DL 125 (using an 18-47 sprocket set-up) and a flywheel with a thicker taper and a wider bearing to give more support to the crankshaft. As far as badges go, the DL/GP 200 Electronic had an 'Electronic' sticker on the right-hand side of the leg shield. The scooter was available in white, red and yellow ochre. The hubs, wheels, stand and splash plate were all painted silver.

April 1971 saw the end of the GP 200 Electronics production run and it is not known how many were built.

Production changes

No known production changes.

diciotto

18

Dealer specials

Who presented the first dealer special to the scootering masses is probably open to speculation. Lambretta Concessionaires brought the Rallymaster to the Lambretta buying public in 1961 and, prior to that, had built the three machines for use in the Scottish 6 Days Trials in 1959 (though these were never available for the public). Essex scooter dealer Eddy Grimstead offered his Lambrettas in a choice of paint schemes and his dealerships would do some engine conversion work, too. His 'Lambretta Imperial' was advertised in 1964 and was based on the TV 200, then the SX 200, with a boast that it could be offered in over 1000 colour combinations and also as a 225cc model. Prior to 1964 there were no dealer specials advertised. However, the Brighton Show of 1965 saw Arthur Francis showing his 'S Type' conversion based on a Lambretta TV 200.

1966 would see other dealers join the fray, and it was during this year that the 'Supertune SX 200 Rallye' and the 'Woodford Z Type' were offered to Lambretta riders. The Rallye was a full-on dealer special with numerous modifications. The Woodford Z Type, offered by Woodford Scooters, was a Lambretta with a powerful 48w Lucas matched spotlamp and foglamp. A legshield glovebox was fitted, along with an ammeter. A special handlebar switch was fitted so that all the lights could be operated from it.

By 1967 Leicester-based PJ Oakley introduced its 'Mark Three SX 200' machine which, like the

The Harlequin dealer special by Wandsworth Bridge Autos. (Courtesy Practical Scooter & Moped)

Supertune machine, had numerous modifications. London-based Supreme Motors, however, chose to simply offer the SX 200 in a choice of colours and called it the 'Lambretta Supreme.' Not to be outdone, Wandsworth Bridge Autos in London offered those who couldn't make their minds up about colour a Lambretta called the 'Harlequin.' The Harlequin was a TV 200 Lambretta with over 30 colours sprayed on its entire bodywork, inside and out!

Paint schemes may have been the limit for some dealers but others kept on producing modifications for a number of Lambretta models. 1968 saw Scoota-Mobile offering a 225cc Lambretta conversion, along with a hyper-performance 30mm inlet manifold for use with Amal carburettors, while Portsmouth based Rafferty Newman introduced their Wildcat conversions along with a five port induction barrel.

Five years on from the adverts for Eddie Grimstead's Imperial, saw Eddie now offering the 'Tornado.' The scooter was based on the SX 200 and came in a two-tone paint scheme along with a 225cc version. The early 1970s saw many dealers stop producing dealer specials, among them Supertune which closed in 1971. This didn't stop new dealers offering machines or conversions, amongst them Roys of Hornchurch who under their Royspeed banner offered a 44mm exhaust, racing barrels (from 125cc to 200cc versions), double engine mounts and bars, transistorised ignition kits and 12 volt conversion kits.

Despite all of this, sales of Lambrettas dropped in the late 1960s and early 1970s, and the closure of the Innocenti works didn't do much to help matters. That setback didn't stop some dealers and it is all credit to Ray Kemp, who took over the mantle from Arthur Francis, that he is still going strong and still producing 'S Type' Lambrettas.

The main dealer specials of the 1960s and early 1970s will now be looked at in detail.

A Royspeed machine ridden by Doug May. (Courtesy Mick Murphy)

Doug Miller aboard his SX 200 S Type on the Isle of Man. (Courtesy Doug Miller)

Arthur Francis, New Road, Lower High Street, Watford

In 1963 and 1964 Arthur Francis spent most of his spare time experimenting with his own Lambretta TV 200, doing some mild tuning to the scooter. The work that was carried out produced definite improvements. He then asked a design expert to produce a paint scheme and a sports rear carrier for the scooter: the result was the Sebring rear carrier and the two-tone AF paint scheme.

In November 1965 Arthur had a stand at the Brighton show. On the stand was displayed one of his TV 200 S types. Following the show, Arthur got a fantastic response to the scooter and he received numerous enquiries from as far afield as America.

The S Type TV 200 was based on a standard Lambretta TV 200. However, the 198cc engine had been stripped and rebuilt to exact tolerances. Whilst rebuilding the engine the ports were cleaned up and the gear ratios were modified by fitting lower gears.

Aesthetically, to the causal observer, the TV 200 was recognisable by the addition of ball end levers, a 100mph speedometer, a sports flyscreen, Sebring rear carrier and a lockable legshield mounted spare wheel. Topping off all of this was a two-tone paint finish and the addition of an 'S' symbol on the legshields and side panels. The 'S'

The AF 250 was tested in 1967 at Brands Hatch. (Courtesy Practical Scooter)

badges being sourced from the then popular Mini Cooper S. Extra touches to the scooter were: 12volt lighting and Maserati air horns. The 12 volt lighting giving a vast improvement over the normal 6 volt set-up. Mounted on the legshields were two Lucas spotlamps, which had had a quartz iodine bulb conversion. These gave a 160 watt beam when used. These lights could be used with the normal main/dip beam or dip/spots with the dip/main cutting out when the spotlights were used. Also added to the engine unit was a Wal Philips fuel-injector. Although the latter was much maligned by many scooterists, a road tester from *Scooter & Three Wheeler* magazine noted that the fuel-injected machine seemed somewhat smoother, with a quicker and cleaner pick-up on an opened throttle. The 100mph speedometer was calibrated and claimed to have better accuracy than the standard item. Arthur did offer the option of a rev counter, which could be mounted neatly in the spare wheel boss. The machine cost an extra £40 for the modifications (not including the fuel-injector, air horns and 12 volt lighting). The fuel injection cost an extra £10, the 12 volt lighting an extra £12 and the air horns an extra £5 19s 6d.

By 1967 the number and variations of machines offered by Arthur was phenomenal with the following options being offered:

200 S Type: Based on the SX 200 only, the engine was stripped for stage one exhaust port and piston modification, compression was raised and the engine was rebuilt to exacting tolerances. The bodywork was painted in the S type scheme to the customers choice. A Sebring rear carrier was fitted, along with ball end levers, legshield-mounted spare wheel, damper gaiters and S type badges.

150 S Type: Based on the SX 150 only, the engine undergoing the same changes/modifications as the 200. Specification was as per the 200 less the damper gaiters. It is interesting to note that the SX 150s were offered in the S Type paint scheme. However, the machines had to have their panels and horn casting resprayed white before the S type scheme could be added.

200 Extra S Type: Based on the SX 200, the engine was given a stage 3 tune with extensive modifications to the exhaust and transfer ports, compression was raised along with increased induction overlap. An AF ultra performance exhaust system with a big bore U-bend was fitted with a megaphone tail silencer. The specification was as per the 200 S Type with double engine mounts also being fitted, a disk brake modification and S type badges.

150 Extra S Type: Based on the SX 150, the engine received the same modifications as the 200cc machine. This machine's specifications being the same as the 200cc scooter, less the damper gaiters. 'S' badges were fitted to the panels.

225 S Type: The cylinder was precision bored and then fitted with a high performance 70mm piston. The exhaust and transfer ports were reshaped and the inlet port was polished and matched. A 71mm squish head was fitted along with an AF manifold and 26mm carburettor. An ultra-performance exhaust was also used. Double engine mounts were fitted, the disk brake was modified, 'S' badges together with a '225' legshield badge.

Arthur also supplied a 12 volt pathfinder light set-up which included Lucas spotlamps and foglamps mounted on the legshield, new handlebar end, and switchgear for fingertip control and concealed wiring. A deluxe pathfinder set-up was also offered which involved modification of the toolbox and extending of the battery tray to create a 12 volt battery system, with the second battery being mounted inside the toolbox.

In a January 1967 road test in *Practical Scooter* the test machine was an SX 200 Extra S Type finished in metallic orange and white. The engine had been fitted with the thinner TV 200 head gasket and the carburettor had been opened out to 21.7mm with the main jet being increased from a 103 to a 120 item. The exhaust was an Ancillotti unit with a second fixing bracket welded on to prevent any fracturing of the bracket. The handlebar switches were from an Li 150 (Series 3). A zener diode was fitted in order to prevent over-charging. The Sebring rear carrier was sprayed to match the metallic orange of the scooter. The braking set-up was converted to a reverse pull system. A 100mph speedometer was fitted, with the machine attaining 70mph down a slight incline, average top speed being 68mph. The air filter box had also been drilled to allow more air to the filter.

Another test in the March 1967 edition of *Practical Scooter* concerned a 250cc S Type at Brands Hatch. To achieve the 250cc conversion Arthur had tried various barrels with an SX 200 bottom half and cylinder head, eventually settling on an alloy barrel. The scooter that featured in the test had a concentric Amal 1 3/16in carburettor fitted. The gearing had been changed to that of the Li 125 Special and the tester felt that the scooter was under geared, though the scooter did manage to top 80mph. The scooter on test was set-up for track use as a solid rear suspension had been fitted. A long race-style dual seat was also fitted. The scooter was also available for road use in the usual AF S type scheme. The road going version being fitted with a piston that had a deeper skirt than the track version and which provided more power lower down the rev range. It was also equipped with a normal rear suspension unit.

All of Arthur's hard work came to fruition when Team S Equipe (with riders John and Norman Ronald and Neville Frost) came first, second and third at the 1968 Isle of Man Scooter week.

The phasing out of the SX range for the new DL/GP machines saw Arthur Francis continuing to carry out S type conversions on these new machines and racing successes came again with 1st, 2nd and 3rd places for an S Type Lambretta.

Eventually the early 1970s saw Arthur move on from selling Lambrettas to selling the Lotus Super Seven car. However, the tradition of the S Type machines continued under Ray Kemp who had worked for Arthur.

Although it is not known how many S Type machines were sold it was certainly one of the most popular conversions of the 1960s and 1970s.

Ray Towle of the Nottingham & District LC on his Jaguar jewelescent green S Type. (Courtesy Ray Towle)

What the Tester Said

"At night, a quick flash of the two spots was usually enough to encourage centre of the road dawdlers to move over. And if they wouldn't move with a flash of the lights, they would certainly move after a blast from the twin Maserati air horns which proved immensely powerful."
– *Scooter & Three Wheeler* January 1966

"Head down, wind it in third and then snick it into top and take another handful. The scooter surges forward and the long grey ribbon of the main stretch past the grandstand at the famous Brands Hatch leaps up to meet you. At the end of the straight the speedo on the Arthur Francis 250cc Lambretta special is nudging 80mph and

Supertune-built scooters were popular with scooter racers. (Courtesy Mick Murphy)

Ron Moss, racing aboard a Supertune-built GP 200. (Courtesy British Lambretta Archive)

you need that handful of potent front disc to slow it down before you crank it over for the infamous Paddock Hill bend." – *Practical Scooter & Moped* March 1967

"The twelve volt electrics were a tremendous improvement over the original six volt type. This extra capacity made room for a fog and a spot lamp which were firmly fixed on either side of the front shield. These were operated by a handlebar switch from the 150cc slimstyle Lambretta which also included the main headlamp dipswitch and horn button. Ignition, parking light and headlamp were operated with a key switch on the headstock. Charging system was rectifier type with a zener diode system to prevent over-charging." – *Practical Scooter & Moped* January 1967

Supertune – 335 Brighton Road, Croydon

Supertune was set-up by Malcolm Clarkson, who had associations with Lambretta and the British Lambretta Owners Association that went back over a long period of time. Malcolm also having experience in the sporting side of scooter life, including his riding a Lambretta as part of the Lambretta Club of Great Britain team in the 1967 Moto Giro d'Italia. Supertune operated from its Croydon address for five years until the doors finally closed on 21st July 1970. Malcolm Clarkson ran the shop until 1968 when scooter racer Ron Moss took it over after Malcolm left. During the time that Malcolm ran the shop he worked on and produced three dealer specials: 'Avanti,' 'Rallye' and 'Rallye SE.'

Supertune Avanti: '666 CRK' was a standard TV 200 that had been stripped down, bored to 235cc, had its gearing changed, its front end lowered by 90mm and then given a black and white Supertune paint scheme. The forks had a section cut out of them before re-welding, which lowered the main frame and headstock. Consequently, the legshields were reshaped and the horn casting also cut down in size by 90mm: all control cables had to be cut down by the same amount. The standard seat was replaced by a single position low racing seat which hinged backwards to enable the fuel tank to be filled up. The front brake was converted to a reverse pull set-up in order to improve the machine's braking.

The toolbox, battery and air filter had been removed and the ignition coil repositioned on the battery tray to give the shortest possible HT lead to the sparkplug. The stand and anything else not considered necessary were removed.

The 198cc engine had the bore of the cylinder increased to 72mm whilst retaining the standard crank stroke of 60mm. The barrel had been carefully selected for over boring since the wall of the cylinder would become very thin, especially at the lower stud of the barrel. The cylinder head had to be reshaped to a larger diameter bore and then re-flowed to suit the shape of the new piston. The compression ratio was 10:5 to 1. Aluminium head gaskets were hand cut to the new bore diameter. A special dykes piston ring was required for this conversion (Supertune using either GPM or Dinamin) with the gudgeon pin position at the same height as found on a standard Lambretta piston. However, there was a problem with the piston ring retaining pin positions which fell in the

666 CRK was a standard TV 200 that had been stripped down, bored to 235cc, had its gearing changed, front end cut down by 90mm, and then given a black and white Supertune paint scheme. (Courtesy Richard Soloman)

Malcolm Clarkson kept the machine's gearbox ratios a secret, publicly stating that the standard TV 200 gearing with a 16 tooth front sprocket was used. This is thought to be unlikely. It was pretty much accepted that the machine actually used an Li 150 or TV 175 cluster with a 16 tooth front sprocket. The upper chain guide was reinforced by a steel gusset weld and concentric clutch springs were used to boost standard clutch plate pressure. The second springs used were rear brake lever return springs which fitted snugly inside the standard Lambretta TV springs, with added handlebar shims top and bottom on the springs to stop the smaller springs popping into the gearbox.

To further save weight and improve reliability the standard Lambretta clutch backplate shock absorber system was removed and the two clutch back parts welded together. This prevented the lateral springs popping out of the weak cover plate and into the gearbox.

A Wal Philips fuel-injector was tried in the beginning to improve carburation but this was not kept for long since it proved very difficult to set-up and to get the engine started. A new 32mm Amal concentric carburettor on a purpose built, slight downdraught manifold proved to be the most reliable combination. The only problem with the Amal being that it suffered from vibration frothing in the float bowl at high revs.

The engine mount on the offside of the scooter was reinforced to prevent the engine torque twisting the engine under acceleration. This was achieved by cutting a standard

The Supertune Avanti pictured next to an Arthur Francis S Type. (Courtesy Richard Soloman)

wrong place for the transfer/exhaust run. These had to be drilled out and replaced with new pins in more suitable positions. Early attempts to run these pistons without modification caused considerable damage when the dykes ring caught in one of the ports and removed the top edge of the piston. The induction side of the piston skirt was reduced to increase port timing and the inlet/exhaust ports flowed to deal with the extra volume of gases passing through them. The inlet port was carefully matched to the larger, non standard inlet manifold.

Lambretta engine mount in two and welding this section onto a second standard engine mount. Consequently the engine bar had to be replaced with one about 50mm longer.

The Avanti had a large bore exhaust system with a handmade 45mm front pipe and reverse cone into a standard Lambretta exhaust box. The inboard side of the tailpipe section was cut out and the exterior tailpipe was reinforced with a 6mm rod to prevent the pipe fracturing from vibration. The main silencer support had a gusset

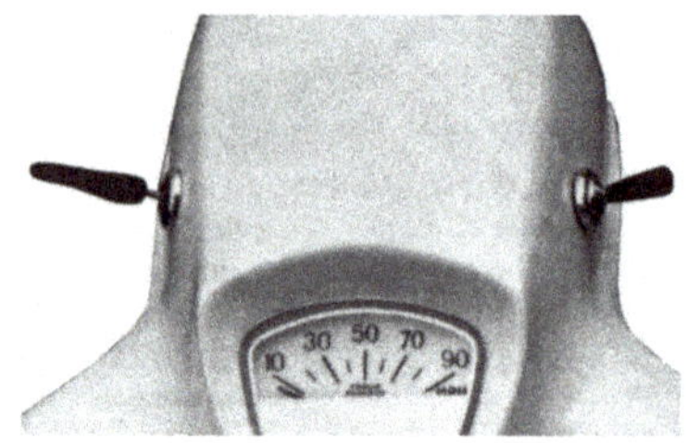

The switches to the quartz iodine lamp, and the headlamp flasher, were located on the headset top of the Oakley Mark 3 SX 200. (Courtesy Scootering & Lightweights)

The PJ Oakley SX 200 Mark 3 had a 12 volt conversion which assisted with illumination of a Lucas quartz iodine spotlamp that was located on the bottom of the horn casting, and also the headlamp flasher unit. (Courtesy Scootering & Lightweights)

welded on to it to reinforce it and the back end of the exhaust box was cut back, raised and re-welded to help ground clearance.

Malcolm Clarkson was convinced that the Avanti machine was a viable machine to sell, however, reliability was not good, and Supertune eventually offered the Avanti as a road going 225 machine, with many of the 235 version's modifications in place. The piston was reduced to 70mm with the standard stroke of 60mm. The 225 configuration meant that the cylinder could be bored safely with less risk of bore distortion or wall collapse. The 225 was offered with a 12 volt conversion, zener diode and large spotlights mounted on the legshields. Only a few of these machines were made – maybe as few as three.

Supertune Rallye: The Rallye was offered by Supertune in 1966, in 150, 200 and 225cc versions. The main changes to the machine being found in the engine: compression ratio changed to 9:1 and the inlet and transfer ports were polished and modified to aid gasflow. Timing was left as standard. 12 volt electrics were fitted, with an extra battery being placed inside the toolbox. A Lucas 12 volt zener diode to regulate the charging system was mounted under the nearside footboard and a 12 volt rectifier was also mounted inside the original Lambretta box. 12 volt bulbs were used for a 45/40 watt headlamp and a 21/6 brake light and rear light. The standard Lambretta disk brake was converted to a reverse pull set-up. Supertune also fitted Nylock nuts to the front and rear brake adjusters. In order to prevent theft the toolbox lid was strengthened to prevent any forcing of the lock. Panel locks were also fitted to prevent theft of the side panels. A Rallye was tested by *Scootering and Lightweights* magazine in 1969. The tester noted that in fourth gear the Rallye got to 40-60mph in 9.2 seconds with a maximum speed of 77mph being achieved. The Rallye came equipped with a legshield mounted spare wheel, 12 volt lighting with Lucas rectifier and Zener diode, an extra 6 volt battery mounted in the toolbox, reinforced toolbox door, reverse pull front brake, high compression cylinder head, gaiters on the front dampers and two-tone paintwork.

Supertune Rallye SE: The Rallye SE was introduced during 1969 and had a carefully rebuilt engine with higher compression ratio, a machined cylinder head and port improvement work.

By July 1970 Ron Moss decided to close Supertune, not because there was no work, but simply because there was too much work for him to run the shop single handedly. It is not known how many Supertune machines were produced.

What the tester said

"The top speed of just over 70mph is a noticeable improvement on the standard SX, which normally clocks a modest 60 to 64 flat out. The acceleration figures are the most impressive results, however, with the outstanding 0-30 in 5 seconds – all without a gear change – being the most impressive. Handling of the Rallye was fair without being outstanding. In the wet however it could be rather alarming and frankly I would have preferred the more progressive old fashioned drum brake at the front end."
– *Practical Scooter & Moped* November 1966

"With the extra revs comes vibration problems which caused a locknut to unwind. Malcolm plans a double engine mounting bush to cure vibration troubles, which he also hopes will improve handling by stiffening the rear end. Unfortunately there are no high speed scooter tyres made for

track work so he had to make do with a pair of Avon 350x10 ordinary road tyres. These are not too bad in the dry but tend to cut speeds right down in the wet."
– *Practical Scooter & Moped* February 1967

"First thing in the morning the bike was a little hard to start – but this is common to all supertuned bikes. Once warm though the bike purred into life first kick. The scooter we used had a 1¼ inch Amal concentric carburettor fitted, instead of a fuel-injector, for easier starting and use in heavy traffic. When I climbed aboard the scooter its throbbing pulse gave that 'feel' of power, its acceleration times proved it. It took two and a half seconds to reach 20mph, three and half to reach 30mph, five seconds to 40mph and six point two seconds to reach 50mph which is good going for a sports car, let alone a scooter."
– *Practical Scooter & Moped* September 1967

"Nothing other than the alterations to the jetting is done to the carburettor but Supertune make up for it when it comes to working on the piston and barrel. This barrel has reshaped transfer ports, the exhaust is opened up and the piston is modified. By substituting the SX head gasket for one from a GT, the compression ratio is raised slightly. A feature of the lighting on this Rallye was the 6 volt system which had been converted to give greater output and yet not blow bulbs when on absolute maximum revs. The power is constant after a third throttle, this being due to a diode fitted into the circuit."
– *Scootering & Lightweights* January 1969

PJ Oakley – 277a Melton Road, Leicester

Hailing from Norfolk, Peter Oakley had grown up with an interest in motorcycles. He moved to Leicester where he worked as a motorcycle mechanic and then, in 1955, set-up his own business. Initially Peter fixed Lambretta scooters as he needed the work, but he gradually built up his business and eventually he took over the Lambretta agency in Leicester. In 1964 he moved to 277a Melton Road, Leicester and it is from there that the Oakley dealer specials emerged.

Oakley's are best known for their Mark 3 Lambretta SX 200, which they described in their adverts as being "for the connoisseur." There wasn't a Mark 1 or Mark 2 machine, the Mark 3 name came about as the badge used on the scooter came from a Mark 3 car. The Mark 3 was based around a standard SX 150 or 200cc Lambretta. With an SX 150 exhaust being fitted to the 200cc model. In the main the Lambretta SX 200 was used as a base and offered with the following modifications: 12 volt lighting, two-tone

Paul Chambers testing the PJ Oakley Mk 3 SX 200. (Courtesy *Scooter World*)

Wildcat
CONVERSIONS and ACCESSORIES
Suitable for:

LAMBRETTA		VESPA	
150 to 175	99/6	160 to 180	99/6
175 to 200	99/6	180 to 200	99/6
200 to 225	110/–		

Special Announcement
FANTASTIC POWER INCREASE with our
"5-PORT INDUCTION" BARREL
Suitable for LAMBRETTA
Returning up to 30% POWER INCREASE
Also available: 'Multi-Port' Barrels (Suitable for Vespa)
Send SAE for FREE *Illustrated Catalogue*
RAFFERTY NEWMAN
(Incorporating WILDCAT equipment)
260-262 West Street, Fareham, Hants
Telephone 5039

A late 1960s advert detailing the Wildcat conversions on offer from Rafferty Newman. (Courtesy *Scootering & Lightweights*)

The X5 5-port barrel was a brilliant piece of engineering by Les Rafferty. However, the drawback was that producing one was a time-consuming exercise of drilling and grinding all of the new ports. (Courtesy Scootering & Lightweights)

paint scheme to customers own choice, Lucas quartz iodine 55 watt spotlamp; legshield toolbox, Avon cling tyres, headlamp flasher with indicator light, ball end levers, front fork damper gaiters and a reverse pull disc brake. Optional extras were a fuel-injector, 32mm Amal carburettor, Ancilotti exhaust, racing seat, a 4.00x10 inch rear tyre, suspension bush modification, 12 volt ignition, engine heat dissipation treatment and side panel locks.

In 1967 Peter Oakley hired the Silverstone race circuit for the day, taking along a Mark 3 SX 200, his rider and mechanic Paul Chambers and a truck full of equipment. During the day Wal Phillips (maker of the Wal Phillips fuel-injectors) rode the scooter and he stated that "it made 70mph with the wind but against it you had to get down behind the screen. The fuel-injector is our standard one-inch bore with a 0.43 jet. It seems to be clean all the way up, no hanging at all." Paul Chambers then took over completing many test runs on the scooter. He managed to record a time of 19.05 seconds over the standing quarter mile. Interestingly enough, after the runs where the Wal Phillips fuel-injector had been fitted an Amal 900 series Concentric 1¼ bore choke carburettor was fitted. The test machine had a 12 volt conversion with a 9amp charge rate. The lighting was a 45watt headlamp with a 55watt quartz iodine spotlamp. The ignition was a special set-up with either a 6 volt flywheel magneto ignition or, at the flick of a switch, a change could be made to 12 volt coil ignition. The switch being fitted just below the seat. The scooter's standard disc brake was retained though it had been changed to a reverse pull system. A front air scoop was also fitted to aid cooling of the brake. On the test scooter a larger 4.00x10 inch rear tyre was fitted. The 200cc engine unit had been painted black in order to aid heat dissipation and the cylinder head used was a high compression item giving a compression ratio of 10:1. An electronic rev counter was used which was operated from the contact breaker unit. The standard exhaust system was fitted.

Testing and refining the Mark 3 SX 200 with the results was all that Oakley's did. Peter Oakley and Paul Chambers believed strongly in the modified machine and Paul rode a Mark 3 SX 200 in many scooter sport events including the 1968 Moto Giro d'Italia.

Although the Mark 3 SX 200 is the machine that appears in all of the Oakley advertisements, they also produced a modified Lambretta GP. Introduced in 1969 the PJ Oakley GP had many modifications like the SX 200. The 200cc engine was tuned to a stage 3 specification and, again, was painted black to aid heat dissipation. A 32mm Amal carburettor was used with the spent engine gases exiting through an Ancilotti exhaust. A 12 volt conversion was employed which aided the lighting of a Lucas quartz iodine spotlamp that was fitted on the bottom of the horn casting. A toolbox was fitted inside the legshields and the side panels had locks. On the handlebars ball end levers were fitted in place of the standard items. Avon cling tyres were supplied with the rear tyre being a 4.00x10 inch item. Fork damper gaiters were fitted and the suspension bushes were modified. Details of the GP paint scheme are scant, however a picture of a yellow ochre GP shows the application of a second colour, in this instance black, to the main part of the side panels, the horn casting and the front mudguard. On the right-hand legshield a 'Mk 3' badge was fitted.

There are no available figures to say how many Oakley specials were produced.

What the tester said

"The scooter being used at Silverstone had the engine painted black, giving a fantastic improvement to the heat dissipation. The treatment is a special and it was found that even after many laps of hard thrashing the clutch case, inlet manifold and suspension bushes were quite cool – of great value to machines used for fast touring or competition use. The engine must be removed and partially stripped for this treatment." – *Scooter World* September 1967

"The Mk3 is built round the standard 150 or 200cc Lambretta, the extras are optional to the individual customer but full specification includes 12 volt lighting, two-tone paint scheme, headlamp flasher, internal engine modifications, ball end levers and substitution of a SX 150 exhaust on the

Wilcat race scooters were raced by the Hampshire Union race team. (Courtesy Scootering & Lightweights)

A full racing Wildcat in blue and yellow livery. (Courtesy Neil Brooks)

200cc model. The resulting machine has plenty of power, at top and bottom end, making a fully tractable machine which will perform adequately on the track yet be docile in and around town." – *Scootering & Lightweights* May 1969

Rafferty Newman 260-262 West Street, Fareham

Set-up in May 1966 by Les Rafferty and Ian Newman, who had previously worked at a motorcycle dealers Lawton and Wilson. When Lawton and Wilson closed, the duo bought all of their Lambretta stock and inherited many of the shop's old Lambretta customers. One of Les Rafferty's main interests was that of tuning 2-strokes, and he started to use this experience on scooter engines. The original 5-port idea was hatched by Les after he had seen a similar 5-port set-up on a Yamaha YAS 1 125cc twin, so Les looked to modify a 150cc Lambretta barrel. Ian's job was to market the barrel and try and make some money out of it.

The Wildcat name came from the term wildcat strikes that were organised by many of the trade unions in Britain in the 1960s. It was a name that Ian Newman thought would be a good name for the tuning part of their business. Newspaper headlines at the time talked about instant wildcat strikes, therefore wildcat conversions were meant as instant conversions. The name also came after fast predatory big cats such as Jaguars, Panthers etc. Les agreed with Ian's idea and Wildcat Tuning was born.

In April 1968 they opened a new workshop fully equipped with a lathe, boring jig and other machinery. This was staffed by six engineers who regularly rode, tested and proved the modified scooters. The shop offered many innovative items:

Primary compression plate: a flat plate that sat under the spigots of the barrel, with a hole for the con rod to pass through. Although the shape and form of each plate was identical, the thickness of the plate had to be varied to suit different machines. The principal idea of the plate being to fill up several thou of space in the crankcase neck and at the same time to ensure that gas flow was smooth.

5-port barrel: Les Rafferty would work late nights in order to produce the 5-port barrel. The X5 5-port barrel was a brilliant piece of engineering by Les Rafferty. However, the drawback was that producing one was a time consuming exercise of drilling and grinding all of the new ports into a blank Fiat 500 cylinder liner which Les pressed into a standard Lambretta 150cc barrel after cutting two troughs from the existing transfer ports to the rear of the barrel, this was after he had bored out the 57mm 150cc barrel to accommodate the liner. Then by precision measurement he had to re-cut every port into the new blank lining including the two extra inlet/transfer ports. No mean feat when all Les had was an electric drill and a flexy-drive with a quarter inch jaw drill head to fit the mini grinders and drills. Rafferty Newman could only do barrels up to 150cc as the walls had to be thick enough to allow boring out to accept the liner and, of course, to cut the trough to the new ports. A limited number of Wildcat 5-port barrels with a piston were offered by Rafferty Newman for £20. But as each barrel took Les a week of evenings to hand bore, cut ports and profile they originally wanted to supply them in a custom-built new scooter to make it economically viable.

Induction stub: In order to enable Lambretta owners the choice of converting their scooter's carburettor to either a concentric or mono bloc, Rafferty Newman designed their own finned induction manifold.

Wildcat dykes racing pistons: Rafferty Newman had these pistons specially produced by Gandini and Figlio in Italy to their own specification. The dykes rings located on sunken pegs, allowing the ring gap to completely close, which stopped gas escaping and thus improved compression. The top ring being located very close to the piston crown thus further increasing compression.

Wildcat kit: Consisted of a 5-port barrel, piston (complete with rings and gudgeon pin), Ancillotti racing seat, Ancillotti exhaust, damper gaiters, ball end levers, headlamp stone guard, nylon cables and 'X5' badge and 'Wildcat' insignia.

Very flexible, Rafferty Newman could supply a standard-looking Lambretta with a 5-port cylinder barrel together with a front panel badge in the shape of a shield, or with any extra fitted such as an Ancilotti seat or exhaust right up to a full racing Wildcat scooter in blue and yellow livery. In essence a scooter custom built to whatever the customer's pocket could afford. When the Luna line machines were produced, Rafferty Newman also produced a Vega conversion that used a barrel from a J125 Lambretta, this being fitted onto the Vega crankcase.

The original Wildcat blue and yellow colour scheme was simply based on the fact that the donor machine used for the first 5-port barrel modification was a blue scooter so they decided to brighten it up a bit by spraying yellow flashes on it: the colour scheme stuck and was continued onto other machines.

The Wildcat logo was Ian's idea, but although he knew what he wanted he was not artistic enough to design it himself so it was down to his brother Barry to come up with the free-flowing design. The Wildcat Equipe logo was also Ian's design, and was based on some tiger stickers which W.E. Wassel were selling at the time. He therefore approached them to produce the stickers for him. Wildcat transfers were made by Philips transfers and metal lapel badges were also made by W.E. Wassell who also made a limited edition set of cufflinks and tie clip in mini presentation boxes. The Wildcat X5 shield featured 'X5' in blue on a silver background.

Success was also found on the track and, in 1969 alone, the Wildcat scooters clocked up 30 wins that season. At the Isle of Man that year a 150cc X5 Lambretta was 1st in the sand race in its class, as was a 200cc X5 machine in its class. At Mallory Park that year Wildcat 225 machines came 1st and 2nd in the Special solo class with the fastest lap being recorded as 1 minute and 12.1 seconds.

Ultimately Rafferty Newman made no profit out of the 5-port barrels. This wasn't just due to the labour cost involved in producing them but also in the tremendous cost of racing scooters, which was something that the firm were keen to invest in to prove their product. Their main benefit was in establishing a good name for Rafferty Newman and a reputation for selling the normal Lambretta conversions 125cc to 150cc etc. They were able to offer a limited number of Wildcat 5-port barrels with a piston for £20.

Scootering and Lightweights magazine evaluated the Wildcat set-up in 1969 and found that the maximum speed in fourth gear of a 150cc machine was 70mph with a speed of 40-60mph being achieved in 8 seconds. The same test on a 175 machine which had been tweaked by opening the porting to maximum and fitting a Monobloc carburettor produced a 0-50mph time of 8.5 seconds. A 200cc machine with a 5-port barrel, standard carburettor and KC Velocita exhaust did the same test in 8.2 seconds. Though the rider felt that the 200cc machine had a slipping clutch.

There are no figures available to say how many Wildcat machines were produced.

WHAT THE TESTER SAID

"The Wildcat five-port system has been developed in a way that allows subsequent reboring without alteration to the advantages obtained by the system. This means new barrels as well as others which have been run in or re-bored can be utilised. With their own equipment for reboring on the premises Rafferty Newman can undertake this work with a fast turn around. For those riders who are keen to convert the carburettor on their scooter to either the concentric or monobloc the firm have designed their own finned induction stub."

– *Scootering & Lightweights* April 1969

RW Horner & Sons – 45-49 Ayres Road, Old Trafford, Manchester

Horner was set-up as business dealing in cycles and motorcycles in 1918, its first shop opening on Princess Road, Moss Side, Manchester. 1926 saw the shop moving to Ayres Road, Old Trafford, Manchester. In 1941 Ernest Horner joined his father in the business followed, in 1945, by his brother Robert and then his brother John in 1953. It was in 1953 that Peter Agg, armed with a demonstration scooter, went to Horner & Sons to see if it would take on a Lambretta dealership. As the Horners were impressed by the Lambretta scooter, they eagerly signed up to be Lambretta dealers there and then. Over the years Horner and Sons sold many Lambrettas with rail trucks often bringing as many as 25 scooters at a time, from Italy, to the Trafford Park depot for the shop.

Horner & Sons concentrated in the main on repair work, spares and accessories and sales of Lambretta scooters, but alongside this they ventured into the world of the dealer special. Based on the Lambretta SX and GP models, the Horner special was called the 'Hornet.' No particular paint scheme was given to the Hornets and they were available in the original factory colours or painted to suit the customer's taste.

So that the scooter could be identified as one of Horners specials, a Hornet badge from the Wolseley Hornet car produced by the British Motor Corporation was used. Outwardly this badge was the only giveaway to the scooter's identity. There were no other set specifications for the scooter.

The scooter's engine would receive tuning modifications with porting and polishing being carried out. Alongside this, either a five-speed or four-speed gearbox was used. However, Horner found that the five-speed box wasn't a reliable item as the width of the gears had to be reduced in order to house them inside the chaincase, and this caused problems. Retaining a four-speed gearbox and using modified porting and polishing gave the best results with Horner's tuned scooters being used in many scooter races. Horner, like many other dealers, also replaced the factory-fitted speedometer with a 100mph item.

The Moto Giro events in Italy proved popular with the British riders and seen here are a Supertune machine, an AF built machine and an Oakley machine. (Courtesy Tony Tessier)

As for any other items on the Hornet scooter, such as the seat or the exhaust, these would be specified by the customer. Horner & Sons were so confident in their product that they did not advertise it or produce any brochures, instead simply allowing word of mouth to spread the news on their dealer special.

In 1966 Terry Colley bought an Li 150 from Horner & Sons. About 18 months later he was introduced to scooter sport by the Manchester Lyons Lambretta Club and he traded up to an SX 200. He was convinced by the Horner brothers not to buy a standard machine, but to buy their dealer special the Hornet, which he remembers had the Hornet badge on the horn casting, just above the horn grille. After having used an Li 150 for nearly two years, he rode away from Horner & Sons open-mouthed at the extra performance that was apparent even at running in speeds. Examining the scooter he discovered that it had a 12-volt conversion and a reverse pull front brake. At that time he was living in Knutsford in Cheshire and worked in Solihull in the West Midlands and, at least twice a week, rode up and down the M6 motorway with the scooter at a steady 70mph, still with extra speed in reserve. He also remembers that the scooter retained its white paint scheme with a black stripe along the top of each side panel.

There are no figures available to say how many Horners Hornets were produced.

Appendices

uno

1

Centro Ricambi

The following details are taken directly from the information sheets sent to dealers by the Centro Ricambi (spares centre) at Innocenti. The production change information contained within the model specifications in the main body of this book gives an overview of the changes made to various Lambrettas. The information here takes this a stage further by giving details of which machines were affected and from what date, though is limited in the main to the Series 1, 2 and 3 machines as no other documents have been found.

Series 1 Li 125 & Li 150

18 July 1958
Li 150
Steering lock replaced, grub screw changed for screw for fixing steering lock from engine number 708821

29 July 1958
Li 125 & 150
Rear brake: in order to prevent dust infiltration, a protective hose between rear brake cable ferrule and brake pedal was used from engine number 502222 (Li 125), 715631 (Li 150)

1 August 1958
Li 125 & 150
Existing chain guide changed for an adjustable one from engine number 503046 (Li 125), 716522 (Li 150)

8 August 1958
Li 150
Electrical equipment updated – new battery specification from 6v4Ah to 6v5Ah; also new junction box used from engine number 719165)

10 September 1958
Li 125 & 150
New spring plate for front brake shoes from engine number 508581 (Li 125), 710871 (Li 150)

27 October 1958
Li 125 & 150
Carburettor air intake fixing grille removed and plastic manifold introduced (from engine number 508590 (Li 125), 727431 (Li 150)

Li 125 & 150
Passenger hand grip changed from rear to front seat from engine number 509266 (Li 125), 728651 (Li 150)

21 November 1958
Li 125
Electrical equipment updated – new junction box; new headlamp from engine number 514081

13 December 1958
Li 125 & 150
New-style choke cable fitted from engine number 518584 (Li 125), 739491 (Li 150)

15 December 1958
Li 125 & 150
New-style exhaust fitted from engine number 518144 (Li 125), 739571 (Li 150)

22 January 1959
Li 125 & 150
To prevent ingress of mud through the footboard opening, a plate was fixed to the brake pedal to act as a mudguard from engine numbers 520810 (Li 125), 742261 (Li 150)

5 February 1959
Li 125 & 150
New-style front forks fitted with new cone for lower ball race, new internal mudguard fitted from engine numbers 523387 (Li 125, 746560 (Li 150)

7 March 1959
Li 125
Headlamp switch replaced by new switch with screws which not only fixed it to the handlebars but also the cover from engine number 524542

7 March 1959
Li 125 & 150
Handlebar levers modified to eliminate vibration from engine numbers 528442 (Li 125), 753860 (Li 150)

9 March 1959
Li 125 & 150
Grease nipple added on backplate of front brake cam and cam pin diameter reduced from engine numbers 527211 (Li 125), 751436 (Li 150)

Li 125 & 150
New-style fuel filler cap fitted with breather from engine numbers 528176 (Li 125), 751591 (Li 150)

12 March 1959
Li 125 & 150
Toolbox changed and single gasket used instead of four from engine numbers 529270 (Li 125), 754550 (Li 150)

24 March 1959
Li 150
New speedometer drive, cable and fixing ring fitted from engine number 751201

3 July 1959
Li 125 & 150
Gasket for air intake removed due to modification of filter plastic section, and addition to pipe of two filter cover centring tongues from engine numbers 534176 (Li 125), 775198 (Li 150)

4 July 1959
Li 125 & 150
Fitted with RIV shock absorber (one ring) from engine number 533991 (Li 125), 778058 (Li 150)

10 July 1959
Li 125 & 150
Sparkplug changed from Marelli CW225c from engine numbers 533994 (Li 125), 781260 (Li 150)

16 July 1959
Li 125 & 150
Front brake cable passes outside, instead of inside, fork steering tube from engine numbers 537137 (Li 125), 790650 (Li 150)

Series 2 Li 125 & 150

16 October 1959
Li 125 & 150
Lower and upper handlebar, horn casting, frame, headlamp, headlamp rim and rear light unit updated from engine numbers 547748 (Li 125), 808963 (Li 150)

19 April 1960
Li 125 & 150
Front fork changed from engine numbers 730679 (Li 125), 849715 (Li 150)

10 November 1960
Li 125 & 150
Legshields changed from engine numbers 761126 (Li 125), 900682 (Li 150)

12 November 1960
Li 125
Kick-start changed from frame number 761126

28 February 1961
Li 125 & 150
Rear light with brake light fitted (from frame numbers 777544 (Li 125), 921665 (Li 150)

6 March 1961
Li 125 & 150
Airbox and air intake changed from frame numbers 780906 (Li 125), 923214 (Li 150)

28 April 1961
Li 125 & 150
MA 18 BS5 carburettor (on the Li 125) changed to MA 19 BS 7; MA 19 BS5 carburettor (on the Li 150) changed to MA 19 BS7 from frame numbers 784443 (Li 125), 919525 (Li 150)

Series 2 TV 175

11 June 1959
Handlebar changed from engine number 103459

16 October 1959
Tail light, frame and toolbox door changed from engine number 109375

30 January 1960
MB 23 BS5 carburettor changed to MB 21 BS5; air intake and air filter housing also changed (from engine number 204492

1 September 1960
Front forks changed from engine number 209104

10 November 1960
Legshields changed from engine number 221911

28 February 1961
Rear light – including brake light – fitted from engine number 224376

6 March 1961
Air intake and airbox changed from engine number 224886

28 April 1961
MB 21 BS5 carburettor changed to MB 21 BS7 from engine number 227928

Series 3

Series 3 frame change: modification sheet S/40 of 12 May 1965 deals with the changeover of the old chrome ring frames to the new non-chrome versions. Also changed at the same time were the headset bottoms and legshields. These modifications are relevant to the Li 125, 150, TV 175, and Li 150 Special models.

Four pole to six pole magneto: on 26 September 1962, Innocenti switched from four to six pole magnetos. Machines affected were:
Li 125 (Series 3) from frame number 036626
Li 150 (Series 3) from frame number 631475
TV 175 (Series 3) from frame number 507945

Anti-vibration plugs: from 2 September 1962, the Series 3 machines had four anti-vibration plugs fitted to the flywheel cowling, as follows:
Li 125 (Series 3) from frame number 038839
Li 150 (Series 3) from frame number 633086
TV 175 (Series 3) from frame number 508889

TV 175 (series 3) & TV 200 side panel change: from 9 December 1963 Innocenti swopped the Li-style side panels on the TV 175 & TV 200 for the Li 150 Special-style side panels

Golden & Silver badges: modification sheet T/73 of 5 May 1965 deals with the introduction of two new badges for the Li 150 Special, the silver and gold badges located on the legshields

Lambretta concessionaires information

To keep the UK Lambretta dealer network informed of the various machine updates, part changes and new models, Lambretta Concessionaires issued information sheets for dealers.

Initially these sheets contained all the information grouped together, irrespective of whether the matters discussed were technical or related to things such as accessories. Over time the information was refined and the sheets were issued in a more logical, ordered way. The sheets provide information on the specifications and colours of the Lambrettas launched onto the UK market.

Model D & LD

August 1956 saw dealers being advised that forks and frames sent back under the S.E.P (Service Exchange Plan) were to be left bare and Concessionaires would accept no responsibility for any parts left on.

Side panniers

Concessionaires introduced side pannier bags and frames for the Lambretta LD, in July 1956, to be used in conjunction with rear carriers. The pannier brackets clamped to the carrier (no drilling required) and allowed access to the side panels. For security the pannier bags were able to be locked to the frames and costs were £2 0s 0d for the frames (per pair) and £2 12s 6d for the pannier bags.

Non-standard items

In 1956 dealers were advised that certain parts on the Lambretta scooters were not of Innocenti manufacture. These included; Bosch (batteries, HT coils, suppressors), KLG (spark plugs and suppressors), Pirelli (tyres) and Avon (tyres).

Display stands, radios, panniers and tyre pumps

April 1957 saw the introduction of a display stand for dealers. Made of durable tubular steel and finished in stove enamel the stand raised the Lambretta 14 inches off of the ground but the stand was available in other sizes so that the scooters could be shown in a tiered effect.

In order to clear stocks Concessionaires offered the Faras radio at £9 17s 6d.

To match existing stocks of saddle and spare wheel covers Blue Tartan plastic front panniers were introduced at a cost of £3 3s 0d.

Described by Concessionaires as "a new and novel foot pump" a plastic pump with a self lubricating nylon piston was made available. Small enough to fit in the glovebox or rear toolbox it was available at 8s 9d with Concessionaires stating "it will sell itself."

Non-genuine Lambretta spares

A stern newsletter dated 15th May 1957 informed dealers that Concessionaires had been informed that non-genuine accessories and spares were being sold as Genuine Italian Spares Suitable For Lambretta," an act not authorised by Concessionaires. Dealers were advised that if scooters were found with non-standard spares/accessories fitted and the fitment of them could be traced back to a dealer/sub-dealer then they would be removed from the dealer network.

LDB 150 (Mark 3) front forks

In order to eliminate front fork noise due to rattling suspension springs inside the fork tubes a longer spring guide piston was introduced (now 211mm as opposed to the previous 131mm item). This modification came into effect from engine number 224365.

Re-Introduction of the Model D 150

25th May 1957 saw Concessionaires informing the UK dealer network that the D 150 was being reintroduced, and was to be available from June 1957 onwards, finished in grey and without parking lights, though a pillion seat was to be fitted. The purpose of the reintroduction was twofold, the first being to keep prices down and provide affordable machines and the second was that the Model D was to be available while there was a shortage of LDB machines.

Handlebar cowls modification – LD 125 & 150 (Mark 3)

From engine number 224261 (LD 150) and 240446 (LD 125) the following parts were changed; control cable ring screw and spring washer. Consequently the screw hole in the handlebar cowl was changed from 3mm to 4mm.

Marelli flywheel magneto

On the 30th April 1957, from engine number 123447 (of the Mark 3 LD), a new type of flywheel magneto was fitted with a modified flywheel and fan. The modification consisted of a labyrinth incorporated into the fan to prevent dust from entering the flywheel and thus causing wear.

LDA kick-starts

With the introduction of the LDA, Concessionaires had provided dealers with brochures that stated that the LDA would be fitted with an independent kick-start mechanism. However, when the scooters came into the country it was found that they had no kick-start fitted. Concessionaires were keen to advise dealers that the electric start scooters were of such high competence that a kick-start wasn't necessary. Rather than alter the price of the scooter they simply offered to supply it without the kick-start. Any owner who wanted a kick-start fitting would be charged £12 12s 0d for this. Anyone who had ordered a machine before 1st July 1957 would be supplied a machine with a kick start due to that being specified in the original brochure.

Mark 1 & 2 LD 150 handlebar covers

In order to allow owners of Mark 1 or 2 LDs to fit a Mk3 Handlebar cover, the Mk3 cover was offered for sale for £2 2s 0d and would be available in three colours grey, red and Winchester Blue. The grey covers were available from stock but dealers were advised that red and blue would be available in four to five weeks. Special covers for the Mark 1 LD 125 were to be made available later at the same price. (8th July 1957).

LDA & LDB Issues

Production of the LDA had been suspended in order to increase output of the LDB which had been in greater demand. Concessionaires had hoped that they could continue with production of the LDA by Easter 1957, this wasn't to be the case as an engineering strike caused a delay in the supply of the voltage control regulators.

The Mark 3 LDB had been delayed in its introduction (at the request of the dealer network, to allow remaining Mark 1 and 2 machines to be sold). March 1957 saw Concessionaires beginning to release of the Mark 3 machine.

Production runs of the various five colours meant that Concessionaires had to organise production colour runs for a whole week to ensure all five colours could be available.

LD colours

Dealers were advised that Concessionaires were organising colour runs by a five week rotational system. This meant that dealers had to order their machines carefully otherwise they had to accept the colours that were in stock.

Model D 150 (reintroduction)

Due to demand, the Model D 150 was reintroduced in June 1957. Finished in grey only and offered with a pillion seat but without parking lights the scooter sold for £122 10s 0d. Concessionaires were keen to get the Model D out and on sale as there were shortages of the LDB.

Mark 2 LD frames cracking

In August 1957 Concessionaires advised dealers that a small percentage of Mark 2 frames were developing a crack on the main frame cowling between the saddle mounts, adjacent to the pressing for the side panel rubber. Dealers were advised not to repair the frame but to get it replaced.

Introduction of the Series 1 TV 175

Dealers were advised in august 1957 that a new 175cc scooter was being built. However, Concessionaires were keen to point out that they would not introduce a new machine until they were ready to provide a speedy after sales service and, as such, they were not able to give a date when the new TV scooter would be available to the UK dealer network.

LD & LDB repair times

To fit a complete engine was listed as taking 10 hours and 20 minutes at a cost of £7 15s 0d, with a gearbox overhaul taking 5 hours and costing £3 15s 0d. Torsion bar replacement took 2 hours at a cost of £1 10s 0d. (1st August 1960)

Mayfair & Riviera models

Concessionaires advised dealers that they were unable to carry out the fitment of all the relevant accessories to the LDA and LDB machines in order to make them Mayfair and Riviera models. Dealers were asked to undertake the fitment of all accessories and were informed that they should only fit Mayfair and Riviera badges to machines that were sold as either model.

LDA

Concessionaires wrote to dealers (8th July 1957) about the LDA, making mention that the brochure for the scooter said it would be fitted with an independent kick-start. However, when the LDAs arrived in the UK they were found not to be fitted with one as the self-starter was considered to be "of such high competence" that a kick-start wasn't considered necessary. Anyone buying a machine who wanted one would not only have to pay the £179 10s 0d for the scooter, but a further £12 12s 0d for the kick-start plus 30s 0d to have it fitted. Anyone who had bough their LDA before 1st July 1957 would be given special consideration as to whether they would be given the kick-start.

Accessories for the Series 1 Li

On 3rd December 1958 the Lambretta newsletter introduced the 'Scootboot' by Raydot. A lockable luggage boot that was 20 inches long, 16.5 inches wide and 6.5 inches deep. It had attracted interest at the Earls Court show, and the complete ensemble was £7 17s 6d and was available in grey/ red and grey/blue.
Also introduced were extending carriers by Wistonia which came in red, blue, Li 150 grey and Li 125 grey.

LDB 150

Following the introduction of the Li range at Crystal palace in November 1958, Concessionaires noted the huge response to the new range and dropped the LDB from their range in all colours except an all blue model.

Reduced gear Li 150 model

Due to requests both from customers and dealers alike, Concessionaires offered a lower geared Li for use with sidecars. The solution was an easy one: the gear cluster from the Li 150 was removed and replaced with the gear cluster from the Li 125 thus giving the ideal ratio. Dealers were offered the option of completing the change themselves or of buying such a machine direct from concessionaires. Colour schemes were Grey/ Red, Grey/Blue, Grey/Turquoise and an all red machine.

Introduction of the Series 2 TV 175

May 1959 saw Dealers being informed of the new Series 2 TV 175, a machine described as incorporating improvements over its predecessor. The scooter was to be launched to the Press on Thursday 28th May 1959. Dealers were advised that the scooter would only be available in Glacier Blue at that time with no other alternatives. Along with the scooter came a number of accessories just for it, these were a front mudguard embellisher with 'TV 175' on it, a rear carrier enameled in Glacier Blue, an extending rear carrier in Glacier Blue, a horn cover, a spare wheel in Glacier Blue and a Benzi windscreen.

Li 150 Series 2 colour availability

Dealers were advised that all Series 2 Li 150s would be finished in light grey with a choice then for the dealer to have the side panels sprayed in a colour of their own choice. Dealers were asked to provide colour samples to Concessionaires and the scooters would be sprayed in that shade prior to delivery to the dealer. Minimum order for these paint schemes was 5 machines.

TV 175 colours

Due to enquiries from numerous dealers for additional colour schemes the TV 175 (Series 2) was made available in dual colour schemes, these were Ivory/Ocean Green and Ivory/Winchester Blue. These joined the already available Ivory/ Coffee (coffee & cream scheme).

Touring kit

Concessionaires were keen to capitalise on the increasing number of Lambretta owners who travelled to the continent and to remote parts of the British Isles. To this end they put together a Touring Kit consisting of the spare parts necessary for minor repairs on all Li and TV machines. All of the spare parts were supplied in labelled plastic bags which were then put in a cardboard box. Owners paid their local dealer £7 12s 6d and when returning the kit the owner would get £7 2s 6d less the cost of any spares used.

Test ride scheme

1959 saw Concessionaires launching the first ever Test Ride scheme. Potential Lambretta owners were sent a range of literature on Lambretta scooters, a covering letter and a free test ride voucher which would have had the name of their nearest dealer written on it (these dealers would have licensed demonstration Li models). Dealers were given a PVC Test Ride banner, Test Ride handlebar showcards, a Test Ride window sticker and a Test Ride poster.

Reconditioned service exchange scheme

1960 saw Concessionaires offering items such as LDA regulators, Li (Series 1 & 2) forks, LD (125 & 150) speedometer heads, and frames for the LD 125, Series 1 and 2 Li and Series 1 and 2 TV machines under the S.E.S.

Paint sprays and touch-up paint

Concessionaires were keen to supply spray paint for their available machines and 1960 saw them offering Ivory/Cream which boosted their range of sprays, which was as follows:
Red – suitable for the LDA, LDB and pre-April Li 150
Winchester Blue – suitable for the LDB and Li 150
Mark 3 Off White – suitable for the Mark 3 LD 125 and the LDB
Slate Blue – suitable for the Mark 3 LDA and LDB
TV Ivory/Cream – suitable for the Series 1 TV 175 and the Coffee/Cream LDB 150
Li 150 Grey – suitable for the Li 150
As for touch-up paints three new colours were introduced; Flaminia Grey, Glacier Blue and TV Yellow.

Engine stoppage

Dealers were advised (via Service and Technical sheet 55/60) of the possibility of engine stoppage through the pillion riders clothing covering the carburettor air inlet beneath the saddle. When the air inlet was obstructed the engine died.

Series 2 Li & TV repairtimes & charges

The 1st August 1960 saw Concessionaires providing times and charges for various repair and servicing jobs on the Series 2 Li and TV machines. A frame change was listed as taking 18 hours at a cost of £13 10s and 0d. To renew two main bearing and/or oil seals or crankshaft or drive side bearings and/or oil seal would take 5 hours and cost £3 15s 0d. A 500 mile service of the scooter cost 12s 6d, with a 1500 mile service costing £1 5s 0d and a 3000 mile service would set you back £2 5s 0d. Cable renewal would take an hour (for a complete cable) and cost 15s 0d, whereas changing 2 cables would take and hour and a half and cost £1 2s 6d.

Speedo heads

Under the reconditioned Service Exchange Scheme detailed in November 1960 was a note that both Jaeger and Veglia speedo heads were available for the LD 125 and 150 and the Li and TV machines.

Training school

Dealers were advised via a newsletter dated 13th January 1961 that Concessionaires had (due to increasing demand from dealers) set-up a Mechanics Training School. This included a well-equipped technical workshop, modern lecture theatre and instructors of the "highest calibre." Pupils were given a tour around the works and could inspect the up to date Lambretta Service Station Workshops. Courses lasted a week.

Accident repairs

Due to frequent requests from dealers who sought assistance with crash damaged Lambrettas, Concessionaires set-up a modern Crash Workshop, adjacent to the Lambretta Service Station at Purley Way, Croydon. The procedure to be adopted by dealers was as follows; the scooter was sent to Croydon with a request for an estimate of the work to be carried out, the estimate was then sent back to the dealer and this could then be submitted to the insurance company or owner. Insurance assessors would be told that the scooter was at Croydon if they wished to inspect it. Once the estimate had been accepted work would start on the damaged scooter. Discount was offered to dealers on any spares used but not on labour charges.

Problem starters

Dealers who had machines standing in showrooms during winter would often find a problem when it came to getting the machine started and usually it would only start with the choke on. The problem being identified as corrosion of the brass main jet restricting the aperture. This meant a replacement jet being fitted to the Series 2 machines affected.

2% oil mixture

Following considerable research and improvement in design, dealers were informed that the Series 2 Li 125 (from engine number 560300) and the Li 150 (from engine number 834300) could be used with a 2% oil mixture. Riders who used the 2%

mixture were advised to use 40 SAE specification oil. However dealers were advised that under no circumstances was the 2% mixture to be used on the Series 2 TV 175.

No Series 2 Li 125s
January 1962 saw Concessionaires informing dealers that its stocks of Li 125 scooters were exhausted and would remain that way until March. It had Li 150, Rallymaster and TV 175s in reasonable stock, but it was also concerned that, if there was an increase in demand for these machines, then it would result in exhaustion of these stocks as well.

Stoplights – Series 2 Li 125 and 150
Li 125 and 150 machines initially came into the UK with no stoplights fitted. This was due to a decision not being made on the light unit's reflector by the British standards institute.

Cheaper scooters and the Gran Luxe 150
September 1963 saw the cost of the Li 150 (Series 3) and the TV 175 (Series 3) being reduced so that they were within the reach of more people. Coupled with the price reductions was the introduction of the Gran Luxe 150 which was a standard Series 3 Li 150 which was available with chrome side panels at £140 16s 7d, as opposed to the price of £132 10s 10d for the standard 150 machine.

Ducati flywheel magneto
The TV 200 and Li 150 Special came equipped with a 6 pole magneto. The 6 pole magneto was then introduced for the Series 3 Li 125 (from frame number 036626), Series 3 Li 150 (from frame number 631475) and the Series 3 TV 175 (from frame number 506945). Prior to those machines all Slimstyle machines had a four pole magneto.

SX 200 introduction
Dealers were advised of the launch of the SX 200 in March 1966. Concessionaires called the scooter the Lambretta 'SX Grand Prix 200,' stating it had a complement of power, elegance, aerodynamic styling, smooth running and a 25% increase in mpg. They also stated that it could cover a distance of 110 yards from a standing start in 8.8 seconds.

Starstream introduction
June 1966 saw dealers being advised of the new Starstream, available in Roman Blue only. Quoting that its performance was approaching that of the Li 150, dealers were told that it had a restyled body and lower riding position and told to think of short, slim ladies! To start sales off dealers were given the incentive of buying SX 200s (in equal numbers to any Starstreams they ordered) at a lower net price.

Luna Line introduction
Dealers were advised that the Luna line machines would be launched on the 26th November 1968. They were told that the Luna 50 wouldn't be available until March/April 1969 and that the first Vega available would have the frame number 650310 and the first Cometa available would have the frame number 650016.

1968 colours
The Lambretta range for 1968 were listed as being available in the following colour schemes:
Starstream – Light Blue
Super Starstream – White/Winchester blue, White/Flame Red
Li 150 Special – Hawthorn White/Scarlet Red, Hawthorn White/Ocean Blue
SX 150 – Hawthorn White/scarlet red, Hawthorn White/Ocean Blue
SX 200, Hawthorn White/Lemon, Hawthorn White/Lemon & Black, Hawthorn White/British Racing Green, Hawthorn White/orange, Hawthorn White/Lime Green, Hawthorn White/Royal Blue, Hawthorn White/Black, Hawthorn White/Polychromatic Blue, Hawthorn White/Polychromatic Red, Hawthorn White/Polychromatic Pink

SX 200 & SX 150 fork links
In November 1968 dealers were informed that SX 200 fork links would now only be available as modified items. Stocks of pre-modified fork links were exhausted. By December 1968 dealers were told that stock of pre-modified SX 150 fork links was also exhausted and only modified items were available.

Grand Prix launch
Shown on the Concessionaires stand at the Brighton Show in 1969 were two new scooters to be known as the Lambretta 'Grand Prix,' 'Formula 150' and 'Formula 200.' Dealers were informed that the Formula 150 would be available in white with black body flashes and trim, white with red and white with blue. The Formula 200 was offered in ochre or red. Due to the Lambretta-Trojan Group building racing cars for Bruce McLaren, the new scooters would be shown against a backdrop of a motor racing circuit.

Series 3 exhaust
January 1969 saw a new, more robust exhaust being made available. Fully interchangeable with

previous exhaust and suitable for the SX 200. 69s 6d was the recommended retail price.

Colours for 1969

The colour lists for models available in April 1969 was as follows:
Vega – orange, yellow, red, turquoise.
Cometa – orange, yellow, red, turquoise.
Startsream & Cento – Light Blue.
Superstarstream – SX 200 White/Flame Red, SX 200 white/Winchester Blue
Li 150 Special – Hawthorn White/scarlet red, Hawthorn White/Ocean Blue
GP 150 – Hawthorn White, Hawthorn White/Scarlet Red, Hawthorn White/Ocean Blue, orange, turquoise
GP 200 – red, yellow

Luna clutch disc

Dealers were advised that the clutch disc on the Luna line was interchangeable with that of the Cento and the J125.

Grand Prix 200 technical details

The 17th March 1969 saw a 'Technical Details and Specification Sheet' being issued for the GP 200. The sheet detailed the maximum speed as 69mph with a cruising speed of 47mph and the completion of a standing quarter mile in 21.1 seconds. Electrics were given as a Ducati 6 pole flywheel magneto and an Exide 3EV9.11 battery. The oil mix ratio (SAE 40 or SAE 30) was 5% for the first 900 miles and then at a 4% mix after 900 miles. The tool roll was listed as containing a sparkplug spanner, an 8x10mm spanner, a screwdriver and a 10mm Allen key.

SX 150 Superseded by the GP 125

December 1969 saw the GP 125 launched onto the UK market in place of the SX 150. Concessionaires were happy to showcase the GP 125 as having the latest body styling and improved technical specification with the scooter being available in white or turquoise.

1969 touch-up paints

The list of touch-up paints available in 1969 was staggering, with a vast array of colours available. It shows the various shades that had been and were being used on Lambrettas in the UK. The list is as follows: Li 150 grey, orange, royal blue, lemon, British Racing Green, Lime Green, Orbit Orange, Astral Blue, Venus Green, Yellow Ochre, 150 grey, 125 grey, Flame Red, Winchester Blue, turquoise, SX 200 white, Cento ivory, Cento yellow, Metallic Gold, Metallic Blue, Cento light blue, Polychromatic Peacock Blue, Polychromatic Emerald Green, Polychromatic New Gold, Polychromatic Copper Pink, Polychromatic Red, Polychromatic Blue, Polychromatic Purple, Polychromatic Green, Polychromatic Gold, SX 150 grey, Hawthorn White, Scarlet Red and Ocean Blue.

Luna footrests

Introduced in June 1970 were footrests for the Luna line, available at 10/6d each.

1970 colours

September 1970 saw Concessionaires advising dealers that the available colours for the current range of scooters was as follows:
Vega – red, yellow, turquoise and orange
Cometa – red, yellow, turquoise and orange
GP 125 – white and turquoise
GP 150 – white, white/blue, white/red, orange, turquoise
GP 200 – white, yellow and red

Vega/Cometa speedo modification

February 1971 saw dealers being advised that Concessionaires were still be able to supply both pre- and post-modified cables.

GP bulb blowing

In order to eliminate bulb blowing on the GP range, the rear light was now rubber mounted (February 1971). The new modification for the GP incorporated a grommet, sleeve nut, light gasket, washers, earth wire bolt, spring washer and a 6v 5/20w bulb.

tre

Frame numbers

The following information shows the frame number sequences (as far as they can be ascertained) used during the various years of manufacture of the Lambretta scooters described in this book. Where relevant, the frame prefixes are shown. It needs to be borne in mind that the figures shown here are a guide, and not a definitive list of Innocenti-produced frame numbers.

Also included, where relevant, are the IGM (DGM on some models) numbers for specific models. These were used from the Li 125 (Series 2) onwards. However, some Series 2 machines do not have them; yet another example of the changes implemented by the factory and the Italian government. IGM stands for Ispettorato Generale Motorizzazione. The Motorizzazione (whose extended name is Motorizzazione Civile e Trasporti in Concessione) is a branch of the Ministry of Infrastructures and Public Transportation in Italy, and the IGM is the office that certifies a vehicle is legal. Not only the vehicle, but its most important parts too, such as the engine, the exhaust system, the carburettor, the lights, and so on.

Model A
Frame prefix Tipo 2* followed by the frame number
1947: 5001 – 5153
1948 – 5154 – 14,670

Model B
Frame prefix Tipo 3* or Tipo B* followed by the frame number
1948: 00,001 – 01,854
1949: 01,855 – 33,175
1950: 33,176 – 35,015

Model C
Frame number followed by 125 C
1950: 50,001 – 84,757
1951: 84,758 – 137,501

Model LC
Frame number followed by 125 LC
1950: 400,001 – 416,813
1951: 416,814 – 442,501

Model D 125 (Mk 1)
Frame prefix 125 D followed by the frame number
1951: 00,001 – 03,865
1952: 03,866 – 68,541
1953: 68,542 – 69,000

Model D 125 (Mk 2)
Frame prefix 125 D followed by the frame number
1953: 69,001 – 91,565
1954: 91,566 – 122,641

Model D 125 (Mk 3)
Frame prefix 125 D followed by the frame number
1955: 122,642 – 122,991
1956: 122,992 – 123,141

LD 125 (Mk 1)
Frame prefix 125 LD followed by the frame number
1951: 00,001 – 00137
1952: 00,138 – 29,608
1953: 29,609 – 53,197

LD 125 (Mk 2 includes Elecstart version)
Frame prefix 125 LD followed by the frame number
1953: 53,198 – 75,405
1954: 75,406 – 107,026
1955: 107,027 – 119,029
1956: 119,030 – 140,360

LD 125 (Mk 3 includes Elecstart version)

Frame prefix 125 LD followed by the frame number
1957: 500,001 – 526,716
1958: 526,717 – 543,637

Model D 150 (Mk 2)
Frame prefix 150 D followed by the frame number
1954: 5,001 – 5,611
1955: 5,612 – 38,759

Model D 150 (Mk 3)
Frame prefix 150 D followed by the frame number
1956: 38,760 – 59,594

LD 150 (Mk 2 includes Elecstart version)
Frame prefix 150 LD followed by the frame number
1954: 105,001 – 105,442
1955: 105,443 – 157,801
1956: 157,802 – 212,350
1957: 212,351 – 217,228

LD 150 (Mk 3)
Frame prefix 150 LD followed by the frame number
1957: 208,000 – 293,946
1958: 293,947 – 325,929

Model E
Frame prefix 125 E followed by the frame number
1953: 000,001 – 034,650
1954: 034,651 – 042,352
Note: Frame numbers started either 000,001 or 100,001

Model F
Frame prefix 125 F followed by the frame number
1954: 042,065,702
1955: 065,702 – 075,042
Note: Lower frame numbers have been found where Model Es were changed to Model F machines.

Li 125 (Series 1)
Frame prefix 125 Li
1958: 505,421 – 562,734
1959: 562,735 – 658,692
Note: Frame numbers follow the sequences for the Li 150 as they were built together from June 1958.

Li 150 (Series 1)
Frame prefix 150Li* or Li 150 (both of these were used and the prefix can appear before or after the frame number)
1958: 500,001 – 562,734
1959: 562,735 – 658,692
Note: Frame numbers follow the sequence for the Li 125 as they were built together. Some late models have been seen with frame numbers starting with an 8 – there is no known reason for this jump.

TV175 (Series 1)
Frame number followed by *175TVS
1957: 001,001 – 002,126
1958: 002,127 – 011,088

Li 125 (Series 2)
Frame prefix: 125Li* followed by frame number, IGM 0902 OM
1959: 703,001 – 712,839
1960: 712,840 – 772,060
1961: 772,061 – 799,999
1961: 300,001 – 311110
Note: Frame numbers started at 300,001 in late 1961 so as not to cause confusion with the 800,001 series used on the Series 2 Li 150.

Li 150 (Series 2)
Frame prefix: 150Li* followed by frame number, IGM 0903 OM
1959: 800,001 – 823,646
1960: 823,647 – 906,185
1961: 906,186 – 962,041

TV 175 (Series 2)
Frame prefix: 175TV2* followed by frame number, IGM 0904 OM
1959: 100,001 – 108,773
1959: 200,001 – 203,261
1960: 203,262 – 222,718
1961: 222,719 – 234,055

Li 125 (Series 3)
Frame prefix: 125Li* or 125Li3* (both types used on this model) followed by frame number, IGM 0902 OM
1961: 001,001 – 003,125
1962: 003,126 – 051,476
1963: 051,477 – 101,941
1964: 101,942 – 127,288
1965: 127,289 – 143,240
1966: 143,241 – 145,262
1967: 145,262 – 146,734

Li 125 (Series 4)
Frame prefix: 125Li4* followed by frame number, IGM 0902 OM
1967-1968: 148,001 – 149,400

Li 150 (Series 3)
Frame prefix: 150Li3* followed by frame number, IGM 0903 OM
1962: 600,001 – 648,718
1963: 648,719 – 696,739
1964: 696,740 – 714,018
1965: 714,019 – 731,133
1966: 731,134 – 742,064
1967: 742,065 – 743,092

TV 175 (Series 3)
Frame prefix: 175TV3* followed by frame number, IGM 2515 OM
1962: 500,001 – 513,950
1963: 513,951 – 531,506
1964: 531,507 – 545,183
1965: 545,184 – 552,778
Note: As the TV 200 entered production in April 1963 both machines were built together, and the frame sequences are for both machines.

TV 200
Frame prefix: TV3* followed by frame number
1963: 520,000 – 531,506
1964: 531, 507 – 545,183
1965: 545,184 – 552,778
Note: The TV 200 did not have an IGM number. As with the TV 175 (Series 3) the frame sequences reflect that both machines were built together.

Li 150 Special
Frame prefix: 150LiS* followed by frame number, IGM 3316 OM
1963: 200,001 – 207,953
1964: 207,974 – 242,975
1965: 242,976 – 259,280
1966: 259,281 – 268,831

Li 125 Special
Frame prefix: 125 LiS* followed by frame number, IGM 4190 OM

1965: 850,001 – 854,197
1966: 854,198 – 867,375
1967: 867,376 – 875,817
1968: 875,818 – 879,827
1969:879,828 – 879,842

SX 150
Frame prefix: SX 150* followed by frame number, IGM 4470 OM
1966: 750,001 – 753,571
1967: 753,572 – 767,228
1968: 767,229 – 781,072
1969: 781,073 – 781,239

SX 200
Frame prefix: SX200* followed by frame number, IGM 4355 OM
1966: 830,001 – 842,642
1967: 842,643 – 847,274
1968: 847,275 – 850,774
1969: 850,775 – 850,784

DL/GP 125
Frame prefix: 22/1* followed by frame number, DGM 6439 OM
1969: 001,001 – 008,450
1970: 008,451 – 014,891
1971: 014,892 – 016,301

DL/GP 150
Frame prefix: 22/0* followed by frame number, DGM 6437 OM
1969: 200,001 – 210,704
1970: 210,705 – 220,210
1971: 220,211 – 221,451

DL/GP 200 & 200 Electronic
Frame prefix 22/2* followed by frame number, DGM 6441 OM
1969: 250,001 – 254,778
1970: 254,779 – 258,602
1971: 258,603 – 259,351
Note: It is not known exactly how many DL/GP 200 Electronics were built, but it is believed that they numbered no more than 500 machines and their production numbers are included with those of the standard DL/GP 200.

Cento
Frame prefix: 100LB* followed by frame number, IGM 3484 OM
1964: 800,001 – 814,085
1965: 814,086 – 817,643

J 50 (3 Speed)
Frame prefix: j50* followed by frame number, IGM 3687 OM
1964: 400,001 – 402,799
1965: 402,799 – 421,383
1966: 421,384 – 431,022

J125 (3 Speed)
Frame prefix: j125/3* followed by frame number, IGM 3689 OM
1964: 600,001 – 606,484
1965: 606,485 – 616,863
1966: 616,864 – 621,652

J50 (4 Speed)
Frame prefix: j50* followed by frame number, IGM 3687 OM
1966: 431,022 – 437,102
1967: 437,102 – 468,004
1968: 468,005 – 469,989

J125 (4 Speed)
Frame prefix: j125/4* followed by frame number, IGM 3689 OM
1966: 150,001 – 158,811
1967: 158,812 – 161,541
1968: 161,542 – 166,952
1969: 166,953 – 166,053

J 50 Deluxe
Frame prefix: j50* followed by frame number, DGM 5520 OM
1968: 450,000 – 485,097
1969: 485,098 – 494,142
1970: 494,143 – 508,170

J 50 Special
Frame prefix: j50* followed by frame number, DGM 5520 OM
1970: 507,001 – 510,299
1971: 510,300 – 512,452

Lui 50 C, CL & S
Frame prefix: 20/9* followed by frame number, DGM 5629 OM
1968: 575,001 – 595,666
1969: 595,667 – 602,813

Vega & Cometa
Frame prefix: 20/8* followed by frame number, DGM 6216 OM
1968: 650,001 – 654,543
1969: 654,544 – 658,872
1970: 658,873 – 659,403

quattro

4

Paint schemes

The following information relates to the paint schemes used by the Innocenti factory, but, as variations do occur, it is intended as a guide only. All of the codes listed are for Lechler brand paints.

Model A

Dark Olive Green – 8022
Dark Red – 8020
Light Blue – 8017
Ivory – not known

Model B

Metallic Blue – 8024
Metallic Red – 8023
Metallic Green – 8025
Metallic Bronze – 8053

Model C & LC

Light Olive Khaki – 8027
Chamois – 8011
Blue – code not known; used only on early Model Cs
Red – code not known; used only on early Model Cs
Special Blue – code not known; used only on early LC 125s

Model D & LD 125

Olive Green – 8021
Light Chamois – 8055
Sand Beige – 8029
(From 1953 the LD 125 was available in sand Beige only)

Model E

Olive Green – 8021

Model F

Olive Green – 8021
Sand Beige – 8029
Light Grey – 8012

D & LD 150

Sand Beige – 8029
Light Grey – 8012*
*(*This colour was used only on a number of 1956 machines)*

1957 LD 125

Earth Grey – 8041

1957 LD 150

Earth Grey – 8041 (used on all bodywork except the headset, horn casting and side panels, which were painted as follows):
Maroon – 8020
Emerald Green – 8051
English Blue – 8031

TV 175 (1)

Ivory – 8028

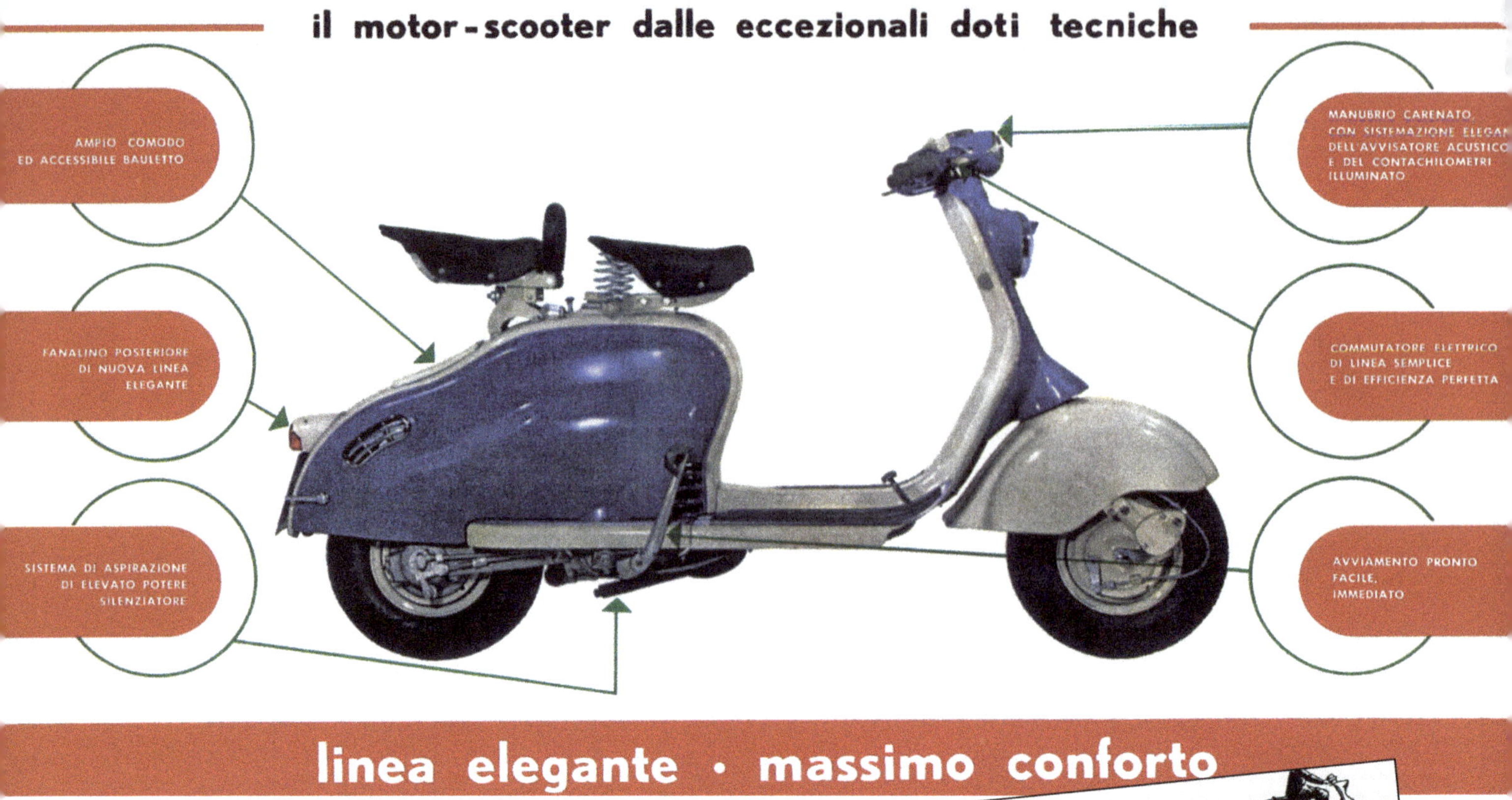
il motor-scooter dalle eccezionali doti tecniche
AMPIO COMODO ED ACCESSIBILE BAULETTO
FANALINO POSTERIORE DI NUOVA LINEA ELEGANTE
SISTEMA DI ASPIRAZIONE DI ELEVATO POTERE SILENZIATORE
MANUBRIO CARENATO, CON SISTEMAZIONE ELEGAN DELL'AVVISATORE ACUSTICO E DEL CONTACHILOMETRI ILLUMINATO
COMMUTATORE ELETTRICO DI LINEA SEMPLICE E DI EFFICIENZA PERFETTA
AVVIAMENTO PRONTO FACILE, IMMEDIATO
linea elegante • massimo conforto

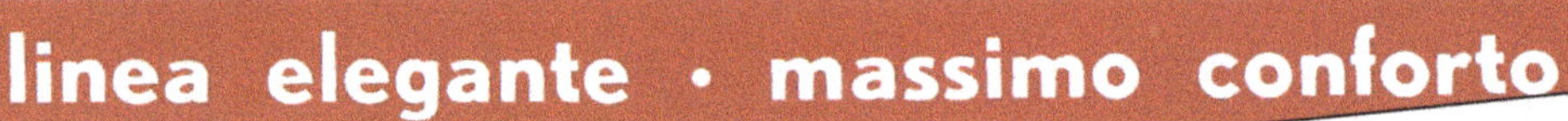

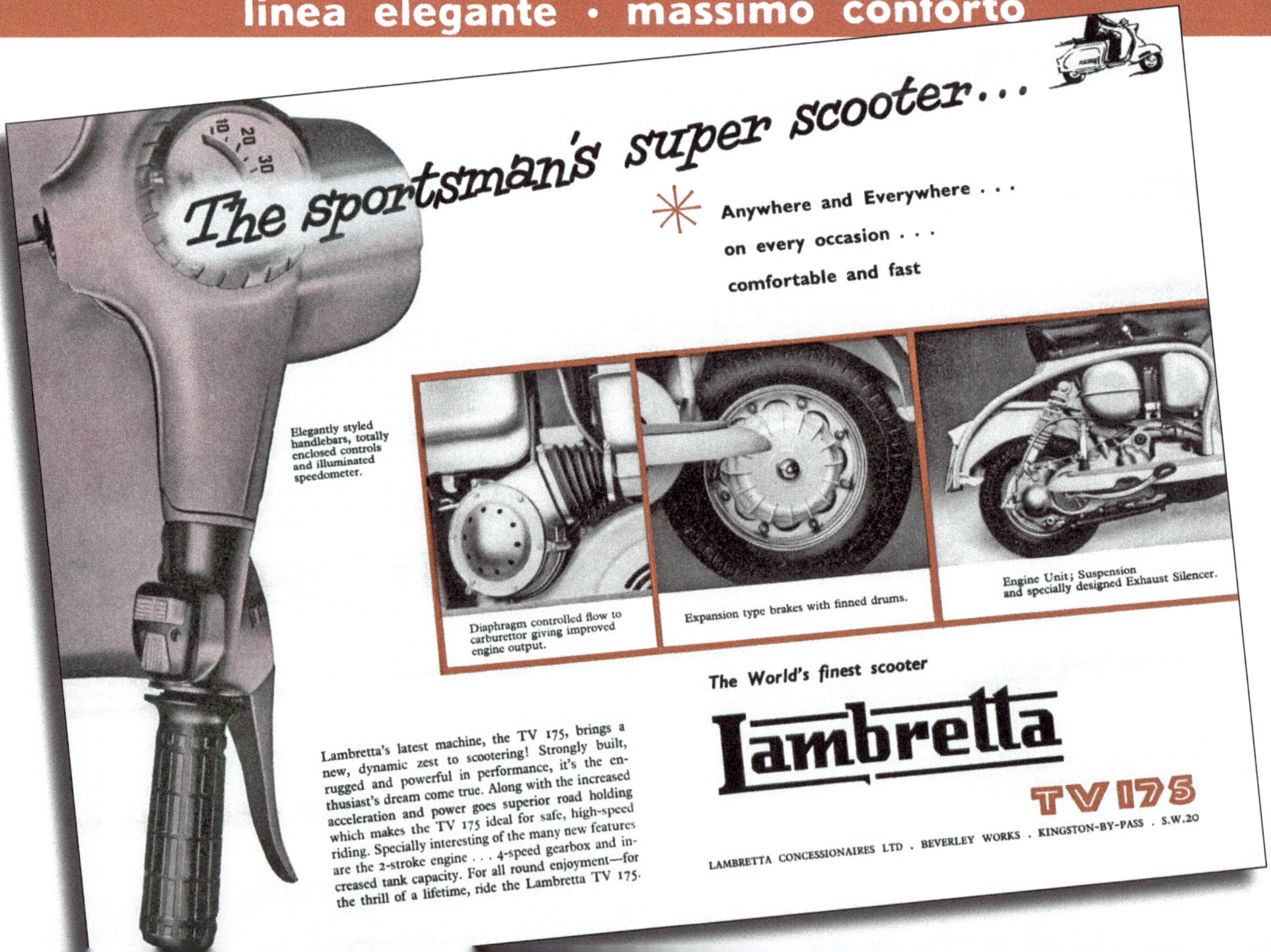
The sportsman's super scooter...
Anywhere and Everywhere . . .
on every occasion . . .
comfortable and fast
10 20 30
Elegantly styled handlebars, totally enclosed controls and illuminated speedometer.
Diaphragm controlled flow to carburettor giving improved engine output.
Expansion type brakes with finned drums.
Engine Unit; Suspension and specially designed Exhaust Silencer.
Lambretta's latest machine, the TV 175, brings a new, dynamic zest to scootering! Strongly built, rugged and powerful in performance, it's the enthusiast's dream come true. Along with the increased acceleration and power goes superior road holding which makes the TV 175 ideal for safe, high-speed riding. Specially interesting of the many new features are the 2-stroke engine . . . 4-speed gearbox and increased tank capacity. For all round enjoyment—for the thrill of a lifetime, ride the Lambretta TV 175.
The World's finest scooter
Lambretta
TV 175
LAMBRETTA CONCESSIONAIRES LTD . BEVERLEY WORKS . KINGSTON-BY-PASS . S.W.20

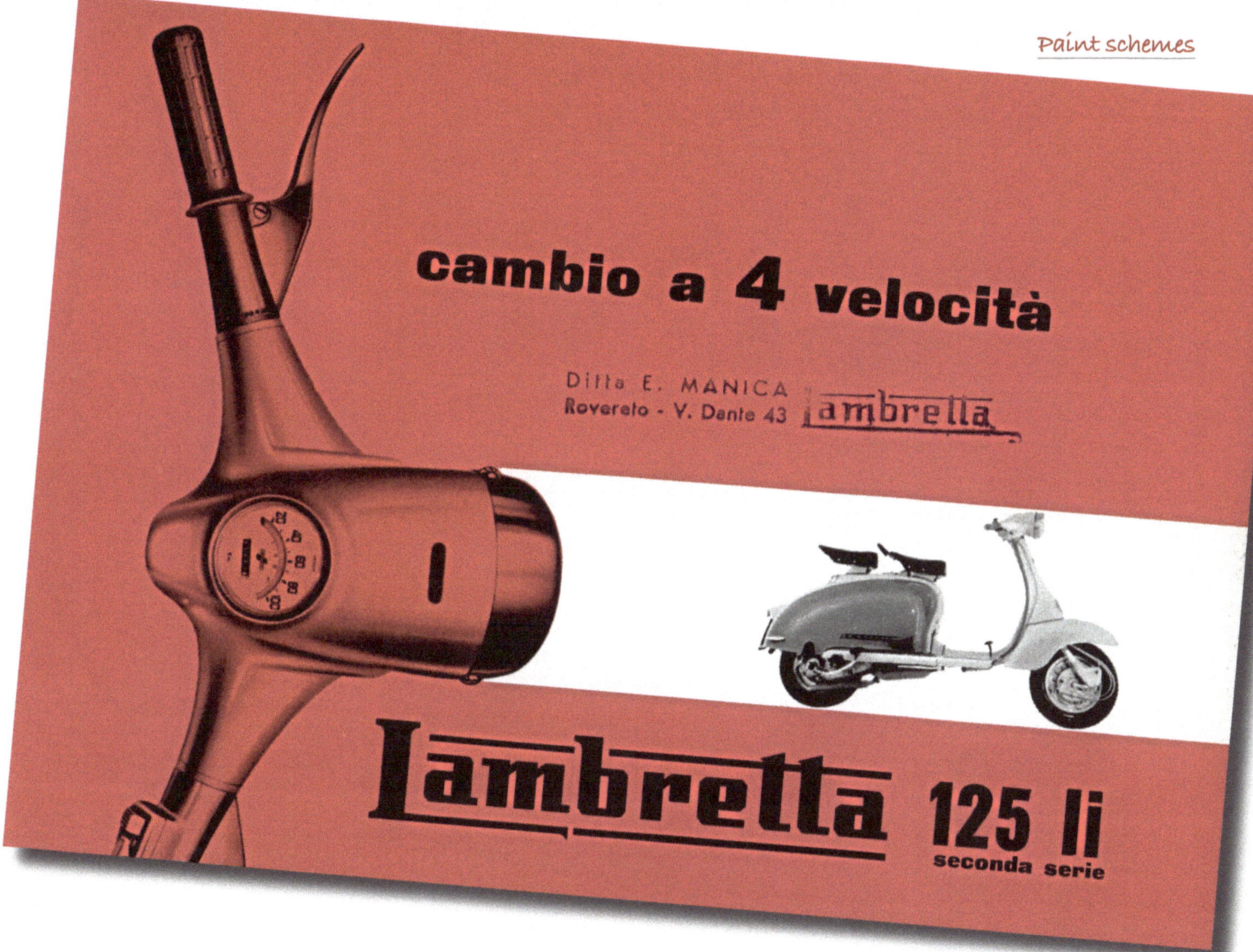

Li 125 (Series 1)
Dawn Grey – 8019
Dark Steel Grey – 8040 (used on Li 125 side panels only)

Li 150 (Series 1)
River Grey – 8014 (used on machines with single colour bodywork)
Dawn Grey – 8019 (used on machines that had side panels, horn casting and headset top painted as follows):
English Blue – 8031
Flaminia Blue – 8032
Nile Green – 8015
Ruby Red – 8047
Coral Red – 8046

TV 175 (Series 2)
Tyrrhenian Blue – 8042
Oriental Yellow – 8049

Li 125 (Series 2)
Dawn Grey – 8019
Dark Steel Grey – 8040 (used on side panels only)

Li 150 (Series 2)
Dawn Grey – 8019
River Grey – 8014 (used on some of the machines produced up to mid-1960)
Hawthorn White – 8082 (used on some machines produced between mid-1960 and January 1961)
Horn casting, side panels and headset tops painted in any of the following colours:
English Blue – 8031
Flaminia Blue – 8032
Nile Green – 8015
Ruby Red – 8047
Coral Red – 8046

This is SLIMSTYLE, the last word in scooter design and workmanship, produced especially for you, the **discriminating** scooterist.

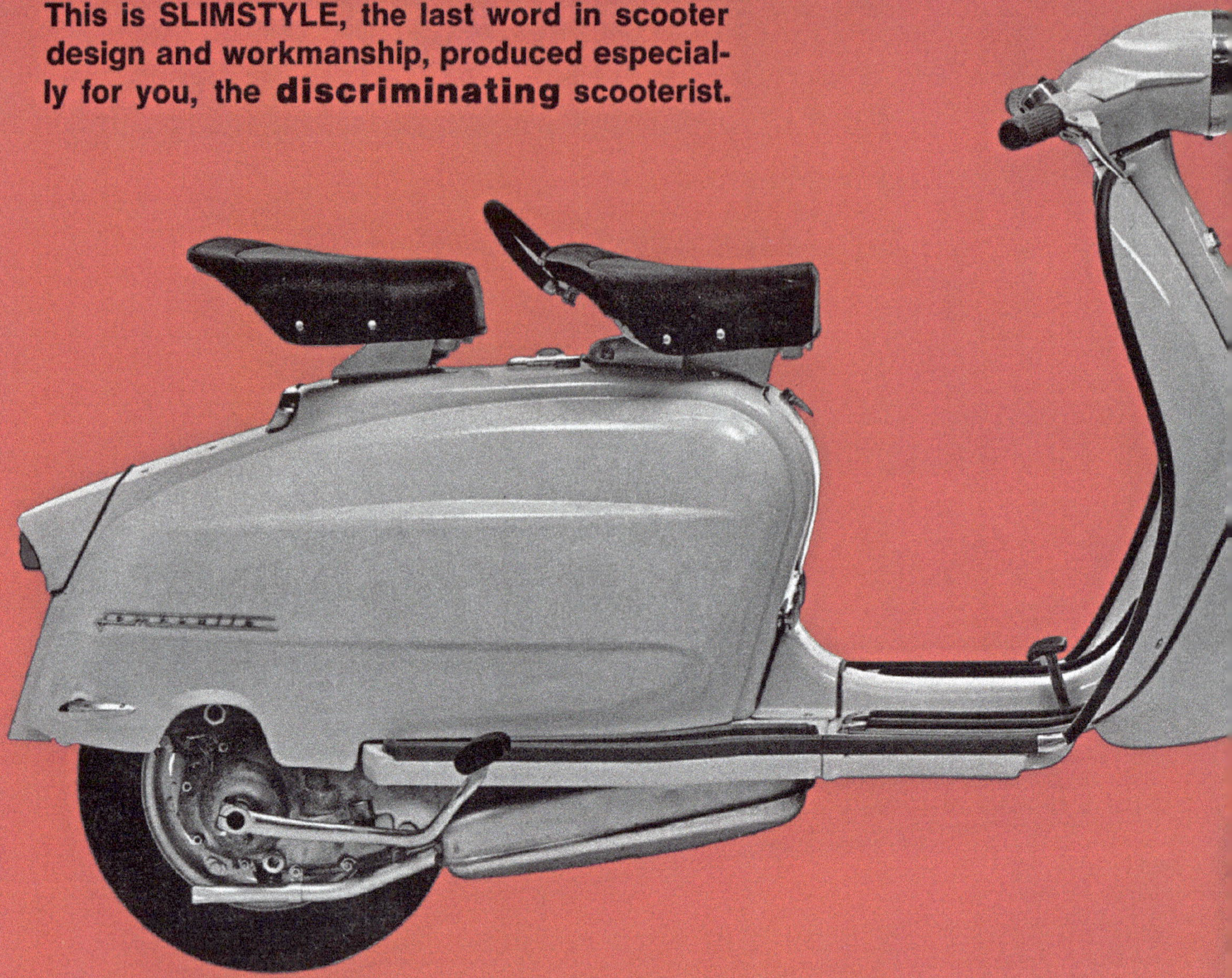

Your good taste is reflected in every line of these elegant machines, available in co

Li 125 (Series 3)
Grey – 8068
Iseo Blue – 8035
Beige – not known

Li 150 (Series 3)
Grey – 8068 (used on early models only)
New White – 8059
Side panels, horn casting and headset top as follows:
New Blue – 8038
Nile Green – 8015
Ruby Red – 8047

Li 125 (Series 4)
Aquamarine Blue – 8030
New White – 8059 (used on internal parts only)

TV 175 (Series 3)
New White – 8059 (used on machines built between 1962-63)
Side panels, head set top, horn casting and mudguard as follows:
Dark Grey – 8071
Coral Red – 8065
Ruby Red – 8047
Light Yellow – 8064
Metallic Blue – 8062 (used on machines built from Dec 1963 to end of production)
New White – 8059 (used on internal parts)

TV/GT 200
New White – 8059
The TV 200 was supplied by Innocenti in an all-white paint scheme. Lambretta Concessionaires then repainted the side panels in a contrast colour. On the early machines that were supplied with Li-style panels, the centre strip was left white whilst the top and bottom strips were painted in a contrast colour. On later models supplied with the Special-style side panels, the 'gullwing' part of the panel was painted in a contrast colour. Colours used included green, blue, black, gold, and red.

SX 150
Spring Grey – 8070
Apple Green – 8039
New White – 8059 (used on internal parts only)
Hawthorn White – 8082 (used on last models only)

Cento
Light Ivory – 8054

J 125 (3 speed)
Metallic Grey – 8060
Metallic Blue – 8062

ours to suit your personality.

J 125 (4 speed)
Roman Blue – detail not known

J50
Machines built between 1964 and mid-1966
New White – 8059
Ruby Red – 8047
Light Olive Green – 8079
Dark Olive Green – 8078 (used on side panels of the light Olive Green machines)
Machines built between mid-1968 and end of production
New White – 8059
Aquamarine Blue – 8030
Purple – 8069
Apple Green -8039

J 50 De Luxe
New White – 8059
Aquamarine Blue – 8030
Apple Green – 8039

J 50 Special
Turquoise – 8016
Red – 8073
Ochre – 8080

Li 125 Special
Metallic Blue – 8061
Hawthorn White – 8082
New White – 8059 (internal parts only)

SX 200
New White – 8059
The SX 200 was supplied by Innocenti in an all-white paint scheme. Lambretta Concessionaires then repainted the side panels in a contrast colour. The top part of the side panel was painted in a contrast colour. Colours used included green, blue, black, gold, and red.

Lui 50C
Hawthorn White – 8082

Marketing Pubblicità Generale 275/LC

TECHNICAL SPECIFICATIONS:	LUNA	VEGA	COMETA
Cubic capacity	50	75	75
Maximum power	2.5 b.h.p.	5.5 b.h.p.	5.5 b.h.p.
Consumption (per gallon)	180	130	130
Weight	144 lbs.	146 lbs.	146 lbs.
Gear ratios	1st - 27.53:1 2nd - 15.10:1 3rd - 9.83:1	1st - 19.27:1 2nd - 12.52:1 3rd - 9.29:1 4th - 6.90:1	1st - 19.27:1 2nd - 12.52:1 3rd - 9.29:1 4th - 6.90:1
Tyres	3 x 10	3 x 10	3 x 10
Lubrication	through petrol mixture at 2 % of oil	through petrol mixture at 2 % of oil	through Lubematic oil injection system

Common dimensions: 65 1/2"; width and handlebars 26" height 42 1/2" seat height 31 1/2"; wheelbase 47 1/2.

LAMBRETTA CONCESSIONAIRES LTD. Lambretta House, Purley Way, Croydon, Surrey.

INNOCENTI

SOC. GENERALE PER L'INDUSTRIA METALLURGICA E MECCANICA

MILANO ROMA NEW YORK PARIS LONDON CARACAS DÜSSELDORF

Lui 50CL
Turquoise – 8016
Orange – 8037
Apple Green – 8039

Vega (75S) & Cometa (75SL)
Metallic Grey – 8060
Ochre – 8080

DL/GP 125
Hawthorn White – 8082
Turquoise – 8016

DL/GP 150
Red – 8073
Hawthorn White – 8082

DL/GP & 200 Electronic
Ochre – 8080

cinque

5

Carburettors

The information given here relates to the Dell'Orto carburettors that were fitted to various Lambretta scooters. In brackets are the numbers of the variant that the information relates to: for example. '1' equals a Mark 1 or Series 1 machine. Some machines, for example, the Series 2 TV 175, used two different carburettors during its production run, so details of both are given.

Scooter	Carburettor	Choke	Slide	Needle	Atomiser	Main jet	Pilot jet	Starter	Float (in grams)
Model A	MA 16	16mm	55	C9	260	65	45	n/a	7.5
Model B	MA 16	16mm	55	C9	260	65	45	n/a	7.5
Model C	MA 16	16mm	55	C9	260	65	45	n/a	7.5
LC	MA 16	16mm	55	C9	260	65	45	n/a	7.5
D125 (1)	MA 18 B2	18mm	75	D1	255b	70	45	n/a	6.5
LD125 1	MA 18 B2	18mm	75	D1	255b	68	45	50	6.5
Model E	MA 18 B2	18mm	75	D1	255b	70	45	n/a	6.5
D125 (2)	MA 18 B2	18mm	75	D3	255b	70	40	55	6.5
LD 125 (2)	MA 18 B3	18mm	75	D1	255b	70	45	50	6.5
LDA 125(2)	MA 18 B4	18mm	75	D3	255b	70	40	55	6.5
Model F	MU 14 C1	14mm	40	F3	270-35	72	n/a	n/a	5
D150 (2)	MA 19 B4	19mm	75	D3	255b	72	40	55	6.5
LD150 (2)	MA 19 B4	19mm	75	D3	255b	72	40	55	6.5
D125 (3)	MA 18 B3	18mm	75	D1	255b	68	40	55	6.5
LDA 150 (2)	MA 19 B4	19mm	75	D3	255b	72	40	55	6.5
D150 (3)	MA 19 B4	19mm	75	D3	255b	72	40	55	6.5
LD125 (3)	MA 18 B3	18mm	75	D1	255b	68	40	55	6.5
LD150 (3)	MA 19 B4	19mm	75	D1	255b	75	40	55	6.5
LDA 125 (3)	MA 18 B4	18mm	75	D1	255b	68	40	55	6.5

Scooter	Carburettor	Choke	Slide	Needle	Atomiser	Main jet	Pilot jet	Starter	Float (in grams)
LDA 150 (3)	MA 19 B4	19mm	75	D1	255b	75	40	55	6.5
TV 175 (1)	MB 23 BS	23mm	70	E15	260b	105	45	60	6.5
LI 150 (1)	MB 19 BS5	19mm	65	D18	260b	95	40	55	6.5
LI 125 (1)	MB 18 B5	18mm	50	D16	260b	92	35	55	6.5
LI 125 (2)	MA 18 BS5	18mm	50	D20	260b	73	35	55	6.5
	MA 18 BS7	18mm	50	D20	260b	73	35	55	6.5
LI 150 (2)	MA19BS5	19mm	50	D21	260b	78	40	55	6.5
	MA19 BS7	19mm	50	D21	260b	78	40	55	6.5
TV175 (2)	MA 23BS5	21mm	70	E15	260b	88	40	60	6.5
	MA23 BS7	21mm	70	E21	260b	110	40	60	6.5
LI 125 (3)	SH 1/18	18mm	5914/1	n/a	5899/1	99	45	50	5
LI 150 (3)	SH 1/18	18mm	5914/2	n/a	5899/1	105	45	50	5
TV 175 (3)	SH 1/20	20mm	5914/1	n/a	5899/2	106	50	50	5
TV 200	SH 1/20	20mm	5914/1	n/a	5899/2	108	48	50	5
LI 150 S	SH 1/18	18mm	5914/1	n/a	5899/2	101	45	50	5
Cento	SHB18/16	16mm	6492/1	n/a	n/a	70	40	50	3.5
J125 (3 spd)	SHB 18/16	16mm	6492/1	n/a	n/a	75	40	50	3.5
J50 (3 spd)	SHB 18/12	12mm	n/a	n/a	n/a	62	40	50	3.5
Li125 S	SH 1/20	20mm	n/a	n/a	n/a	107	45	50	5
SX 200	SH 1/20	20mm	5914/1	n/a	5899/2	103	48	50	5
J125 (4 spd)	SHB 18/16	16mm	6492/1	n/a	n/a	72	40	50	3.5
Super Starstream	SHB 18/16	16mm	6492/1	n/a	n/a	72	40	50	3.5
J 50 (4 spd)	SHB 18/12	12mm	n/a	n/a	n/a	62	40	50	3.5
SX 150	SH 1/20	20mm	5914/2	n/a	5899/2	102	45	50	5
Li125 (4)	SH 1/20	20mm	5914/2	n/a	5899/2	102	45	50	5
J50 dl	SHB 18/12	12mm	n/a	n/a	n/a	62	40	50	3.5
Lui 50 C	SHB 14/12	12mm	n/a	n/a	n/a	52	n/a	n/a	n/a
Lui 50 CL	SHB 14/12	12mm	n/a	n/a	n/a	52	n/a	n/a	n/a
Lui 50 s	SHB 14/12	12mm	n/a	n/a	n/a	52	n/a	n/a	n/a
Vega	SHA1/20	20mm	5914/1	n/a	5899/6	68/100	45	n/a	n/a
Cometa	SHA1/20	20mm	5914/1	n/a	5899/6	68/100	45	n/a	n/a
GP 125	SH 1/20	20mm	5914/2	n/a	5899/4	98	45	50	5
GP 150	SH 2/22	22mm	7895/1	n/a	5899/2	118	45	50	5
GP 200	SH 2/22	22mm	7895/1	n/a	5899/2	118	45	50	5
GP 200 Elec	SH 2/22	22mm	7895/1	n/a	5899/2	118	45	50	5
J50 S	SHB 18/12	12mm	n/a	n/a	n/a	62	40	50	3.5

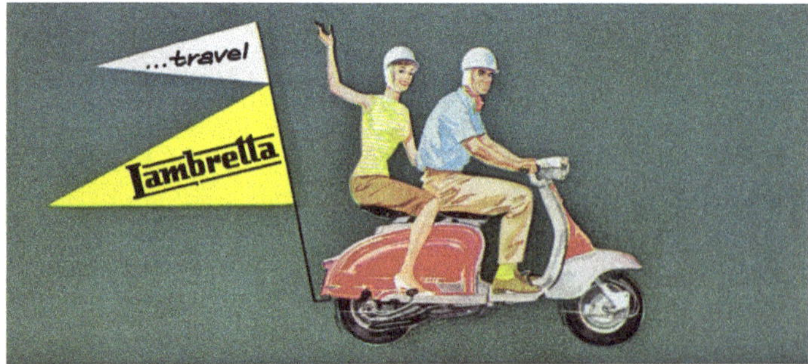

...travel
Lambretta
GET OUT...
GET AROUND
Life can be so full . . . so entertaining . . .so packed with new friends . . . new interests . . . new excitements.
It can also be deadly dull . . . humdrum ! Which life will yours be !
The answer depends very much on your ability to move easily from place to place without suffering the obvious limitations of public transport.
Think ! With your own vehicle you can be as much as 20 miles away in little more time than it takes to get to station or bus stop . . . and without anything like the same effort.

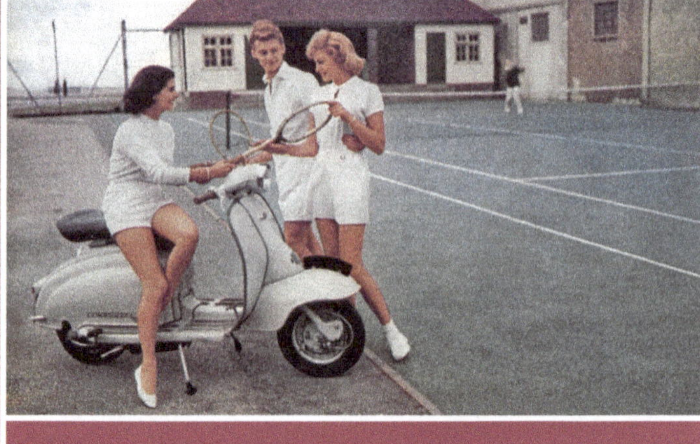

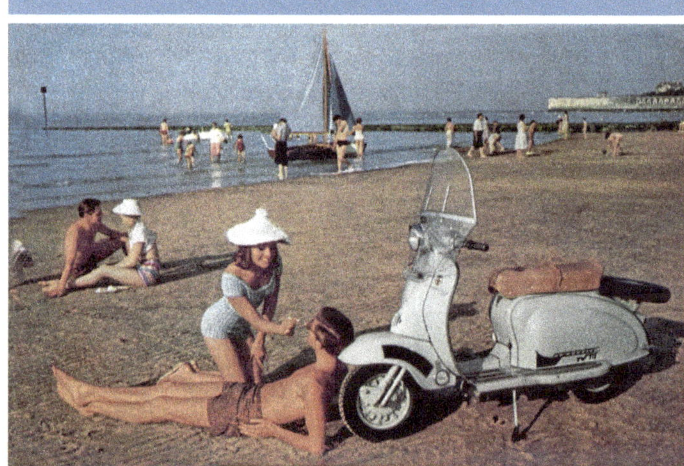

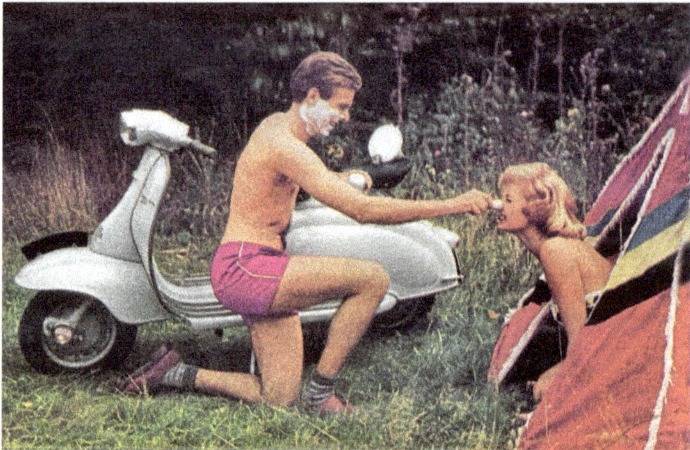

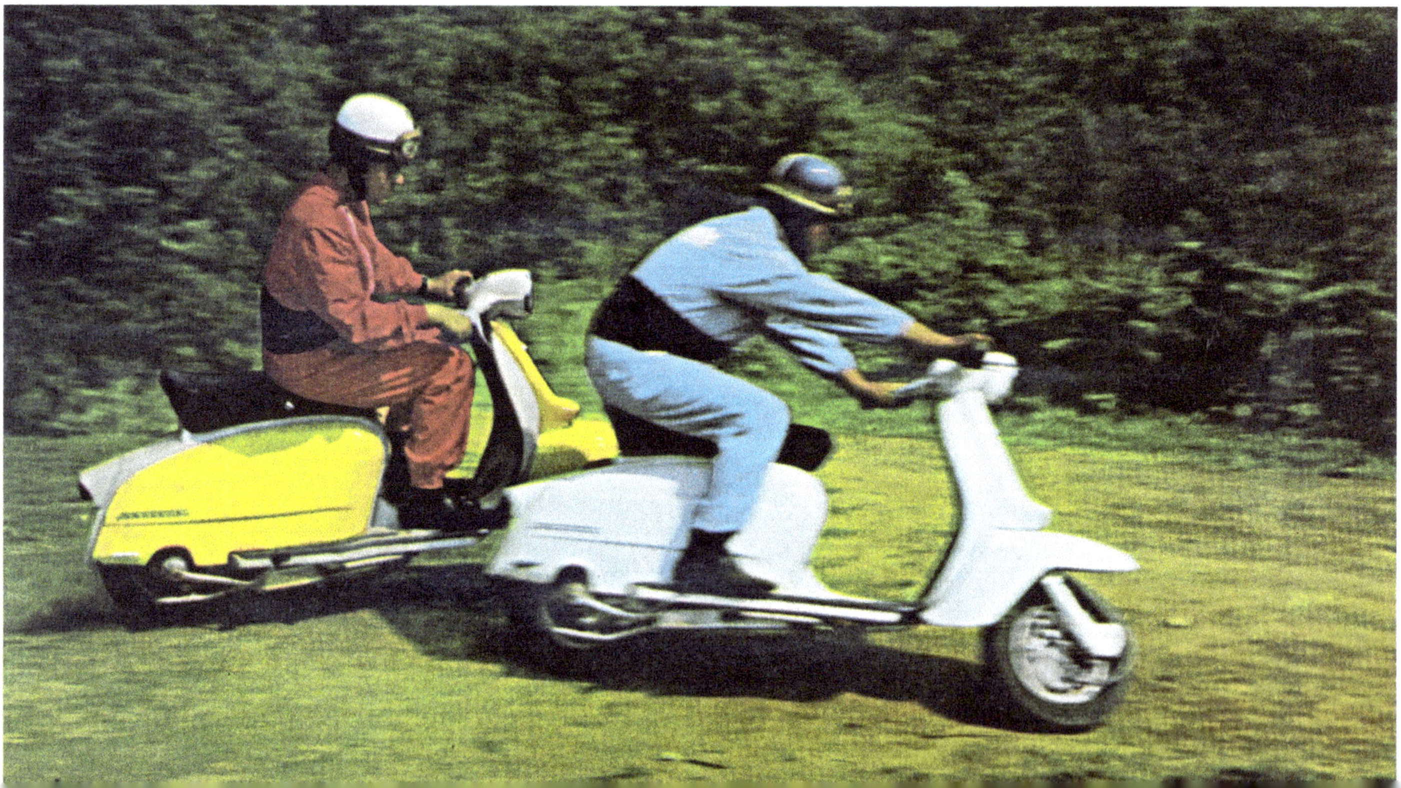

Gear ratios

Gear	Cluster teeth	Gear teeth	Drive sprocket	Crownwheel	Overall ratio
Li 125 (Series 1)					
1	9	51	15	46	17.40
2	12	42			10.71
3	16	39			7.47
4	19	35			5.65
Li 150 (Series 1)					
1	11	50	15	46	13.95
2	14	42			9.00
3	17	39			6.67
4	20	35			5.22
TV 175 (Series 1)					
1	12	49	15	46	12.52
2	14	40			8.76
3	18	37			6.30
4	21	33			4.82
Li 125 (Series 2)					
1	9	51	15	46	17.40
2	12	42			10.71

Gear	Cluster teeth	Gear teeth	Drive sprocket	Crownwheel	Overall ratio
3	16	39			7.47
4	19	35			5.65
Li 150 (Series 2)					
1	11	50	15	46	13.95
2	14	41			9.00
3	17	37			6.67
4	20	34			5.22
Rallymaster					
1	9	51	15	46	17.40
2	12	42			10.71
3	17	37			6.67
4	20	34			5.22
TV 175 (Series 2)					
1	12	49	15	46	12.52
2	14	40			8.76
3	18	37			6.30
4	21	33			4.82
Li 125 (Series 3) early models					
1	9	51	15	46	17.40
2	12	42			10.71
3	16	39			7.47
4	19	35			5.65
Li 125 (Series 3) late models					
1	11	50	15	46	13.95
2	13	41			9.67
3	17	39			7.04
4	19	35			5.65
Li 150 (Series 3)					
1	11	50	15	46	13.95
2	14	41			9.00
3	17	37			6.67

Gear	Cluster teeth	Gear teeth	Drive sprocket	Crownwheel	Overall ratio
4	20	34			5.22
TV 175 (Series 3)					
1	12	49	15	46	12.52
2	14	40			8.76
3	18	37			6.30
4	21	33			4.82
TV 200					
1	13	47	15	46	11.09
2	15	39			7.97
3	19	36			5.81
4	22	32			4.46
Li 125 Special					
1	10	50	15	46	15.33
2	12	42			10.71
3	15	39			7.97
4	18	36			6.32
Li 150 Special					
1	10	50	15	46	15.33
2	12	42			10.71
3	15	39			7.97
4	19	35			5.65
SX 150					
1	10	50	15	46	15.33
2	12	42			10.71
3	15	39			7.97
4	19	35			5.65
SX 200					
1	12	49	15	46	12.52
2	14	40			8.76
3	18	37			6.30
4	21	33			4.82

Gear	Cluster teeth	Gear teeth	Drive sprocket	Crownwheel	Overall ratio
Cento					
1	10	48	14	45	14.02
2	15	42			8.44
3	21	37			5.66
J 50 early models					
1	10	69	14	45	22.17
2	16	64			12.85
3	19	56			8.18
J 50 late models					
1	9	53	13	46	22.80
2	14	54			13.67
3	19	47			7.72
J 125 3 speed					
1	11	48	14	45	14.02
2	16	42			8.44
3	21	37			5.66
J 125 4 speed					
1	11	48	14	45	14.02
2	14	44			10.11
3	16	37			7.43
4	19	34			5.75
J 50 Deluxe					
1	9	58	11	47	27.53
2	15	53			15.10
3	20	46			9.83
DL/GP 125					
1	10	50	15	46	15.33
2	12	42			10.71
3	15	39			7.97
4	18	36			6.32

Gear	Cluster teeth	Gear teeth	Drive sprocket	Crownwheel	Overall ratio
DL/GP 150					
1	10	50	15	46	15.33
2	12	42			10.71
3	15	39			7.97
4	19	35			5.65
DL/GP 200					
1	10	50	18	47	13.05
2	12	42			9.13
3	15	35			6.79
4	18	30			5.22
Luí 50 C/CL/S					
1	9	58	11	47	27.53
2	15	53			15.10
3	20	46			9.83
Vega/Cometa					
1	9	49	13	46	19.27
2	13	46			12.52
3	26	42			9.29
4	20	39			6.99

Index

www.ingramcontent.com/pod-product-compliance
Lightning Source LLC
LaVergne TN
LVHW060631110826
845147LV00014B/889

* 9 7 8 1 7 8 7 1 1 1 3 9 4 *